Acknowledgements

Designing: A Journey Through Time uses the metaphor of a journey to explore how designing as an ongoing human activity has evolved over time and place. The journey metaphor also applies to my own journey—my forty-years' plus experience in the artificial world, the world of designing. The publication of this book is my opportunity to express my gratitude to my fellow explorers: the people who helped me get from there to here.

I would like to acknowledge my parents, Jeannette and Maxime Giard, both long-since deceased, who, while not fully understanding what I was doing when I chose to study industrial design, supported me in my endeavors. I would also like to thank the steadying influence of my younger brother Claude, our family's silent pillar of strength.

My introduction to the world of professional design was André Jarry, first as a professor and then as a colleague, in the late 1960s—followed by Ian Bruce, designer and boat builder extraordinaire. André and Ian, each in his own way, showed me that designing, making, and using were distinct but inseparable activities.

My introduction to design education occurred several years later at Carleton University, Ottawa, Canada, where I taught industrial design for nineteen years. Two people made that part of the journey memorable. Professor Wim Gilles was the kind of mentor that every young educator and aspiring scholar dreams of. And Barrington Nevitt (or Barry, as he was known to his friends) became my guiding light in the world of design research. I cannot claim to stand on Wim's and Barry's shoulders, but if I could, I would.

Instead, I choose to stand on the shoulders of my students. Their energy and curiosity are contagious. That is why I continue to research and talk and write about design.

Of enormous help to me with my manuscript were Dorset Group, who supported the concept of the book, Flavelle Ballem, who performed a twenty-four-hour editorial turn-around time on my first draft, and Carrie Cantor, who copyedited and proofed the final copy.

When it comes to recording my reflections on designing, I am totally indebted to two people: George Egler, a friend of over thirty years and a fellow industrial designer, and Mercedes Ballem, my partner, soul mate, and wife. This book is dedicated to both of them.

Jacques R. Giard   Scottsdale, Arizona

To Mercedes and George

Contents

Preface

The completion of a book brings a sense of satisfaction and relief. The hours, days, and weeks of researching, writing, and editing are finally over. The manuscript has been put to bed, as they say, and soon a new book will appear on the shelves. This is the author's reality.

Not long thereafter, another reality hits. It can happen quite suddenly while reading the newspaper, for example, or while viewing a favorite web site. It happened to me not long after *Designing: A Journey Through Time* was first published. A group of archeologists at Arizona State University, coincidentally where I work, announced that they had found evidence to prove that the earliest stone tools dated back 3.4 million years, and not 2.5 million years. It's with such discoveries that this other reality hits: the first edition of *Designing: A Journey Through Time* made regular reference to 2.5 million years. The book was now factually incorrect. Add a few more such reality moments in the intervening years and it becomes evident that a second edition of *Designing: A Journey Through Time* is needed.

As important as it is, the discovery of earlier stone tools is not sufficient reason to publish a second edition. There has to be more of these types of changes. When I first wrote the book in 2008, for example, the iPad did not exist; it now needed to be included in the context of the iPod, the iPhone, and other similar artifacts. Similarly, social networking had not evolved to the point that it has in 2012. Today, Facebook has become a regular feature in the lives of millions, but it was also a prime element in the orchestrated uprisings of citizens in the Middle East in the so-called Arab Spring of 2011. Who could have imagined that software meant to connect people in the most innocent of ways could also be used for massive changes in society? Strangely enough, there was a clue and it was in the first edition: the popular uprising in Myanmar in 2007. Cell phones—that was the extent of technology then—were used to broadcast events throughout the world.

That said, a second edition is not published only because of minor editorial changes, no matter how many there are. More significant changes are needed. There is now a revised section on Charles and Ray Eames in which more information is provided about Ray. There is a totally new section on Canadian design in chapter 6 as well as a section on sustainability in chapter 7. Most significantly, there is a new chapter on designing your journey. This chapter has one focus: How do you take what you have learned from the design journey undertaken in chapters 1 through 7 and use it design your own life's journey? The chapter does not offer recipes per se, but it does provide an overview of forces that will shape our Artificial World in the years to come and the role that designing plays.

The creation of a second edition of *Designing: A Journey Through Time* meant that I had to reread it several times. In doing so, I was both comforted and pleased to realize that the information in the book provided remains factual and relevant. This being the case, perhaps more years will go by before I need to consider a third edition.

Jacques Giard
Scottsdale, Arizona 2011

Introduction

This book is about designing. More specifically, it is about what we design and how designing has evolved over millennia. It is not another book about cool stuff or trophy houses or superstar designers. Instead, it is about everyday things: those many things that often go unnoticed and that we sometimes take for granted such as products, buildings, and visual information.

Given the ubiquitous nature of everyday things, writing a book about design should not be an onerous task, if even a necessary one. After all, design is everywhere we look, everywhere we live, and everywhere we travel. Moreover, everyone designs. It is a basic human activity and not unlike our capacity to speak, to read, and to write. Consequently, it would be fair to assume that most people already have a good understanding of designing.

Alas, such an assumption would be wrong. Despite the fact that designing is pervasive and that everyone does it, most people know very little about designing—a fact that is both surprising and perplexing. Surprising because everyone is touched by designing every day, and perplexing because something as pervasive as designing should be understood by everyone, at least at a basic level. Like water to the fish—it appears that design is everywhere but no one sees it. Explaining this contradiction is the mission of *Designing: A Journey Through Time*, as it traces the lineage of everyday things, shows how they have evolved, and situates them in today's world—all because of designing.

There is no shortage of books on design. A visit to a bookstore or a library would quickly confirm this fact. Readers can find hundreds of books on design history as well as limitless how-to books on designing. There are also, of course, countless books on designers and architects as well as innumerable coffee-table tomes on design and architecture—gorgeous books on graphics, products, furniture, homes, and buildings. Quite obviously, there seems to be no limit on design topics either, from early Egyptian architecture to the latest "green" products. Yet despite the quantity of books and the breadth of topics, the majority of design books have one thing in common: they generally deal with design as a noun; that is, design as a tangible, material thing. They rarely deal with design as a verb—that is, the act of designing. How-to books aside, the vacuum in books on the designing process is quite noticeable.

Designing: A Journey Through Time is different. It is about design as a verb and how people have applied this unique human capacity we call designing to create an Artificial World very different from the Natural World. The book is not about all the cool stuff that has become increasingly popular in some of the media and that has situated design as a kind of flavor of the month. From the earliest stone tool to today's space shuttle, things that are designed have played a key role in human evolution, allowing people to advance from using simple cutting tools to cutting-edge technologies. This human capacity to design is one of three themes in *Designing: A Journey Through Time,* with the focus on designing as an activity common to all humans every day of our lives.

A second theme of this book is the evolution of the designing activity—that is, how designing has progressed from a highly integrated pursuit in which the designing, making, and using were embodied in one person to an activity that today permeates the business agenda of global corporations and has split into three distinct and independent activities performed by three different actors: the designer, the maker, and the user. The study of this evolution shows that the principles that underpin designing have not changed fundamentally over the last 3.4 million years. What has changed, however, is its complexity and the magnitude of its impact.

The third theme involves an attempt to demystify designing. Studying design as a noun can provide some insights into design as a verb, albeit only to a modest degree. Such insights are more often than not the result of inference or coincidence and without any direct link to cause and effect. The modes of operation associated with designing are not normally in evidence and are rarely obvious in the design object itself. Consequently, it is almost impossible to understand the designing process that gave us a cell phone, for example, by merely looking at the cell phone. Studying design as a verb, however, avoids this indirect route to understanding designing and examines more directly how people design. There is always method in the designing process. It can range from simple to highly complex, and is not always easily explained. Nevertheless, the designing process is not some form of black magic. Quite correctly, a teenager designing a costume for Halloween is not faced with the same challenges as a naval architect designing a 10-meter yacht. That said, and upon closer examination or demystification, the design processes shared by both designers are quite similar, at least in principle.

Understandably, there are many designing activities that should be practiced by no one other than experts such as architects, designers, and engineers. Frank Lloyd Wright was one such expert designer. His name is known to many people and is synonymous with leading-edge architecture and design in the United States. The American architect Michael Graves has also reached similar preeminence in design circles, first, as a leading proponent of Postmodernist architecture and, second, with his involvement in the design of a product line for Target, the large American retailer. More recently and because of a debilitating illness, Graves has focused his design attention on healthcare. Both Wright and Graves have become exemplars of the designer as creative genius—a phenomenon that can be interpreted to mean that designing is limited to a few select people and no one else. This is the conventional wisdom. But in this case, conventional wisdom is wrong. Exceptional designing may be limited to a few exceptional individuals, but designing as an everyday activity is not. Teenagers often design their own rooms, homeowners design the landscape around their homes, and workers are sometimes invited to design their workspace. It would be like stating that no one but published authors and poets should be allowed to write all the while ignoring the fact that most people can write even if they are not as eloquent as authors and poets.

Designing is a human activity. Everyone is born with the capacity to design and, consciously or not, designs every day. Victor Papanek, the American designer, was certainly of that opinion when he stated that, *"All men are designers. All that we do, almost all of the time, is design, for design is basic to all human activity..."*[i] Some people will elect to enhance this innate capacity to design and, by choice, become architects, designers, and engineers much like some people elect to become authors and poets because of our innate capacity to read and write.

As part of its mission, *Designing: A Journey Through Time* seeks to shed light on designing as a very natural activity in all humans. To achieve this end, it will do so via a three-part journey. The first part will be the planning of the

journey, focusing on the operational parameters implicit in designing. These become a road map for a journey that will begin by exploring the two distinct worlds that we inhabit: the Natural World that we are given and the Artificial World that we create; will then continue with the world of material everyday things that we will encounter along the way, or more precisely, its artifacts—tools, structures, and signs; and end with the visual language that makes it possible for us to understand it all.

The second section of the book is the journey itself. The journey will uncover the everyday aspects of design while examining significant societal changes that impacted the design activity itself. Its primary focus will be place, people, and process—sometimes called the three Ps of designing. How, for example, did the concept of surplus change design as societies went from being hunter-gatherers to farmers? How was design affected when the interchangeability of parts became possible? What impact did the realization of self in modern parlance—as a seventeenth-century phenomenon in Europe—have on designing?[ii]

The third and final part of the book reflects on the journey. It is that point when, on the one hand, we look back on what we have learned while, on the other, we dare to peer into the future in an attempt to discern what could happen next.

A few of the revelations in the book may perhaps displease some readers, designers being certainly among them. The disclosure, for example, that the capacity to design resides within everyone and is not a special gift that only a few fortunate people are born with may be potentially disturb-ing. If we were to believe some designers, their special talent is part of a genetic makeup that is unique to them and is what sets them apart from the masses. As important as the genetic component is, no one can rule out the role of nurturing. The jury is still out in the ongoing debate between nature and nurture as concerns designing, but we do know that good designers are not merely the result of a unique DNA. For other readers, the disclosure that design-ing is neither exclusionary nor elitist may be equally unset-tling, especially with the presence that design has attained in the latter twentieth and early twenty-first centuries. Exclusion and elitism as well as other similar qualities have clearly become part of the myth and culture that has in-fected some attitudes in contemporary design. But design-ing has roots that are much more humble and that are grounded in a much simpler reality.

In the end, this book does not attempt to be everything to everybody. It can't be. What it does strive to do is present the phenomenon of designing as something other than the usual moralistic platform or discourse found in many books on the subject—that is, what con-stitutes good or bad design. If anything, *Designing: A Journey Through Time* provides the reader with a cross between the typical writings on design, with their more subjective platform, and writings in archeology and anthropology, with their more objective perspective. In other words, the material manifestations of design—tools, structures, and signs—are nothing more than mirrors that reflect how humanity has evolved by the creation of an Artificial World within a natural one. *Designing: A Journey Through Time* is for people, in most cases non-designers, who want to get a sense of how humanity has evolved from a material culture of nothing more than stone tools, cliff dwellings, and petroglyphs to one of almost infinite variety of everyday things today, and have done so via designing.

Endnotes
[i] Papanek, Victor. *Design for the Real World.*
[ii] Rybczynski, Witold. *Home.*

Designing:
A Journey Through Time

Part I

Preparing for the Designing Journey

CHAPTER 1

Our Natural and Artificial Worlds

The first three chapters of *Designing: A Journey Through Time* provide a foundation for the premise of the book, which will trace the lineage of certain everyday things, show their evolution, and situate them in today's world. Furthermore, the human process that has made these everyday things possible in the first place will be explained via The Designing Triad, a simplified diagrammatic representation of the designing process. After all, it is designing that has allowed humanity to evolve to where it is today. Quite logically, therefore, the story begins with the Natural World.

The Natural World

As complex as our world appears to be—continents and oceans, lakes and forests, villages and cities, kayaks and cargo ships, language and culture—most everything in it can be neatly placed into one of two camps—it is either natural or artificial. The Natural World comes as a birthright; it is what we are provided. The Artificial World is different; it has been designed. For example, lakes are natural but swimming pools are artificial; sandy beaches are natural but silica glass is artificial; forests are natural but wooden boats are artificial. Fish are natural but not so sushi. (See figures 1.1–1.4.) The list of such natural-artificial integration—a kind of symbiosis of natural material and artificial design—is endless. It provides obvious evidence of not only how people have survived over millions of years in the Natural World but, more significantly, how societies have evolved in an Artificial World of their own creation.

In providing raw material for a range of things, from the first stone tools to today's space shuttles, the Natural World has been a resource bank for humanity. Water is an excellent example and for several reasons. Water covers around 70% of our planet and constitutes about two-thirds of the human body. It also provides life-supporting nourishment—a person can expect to survive no more than a week without water. Therefore, it comes as no surprise that all societies, to one degree or another, developed in close proximity to water. Certainly, native tribes in North America established their villages and camps close to rivers, lakes, or oceans. Even extreme geographical situations followed the same pattern. They, too, were only settled were water was available, no matter how little of it there was. The Sinagua people of Arizona are a good case in point. The presence of these early settlers (ca. 500 BCE to 1425 CE) in this particularly arid area of North America was due in part to the presence of water, however minimal. In fact, the name given to the people, Sinagua, is a reflection of this unusual condition—Spanish for *sin,* meaning without, and *agua,* meaning water. There is also evidence to show that the eventual demise of Sinaguan settlements in the early fifteenth century was because of drought, or lack of water.

As societies developed and international trade and commerce expanded, nature's waterways took up more and more of the burden for providing convenient channels of transportation. Countries and cities, especially in Europe, took advantage of their location by building canals as artificial waterways for the purpose of local transportation. During the Industrial Revolution, England developed an extensive system of inland canals in order to ship goods. Stockholm and Bangkok also benefited from the integration of canals in their city plans. Perhaps more than any other city, Venice stands out as a place built almost exclusively on the concept of water as a mode of transportation. And although their uses have changed over time, Venice remains known for its canals, gondolas, and vaporetti. (See Figure 1.5.)

When natural waterways were not located in the most de-sirable place, human ingenuity intervened and artificial waterways were created. Such was the case with the Panama and Suez Canals. Both were massive construction projects that, in the end, created artificial channels and that totally changed ocean-going transportation.

The Panama Canal, for example, reduced the travel dis-tance from New York to San Francisco from 14,000 miles to a little over 6,000 miles.

The water in flowing rivers has provided yet another bene-fit to mankind: energy, first in the form of water wheels but eventually in the form of hydroelectric dams. Water wheels converted the natural flow of water into a rotary action that then drove all types of machinery, such as grinding stones used to make flour. Water wheels were essential to the industrialization process of Europe during the eigh-teenth and nineteenth centuries but had their origin in societies much earlier, in the eastern Mediterranean region around 150 to 100 BCE.[i] Hydroelectric dams also relied on moving water but used turbines to generate electricity. What were once considered massive structures—such as the Hoover Dam, completed in 1935—are dwarfed by more recent constructions, such as the Three Gorges Dam in China, which is five times the size of the Hoover.

Besides water, other natural materials proved to be instrumental in the evolution of society in the Natural World. Stone is an obvious one—obvious because we associate early human development with the Stone Age and stone tools. The latter certainly qualify as the first designed everyday things.[ii] Flint was particularly important. When skillfully chipped, it provided the earliest cutting instruments and led to other everyday tools such as knives and spears. Stone could be used in other, equally simple ways as well. The Inuit, the early people of Alaska, Canada, and Greenland, used medium-sized stones found at various campsites as weights to secure their tents.

Over time, stone of one kind or another would become the material of choice for many societies and for diverse everyday things. This was certainly the case with early architecture. The Egyptians, Greeks, and Romans all made extensive use of stone in the construction of their pyramids, temples, and important buildings. There was extensive use of marble, for example, and much remains the same today with expensive stone of all types found in many buildings—inside and out. Granite counters, for example, have become de rigueur in many modern homes.

Stone was also one of the earliest forms of mass media. We've all heard the expression 'It is etched in stone.' The saying has its roots in the tradition of chiseling messages in stone and is distantly related to the earliest examples of visual communication, such as those found in Egyptian hieroglyphics. Even Moses carried God's words on stone tablets. Petroglyphs fall into this category of visual communication. They are simple images or symbols scratched or chiseled on rocks, cave walls, or canyons. They exist in many parts of the world as evidence of an early form of visual communication between people, and are the basis of the pictograms that we find today in many of the wayfinding systems in places like international airports and sports stadiums. (See Figure 1.6.)

Nature can be more than just a source for physical matter; it can also be the source for spiritual material. Architects and designers have often looked to nature for imagery and symbolism. This was certainly the case with many of the designers and architects at the center of the Art Nouveau movement in Europe and in the United States in the late nineteenth and early twentieth centuries, who reacted against a built environment created during a period of rapid industrialization that was overly mechanistic, both in form and function. The Eiffel Tower, designed and built to celebrate the Paris World's Fair of 1889, was a perfect example of this tendency. (See Figure 1.7.) Although celebrated today as an icon of Paris, it was considered ugly by many Parisians of the day. In a city brimming with unusually fine examples of classic architecture, Gustave Eiffel's masterpiece seemed like nothing more than a gaudy vertical trestle with no redeeming aesthetic value. It exemplified the triumph of technology over humanity. Not surprisingly, artists, architects, and designers of the Art Nouveau movement reacted against this industrial style and created a visual language derived from nature, the antithesis of mechanization. Hector Guimard, the French architect, was one such proponent of Art Nouveau. His designs for the many entrances of the stations for the Paris metro—larger-than-life lamp standards and entrances that resembled plants and that were devoid of straight lines—remain among some of the best examples of design inspired by nature. (See Figure 1.8.) In some ways, Louis Comfort Tiffany was Guimard's counterpart in America. Much of Tiffany's work expressed a feeling for organic form and color, a direction that was contrary to the engineered look that prevailed in industry.

Nature can also be inspirational in ways beyond mere visual imagery and symbolism. Biomimicry is a good example. It is the art of using models found in nature and then adapting them in ways that can serve humanity. Biomimicry clearly rests with learning from the evolutionary developments that have occurred over millennia—that is, using the 'inventions' of nature as a basis for innovation in technology, engineering, and design. Excellent examples of this interpretive model exist today and include the SCUBA diver's flippers, which are based on fins found on frogs, and Velcro, which is based on burrs and their ability to cling to almost anything.

No better example exists to illustrate biomimicry than the concept of flight. People first began to study flight by observing birds. Watching a soaring eagle is an exhilarating sight and clearly makes the case that modern technology has yet to match the refinement of structural and dynamic principles of birds. Challenges aside, people were not easily discouraged from attempting to fly despite early trials that were at times both comical and disastrous. Eventually, however, early concepts of flight led to the general acceptance of aviation as a common mode of transportation. Nevertheless, the modern and sophisticated jet airplane of today owes all of its attributes to the modest bird.

Early attempts to replicate flight led man to believe that the muscle power of a person could be used to flap artificial wings in much the same way that a bird does. Over time and after a continuous series of failures, it became quite evident that a person could never muster the muscular power that was necessary to create the lift given the weight that had to be overcome. Unlike the bodies of birds, our bodies are too heavy in relation to our potential to generate power. What we did eventually learn from the flight of birds was gliding—that is, how lift could be created in order to achieve flight. Over time, the

science associated with aerodynamic properties was refined, and devices such as tails, ailerons, and flaps found their way into modern aviation. But the flapping of artificial wings was clearly not an option. Artificial power, such as the propeller or jet engine, would ultimately provide the required forward thrust of airplanes.[iii]

Besides adequate power, two other properties were required for flight: rigidity and reduced weight. Wings and bodies—whether for birds or airplanes—must be long yet rigid, and both need to meet some very specific weight limitations. Birds meet these two criteria by using hollow bones and feathers for wing and body; for their part, planes use hollow wings and bodies, and are made from light-weight materials (aluminum and carbon fibers).

Several of the designs and creations of Leonardo da Vinci, the Italian Renaissance man, were among the best early examples of biomimicry. Da Vinci was familiar with nature as a model and as a source of ideas. He studied the musculature of the human body, for example, and applied what he learned to his drawings and paintings. He also observed and analyzed some of the fundamental principles found in nature, some of which became the source of inspiration for his inventions. His study of flight is an example of this acute sense of observation. Da Vinci clearly understood the mechanical and dynamic components inherent in the flight of a bird and attempted to replicate its principles with some of his ideas for flying machines. (See Figure 1.9.)

The Artificial World
The Natural World surrounds each and every one of us; it is difficult to avoid it even in a space as artificial as the

city. Wherever we go, there is always some evidence of the Natural World—the trees in New York City, the Thames River in London, or the blue sky above Phoenix. But the city—its cars, its buildings, and the activities in the buildings—are all part of another world, one that is artificial. And unlike the Natural World, the Artificial World exists because it has been designed. It is the designing activity, or human intervention, that clearly differentiates the two. Often, these two worlds seem inseparable and, to a great extent, they are, but in a kind of interdependent way. We cannot have aluminum for our airplanes, for example, without first mining bauxite. However, the difference between the two worlds is quite obvious: the Natural World operates independently of human beings whereas the Artificial World is totally dependent on human intervention. Trees can grow naturally without our assistance but not so wooden furniture. The latter must be designed, and designing is the one factor that differentiates the Artificial World from the Natural World.

But what is designing? If the opinion of some popular design magazines is to be believed, designing is about two things and two things only: designs—objects, buildings, and other such things; and designers—the individual superstars who design these everyday things. How unfortunate that such a narrow opinion exists. It completely reduces the true impact of designing, which goes well beyond designs and designers. At best, the latter are only the small tip of the proverbial iceberg.

As previously explained, everything in our Artificial World has been designed. Nature certainly didn't provide it. This goes for such obvious everyday things as automobiles, houses, and planes, but also includes other, less obvious designs—artificial systems and methods, from business strategies to legal statutes and political organizations. Moreover, design's pervasiveness is not limited to the industrialized or developed world, although the presence of designing may appear to be more evident in these contexts. It is, in fact, just the opposite. Designing is a universal activity. People design in all cultures—developed or developing, rural or urban—and have done so since the dawn of human civilization. Yet many people fail to make the connection between the built environment in which they live and designing as a part of daily life, as if the latter was not responsible for the former. It never crosses their minds, or so it appears, that iPods don't grow on trees in an orchard somewhere in California, or that it's not some magical trick that makes them suddenly appear on the shelves of a retail store or on Apple's web site. So, why is it that designing remains so invisible and so unknown?

There are several reasons for this perceived lack of knowledge or understanding about designing. First, our fascination for designing is often limited to design as a thing or to designers as gifted individuals, but not with designing as a process. As mentioned earlier, this is certainly the case with the majority of books on design and the popular design media, but it also includes museums that collect things and that honor individual designers. The same can also be said for the more recent phenomenon of business magazines and the interest that they have found with design. In most of these cases, however, design is treated as a noun, not a verb.

Second, designing is not easily understood because it does not occur as the result of a recognizable formula or recipe. That is, it is not an activity undertaken by applying a known set of rules appropriate to a given situation. Calculating the load factor on a roof on a house, for example, may be nothing more than using some basic mathematics to a formula already known to architects and engineers. But the design of the roof, let alone the house, is quite a different proposition. Roofs can differ from one place to the next and from one situation to another. Their designs cannot always be achieved by merely knowing and applying one formula or another.

The lack of formulae leads to a third reason for a general ignorance of designing. When designing, designers sometimes rely on approaches that appear to be intuitive or instinctive. As a result, it may seem that there is something mysterious if not magical about the designing activity, something that is not fully understood and certainly not easily explained. From that perspective, the designing activity is similar to the creative thinking associated with the fine arts, which is not at all surprising given design's direct historical links to painting and sculpture via the applied arts.

Despite these three reasons—design perceived only as a thing, lack of explicit formulae for designing, and the accepted use of intuition—designing remains the only reason that we have an Artificial World in the first place. Automobiles do not make it to market without some very conscious planning, much like skyscrapers do not magically appear on our landscape. Consequently, the lack of

knowledge or understanding about designing should not deter us from attempting to understand designing. This is the next part in this chapter.

What Is Designing?
Agreeing on a definition of design and designing is a logical place to begin. However, it is also the first hurdle. Ask a hundred designers to define designing and you are most likely to receive more than a hundred definitions. Moreover, designers may not be the most appropriate sources for a definition. It is not unusual for experts to not see the forest for the trees. And designers are no different. They, too, are prone to this same type of myopia. Someone outside the profession is often better suited to bring an overarching view to a situation, and Herbert Simon, the American political scientist, was such an outside expert. His definition of design is broad yet simple and to the point. From Simon's perspective, "Everyone designs who devises courses of action aimed at changing existing situations into preferred ones."[iv] In this vein, designing is what made the first stone tool possible some 3.4 million years ago and what makes possible all everyday things in our world today.

In most respects, Simon's definition of designing embraces the phenomenon of the Artificial World in a way that goes well beyond many popular definitions found in the so-called design world. This is especially the case with many Modernist definitions over the last century. Modernist designers were sometimes prone to define design and designing within boundaries that, in retrospect, were narrow and perhaps limiting. More so, many of these definitions, especially the early ones, had a very strong connection to allied disciplines of design, such as painting, sculpture, and the fine arts.

Josef Albers, the German-born painter, proposed one of the first of these early Modernist definitions of designing. Albers was closely associated with the Bauhaus in Germany and taught there from 1923 to 1933. For him, designing was "to plan and to organize, to order, to relate, and to control." In retrospect, two of Albers's key words—*organize* and *control*—came to reflect very much the visual tone of Modernism, especially in architecture, graphic design, and industrial design. In this context, design was essentially about logic and rationalism. As a result, the ability to organize and to control the visual language became paramount.

Some forty years later, Bruce Archer proposed a definition of designing that went well beyond the one offered by Albers, if not in substance then certainly in detail. Archer's definition was more descriptive than Albers's. This may have been because Archer, a British engineer, felt obliged to articulate the nature of designing with precision and detail, as engineers are trained to do. For Archer, design was "a goal-seeking activity, in which a model or prescription is formulated in advance of embodiment of an artifact, which is offered as an apt and original solution to a given problem." Archer made clear that designing was a means to an end as the result of a deliberate process that resulted in a tangible artifact. Beyond these more objective qualities, Archer also acknowledged a more subjective side to design. Words such as *apt* and *original* addressed issues that could not easily be measured objectively. Something is apt and original

according to whom? As we know, absolutes rarely exist in designing.

Working at about the same time as Archer, Charles Eames, the internationally celebrated American designer, was more succinct in his definitions of designing, eliminating everything except what was essential for him. For Eames, one definition of designing was "a method of action"; another was, "Design depends largely on constraints." Clearly, the process and the overt challenges were at the heart of designing; nothing else appeared more important than the designing activity itself, including the limitations. The former was the antidote for the latter. Unlike the reverence that we sometimes have for design as a thing or an object, Albers, Archer, and Eames recognized that it was the designing activity that needed to be understood if we were ever to understand design as an everyday thing.

Intentionally or not, various design professions have also added to the definition of the word *design* by modifying the word with adjectives such as *architectural, interior, graphic* and, more recently, *sustainable, universal*, and *interactive*. Adjectives such as these help to narrow the scope of the meaning of the word *design*, which at times can appear to be limitless. Nevertheless, such combinations do not make it any easier to define design and designing. And neither does the regular use of the word *design* in everyday parlance; if anything, it only makes it more challenging. The word *design* has proliferated in our lexicon, language, advertising, manufacturing, and lifestyles. We read about designer garden tools or we go to design salons or we buy designer jeans. In many ways, the word *design* has gone from being specific and meaningful to vague and meaningless. So, what is designing?

Simon's definition of designing as the act of changing an existing situation to a preferred one is ideal if we wish to address designing as a phenomenon that goes well beyond some of its more obvious territories, such as graphics, architecture, and engineering. And, clearly, designing does go beyond these. The designing activities of the latter are only the thin edge of the wedge when designing is considered in a more holistic way. But Simon's definition is also in need of two provisos that may not be immediately apparent.

First, and as previously mentioned, designing is essentially a human activity and all humans have the capacity to design.[v] It is an error to believe that only a few gifted individuals can design. This belief is unfounded. Second, designing is a universal activity. Designing is not limited to the industrialized or developed countries of the world. Everyone designs everywhere. Consequently, and for the purpose of this book, designing is defined as a universal activity that humans undertake to find the means to deliberately change existing situations into preferred ones.

How Did Designing Evolve?
There is nothing new about designing. Designing has been a human activity from the earliest days of humanity and has helped define *homo habilis* (a term that translates as "handy man" in reference to the use of tools), the first species of the *Homo* genus to appear. Designing has allowed humanity to not only survive but

also to evolve over the last 3.4 million years or so. Humanity would not continue to exist on this planet without designing.

As noted above, the first manifestations of designing were simple stone tools, which were designed, made, and used by our earliest ancestors. These were the hunter-gatherers, who were the designers, makers, and users of their Artificial World. Everyday things were small and transportable, as would be most tools required by nomadic people. As for structures, it was whatever was found that served the purpose such as a cave, or if something had been designed it was portable. Nomads did not require permanent structures or shelters. And signs, which came much later, were often permanent and associated with a specific location or place. This combination of three distinct roles—designer, maker, and user—in the creation of everyday things—in our case, tools, structures, and signs—was at the heart of designing then and remains so even today. It is referred to as The Designing Triad and is explained in more detail below.

Significant societal shifts occurred when people evolved from hunter-gathers to farmers some time after 11,000 BCE. Over the next millennia, people generally ceased to move from one place to another and began to stay in the same locale. Understandably, these changes impacted the designing process and with it The Designing Triad. Two are particularly relevant. For one thing, everyday things no longer needed to be small or transportable. For similar reasons, structures or permanent shelters were created and with them the first examples of architecture as found in villages, towns, and cities.

Moreover, agrarian societies created something even more important: surplus food, something that did not exist for hunter-gatherers, who consumed everything they killed or picked almost immediately. However, farming was different. It often created a surplus. For example, more grain was produced than was needed by the individual farmer. This surplus had to be stored and preserved, leading to a need for containers of one kind or another. Furthermore, surpluses led to trade, first among local groups and eventually between far-flung empires. And along with trade, came outside influences and the exchange of ideas. With the agrarian lifestyle, no longer were the designer/maker/user the same person in The Designing Triad. The user became an entity separate and independent from the designer/maker. And, for the first time, the user neither designed nor made the artifact but still benefited from its availability. This was the first major shift in The Designing Triad.

The second shift—the one that would eventually separate designing from making—occurred with the Industrial Revolution. Over time, everyday things would no longer need a designer/maker, as had been the case with artisans prior to the Industrial Revolution. Designing and making would become separate functions along with using. Not surprisingly, there were certain benefits with the shift. For example, everyday things became more readily available because of the mass production enabled by machines and the distribution enabled by advances in transportation: thus began the consumer society. There were also some difficulties, including the exclusion of the designer from the designing process by most makers. This shift is probed in more depth in chapter 6.

The Designing Process Described

Designing is what is sometimes called a doing activity, an activity that is conditioned by two different actions that work in a complementary way. Thinking is one of these actions; in designing it usually manifests itself as a combination of deductive or inductive thinking. The other action is making. The making action involves the development of the thinking action into some form of artificial everyday thing or artifact, first as a model, then a prototype, and eventually a finished product—furniture, building, video game, or the interior of a restaurant.

However, designing as we know it can go well beyond the obvious, tangible artifacts. Business strategies and governing systems are also the result of a designing process. The thinking and the doing, it should be noted, do not evolve in a linear fashion but more in an iterative manner, not unlike a spiral. Based on this explanation, the designing process found in engineering, architecture, and design—three professions that, at first glance, may appear to be quite different—tend to be quite similar. Automobile transmissions, houses, and MP3 players may be very different in type and scale, but they all share a very similar designing process and, as we shall see below, similar features.

The first set of features in the designing process includes its three aforementioned participants: a designer, a maker, and a user. Designing always occurs as the result of the interaction among the three key participants. At one extreme, the designer, maker, and user are one and the same person, such as we find with a person who designs and builds a house to be used by his family. That person is the designer, maker, and user all in one. At the other extreme, the three participants can be very separate entities, such as an architect (the designer) who designs a house for a client (the user) who then has it constructed by a builder (the maker). Second, the designing process results in an everyday thing or an artifact—a product, an interior, a book, a strategy, a plan, or one of an infinite list of everyday things.

The artifact is the tangible result of the interaction of the designer, the maker, and the user. Lastly, the designing process always occurs in a context—that is, the design process evolves and is conditioned by place, culture, and time, factors well beyond those emanating directly from the designer, the maker, the user, or the artifact. Together, these features constitute The Designing Triad. (See Figure 1.10.)

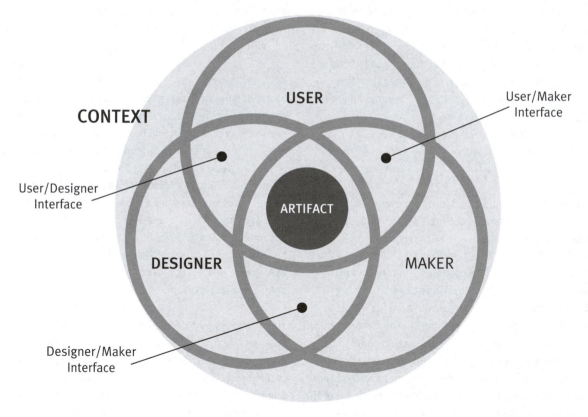

Figure 1.10: The Designing Triad

The Designer

The designer is often perceived to be a single individual but that is not always the case. The designer can just as easily be a team of designers or an interdisciplinary team of creative individuals. In such circumstances, the designer is more often than not anonymous. How many people know of Jonathan Ive or J Mays? We may not immediately recognize these two designers but we certainly know their designs—the iPod and the New Beetle, respectively. Ive is the vice president of design at Apple and responsible for the design of the iPod, iPhone, and iPad, as well as most other Mac products; Mays is vice president of design at Ford Motor Company and was a driving force behind the design of the New Beetle when he worked with Volkswagen. Both designers are totally unknown to most of the users of their award-winning products.

Some designers are more well known. Kmart and Target, for example, have made successful use of two celebrated designers, Martha Stewart and Michael Graves. Each has provided appropriate, albeit different design directions for these companies. The people who frequent Kmart and Target, or the users, are often aware of both designers. Some even go to these retail outlets because of Martha Stewart and Michael Graves.

The Maker

Like the designer, the maker can also be an individual. Jeweler and tailors, for example, are makers. But today most makers are companies—anything from small and local enterprises to very large and international conglomerates—that build or manufacture artifacts of all kinds and often in very large quantities. Some companies are very labor-intensive because only people can actually make the artifact. This is the case in interior design, home building, and construction, which remain essentially craft-based processes. The book-manufacturing and automotive industries, on the other hand, are just the opposite. Most of these operations are highly automated, and labor is kept to a minimum. The result is a making process that can print and bind books in minutes or assemble a complete car in less than twenty-four hours. In comparison, the average house can take months to build.

The maker need not be the actual manufacturer of the artifact. Retailers, such as large department stores, are often intermediaries to manufacturers, or makers, and, as part of the making chain, are considered makers. IKEA, the multinational Swedish furniture retailer, is an excellent case in point. It does not manufacture what it sells, although it designs most of it. IKEA finds manufacturers throughout the world to serve as makers.

The User

The Designing Triad is not complete without the user. The user is the person or persons for whom the artifact is designed. Users come in all ages, shapes, sizes, and dispositions. Determining the needs and wants of the users, let alone their likes and dislikes, is a formidable challenge for both the designer and the maker. Fortunately, most users are the ones who will own or use the everyday thing. This can make the designing and making tasks of the designer and maker somewhat easier than when the end user is not the purchaser. Someone buying a car or a chair, for example, will most likely drive the car or sit in the chair. But that is not always the case. The user is not always the primary purchaser. Such is the case with the grandparent buying a toy for a grandchild or an airline purchasing an airplane. In the first case, the grandchild is the eventual user, much like the passenger is the eventual user for the airline in the second case. When designing, the designer must incorporate both levels of use—as purchaser as well as end user.

The Context

Designing always occurs in a context. In The Designing Triad, the context is the combination of factors that conditions the designing process and, by extension, the artifact and the actions of the designer, the maker, and the user. The context is the ground in what is sometimes called a figure/ground relationship, that is, everyday things are merely figures on a larger background. The letters on this page, for example, are the figures; the page is the ground. The two are interdependent. Much the same phenomenon exists with everyday things. They are the figures and the context is the ground. More importantly, everyday things can never exist outside of a context.

The context has two facets, one explicit, and another more implicit. The explicit context of an everyday thing consists of its tangible features, or those properties that we perceive when we recognize an everyday thing, such as its shape, form, color, material, and texture. There are others, but together they provide the necessary clues to distinguish a pick-up truck from a church. We call these facets the micro-contextual factors.

The implicit facets are the macro-contextual factors. They are not immediately visible in the everyday thing but are its intangible features. Context is explained in more detail below.

The Artifact

Lastly, the artifact is the everyday thing to which we keep referring. It is the result of the design process. The artifact can be big or small, precious or common, one-of-a-kind or one of multiple copies. The possible attributes are infinite. Artifacts can be tools, buildings or communication systems. In every case, they are the artificial inventions made by people as they change an existing situation into a preferred one. For the purpose of our study, artifacts will be tangible everyday things that fall into the categories of tools, structures, and signs. These three categories are explained further in chapter 3.

The Dynamics of The Designing Triad

The five constituent features of The Designing Triad operate in a specific fashion. The Designer, the Maker, and the User are the three participants, hence the triad; these three participants will be regularly identified throughout the book by the use of initial capital letters in their names. The goal of the designing activity is the Artifact, or everyday thing; and the activity always occurs in Context. These five elements manage to work in concert because of a catalyst, and that catalyst is human needs and wants. The latter is discussed further in the next chapter.

As critical as the elements of The Designing Triad are, it is the interfaces—that is, the interaction between and among the various elements—that provide a deeper understanding of the designing process itself. These interfaces exist in three separate sets. The first set includes the interfaces between and among the three active participants—that is, the Designer, the Maker, and the User; the second set includes the interfaces between the Context and the Artifact; and the third set includes the interfaces between the Artifact and each one of the participants.

The Designer/Maker/User Interfaces

The Designer/Maker/User interfaces are those that occur between any two of the participants. There are three such combinations: Designer/Maker; Designer/User; and Maker/User. Of course, when the Designer, Maker, and User are one and the same person, the interfaces are essentially seamless and almost impossible to discern. A person designing and making a bookshelf for personal use will normally play the role of the Designer/Maker/User interdependently and not independently. The interchange between one role and another generally occurs in an unstructured and informal way. Nevertheless, there is a definitive result in the end—a bookshelf is designed, made, and used—although it may be difficult to explain exactly how the designing actually happened.

The designing process becomes more evident and subsequently more describable when two separate participants are involved. At a basic level, it may be simple instructions voiced by the Designer to the Maker; in a more complex situation, those same instructions may be engineering drawings for a new gas turbine. In both cases, the communication principle is the same; the execution and deliverable, of course, are quite different.

The three scenarios that follow will focus on those situations in which the participants—Designer, Maker, and User—are separate and independent entities.

The Designer/Maker Interface. Under almost all circumstances, there are only two kinds of interfaces between the Designer and Maker. The Designer is either in a direct relationship with the Maker, such as an engineer employed by Boeing, the aircraft corporation, or in an indirect relationship, such as the role played by an architect as a consultant to a developer. In the former circumstance, the Designer is employed by the Maker and therefore acts accordingly, balancing the functions of designing with the corporate obligations of the company. Much the same would exist for an exhibit designer working as an employee for a cosmetic company or a graphic designer for a publishing house. The interface in which the Designer acts as a consultant is just the opposite, that is, the Designer has an indirect relationship with the Maker. Most architects and interior designers, for example, act as consultants when they receive a commission to design a building or renovate an interior. They act in the best interest of the Maker but are independent design agents.

The Designer/User Interface. The Designer/User interface is the connection between people who design everyday things and people who use them. In most designing circumstances, the connection is one way—that is, it is essentially about the Designer seeking information about the User because the Designer aims to satisfy the needs and wants of the User. Three significant features condition this Designer/User interface.

First, the Designer/User interface is most often anonymous. There is no identifiable person or individual User, nor is there a continuous contact between the Designer and User. The design of a Web site is a good case in point. The Designer has no idea who the specific visitor or User will be at any given time, although there is often a general sense of who the User should be. Furthermore, the Designer has no control over who will visit the site. In order to compensate for this anonymity, it is not unusual for the Designer to become informed about the User by way of demographics or other statistical information. This is the second feature of the Designer/User interface. It implies a statistical interface in which a User profile is based upon analyses found in marketing techniques or other survey methods. Third, there are occasions when the User can participate more directly with the Designer in the designing process. This is a sampling interface and occurs in circumstances when a new everyday thing can be tested in a specific market, for example, or when a new everyday thing can be evaluated by the use of focus groups or by way of surveys.

It is important to note that there are situations in which the interface between the Designer and the User is a two-way street. This is certainly the case when an architect meets regularly with a client in the design of a private home or when an interior designer develops the design for a restaurant directly with its owner.

The Maker/User Interface. The remaining interface in The Designing Triad is the Maker/User interface—that is, the relationship between the Maker of the everyday thing and its User. Certain features—four of which are particularly significant—condition this interface.

There is an economic interface, which is awareness by both the Maker and the User that the price or cost of an everyday thing is both relevant and pertinent. Most people acquire everyday things with a clear appreciation of their cost, and manufacturers are keenly aware of this feature. Consequently, many everyday things are available in different cost brackets. Digital cameras come to mind as an example. Prices can vary significantly depending on size, image resolution, and other features.

Second, there is a distribution interface. Everyday things are only meaningful if they are available. Quite obviously, Users cannot acquire everyday things if they are not available. Consequently, making everyday things available to the User becomes an essential challenge for the Maker. Imagine what would have happened on June 29, 2007 if the first iPhone had not reached the retail outlets to be available for sale.

The third interface is marketing, which is somewhat similar to the statistical and sampling interfaces with the Designer/User. Whereas the latter is focused more on the needs and wants of the individual User, the marketing interface between the Maker and the User involves knowledge of the marketing environment for the everyday thing, usually identified by way of demographic studies and other methods of analysis such as spending patterns or disposable incomes of Generation X-ers or Baby Boomers.

Lastly, there is a marketplace interface—that is, the clear understanding by the Maker that the decision to acquire an everyday thing is almost always a democratic one, and that it comes as a direct result of a free choice by the User. In general, Makers understand this interface very well, but Designers often do not. At times, there remains a strong desire by Designers to prescribe an everyday thing to the User. This approach is rarely successful in the mass market, although it can happen in the niche markets where Users can be influenced greatly by one trend-setting Designer or other. Fashion design is especially prone to this tendency.

The Context/Artifact Interfaces

In The Designing Triad, the Context is the ground and the Artifact is the figure in the figure/ground relationship previously mentioned. As a result, it is neither unusual nor indeed surprising to find that Artifacts are the embodiment of contextual values. More often than not, these values exist as a combination of explicit and implicit qualities in the Artifact. It is these contextual values—some tangible and others not—that give the everyday thing its visible qualities.

There are two significant types of influencing factors in the Context. As mentioned, one type is explicit, and is referred to as the micro-contextual factors in design. These factors appear as the visible and tangible features, and are normally associated with physical properties of a design such as its color, material, shape, and form. Chairs are excellent examples of Artifacts visibly conditioned by micro-contextual factors. Chairs can be big or small (scale), hard or soft (texture), residential or office (function), wood or plastic (material), and bright or dull (color). (See Figure 1.11.) All of these properties are visible and tangible. They also provide the chair with a general classification or visual identity. For example, we can easily differentiate between a chair and a stool because

of their respective micro-contextual factors much like we can tell the difference between an office chair and a patio chair for the same reasons.

The other type of contextual factors is macro-contextual. These factors are implicit and not immediately visible or even discernible. Typically, these factors are intangible and appear as reflections of value systems such as culture, place (geography and climate), and time or era. The design properties of an Artifact can be greatly influenced depending on whether it is local, national, or global in character because each one of these macro-contexts creates a set of very special design challenges. There is a significant difference between designing an Artifact meant only for a local market and one meant for global consumption. South Korea, for example, produces wonderful ceramic pots or jars for the preparation and storage of *kimchi*, a traditional cabbage dish that is a trademark of Korean cuisine. The Artifacts associated with the making of *kimchi* address a market that is very localized. Place these same pots in a different market, such as the United States, and they become meaningless to the majority of the population no matter how well designed they are. And rightly so. After all, *kimchi* is unknown to the majority of Americans. Appropriateness at the local level does not necessarily translate into appropriateness at the global level. Sometimes it does, but most often it does not. And it is these differences that can contribute to the macro-contextual features of an everyday thing.

Designer/User/Maker and Artifact Interfaces

The interfaces described so far provide a first level of understanding of the designing process. As important as they are, it is equally important to understand the interfaces that exist between the Artifact, on the one hand, and the Designer, the Maker, and the User, on the other. It is at this level that many of the features that define the Artifact are revealed. These revelations occur in three different interfaces.

The Designer/Artifact Interface. The Designer/Artifact interface, the first of these interfaces, includes the features that make it possible for the Designer to design in the first place. This interface has two significant components. The first is design knowledge—that is, a set of theoretically based skills that underpin the validity of the design. These can range from design history and human factors to psychology and mechanics. The second is design skills—that is, the kinesthetic ability that a Designer possesses to take the design from idea to reality. Broadly speaking, design skills include creative thinking, visualization, and model simulation. More specifically, they also include skills such as sketching, mechanical drawing, model making, and computer-aided design. The design of an Artifact cannot easily occur if the Designers do not possess the appropriate knowledge and skills.

The Maker/Artifact Interface. The interface that exists between the Maker and the Artifact is the interface that defines the actual making or production of the Artifact or everyday thing. Yet, it excludes, at least in any meaningful way, issues that are driven essentially by either the Designer or User. The Maker/Artifact Interface has four features that are particularly significant.

First, the Maker must be aware of a resource interface, both in terms of the availability of materials with which to make the Artifact and the requisite level of skills to produce the Artifact. Resources, both materials and skills, are indispensable in all Artifact production. Next, the Maker must contend with a production interface, or the available technology to undertake the making of the Artifact. Materials and a labor pool are only two ingredients in the making process. It is technology of one kind or another that provides the synergy of production from one-off, labor intensive manufacturing of certain exclusive Artifacts to highly automated factories almost bereft of workers for everyday things made in millions. The Maker must also be aware of a User-need interface—that is, the market profile that must be satisfied. This is a third feature of the Maker/Artifact interface. There is no reason to make anything unless there is a User need. Moreover, the better that the User need is defined, the more likely is the chance for success. And in our case, success goes back to the definition of designing—that is, the act of changing an existing situation to a preferred one. Lastly, there is an availability interface that relates to the effectiveness of the distribution system for the Artifact. This has become an important issue as more and more everyday things are designed in one country, made in a second, and sold in a third.

The User/Artifact Interface. The third interface in this group is the User/Artifact interface. It has four significant features, all focused on the direct and indirect relationship between the User and the Artifact. The first of these is a physical interface—that is, the physical fit between the User and the Artifact. Those everyday things that come into close contact with a User, such as door handles or personal floatation devices, must physically and measurably fit a person. In such cases, Designers revert to the study of anthropometrics to determine the optimum physical fit between the User and the Artifact. Similarly, there is a psychological interface. This interface is sometimes referred to as User friendliness—or not—of an Artifact. In this situation, ergonomics and human behavior serve as sources of knowledge and understanding for the Designer. A third interface is a personal one, that is, the emotional connection that a User may develop for an Artifact. Some people develop what would appear to be an illogical bond to an Artifact, such as an old sweatshirt or a ratty pair of bedroom slippers, but do so based on some personal and very real rationale. Lastly, there is a social interface, that is, the cultural identity that an Artifact creates for a User of that cultural group. The use of a Blackberry mobile phone tells a great deal about its User in much the same way that the riding of Harley-Davidsons by weekend Users does. In the end, we are what we use.

Summary

What is evidently clear in the information provided is that designing is a human activity that is natural and universal. People have been designing since the first stone tool, and it is designing that has permitted people to evolve from hunter-gatherers to the developed societies of today by way of the agrarian age and industrialization. Along the way, people transitioned from being Designer/Maker/User to three separate but interdependent entities. As significant as this transition was, the designing process—at least in principle—did not change radically. People were still doing what they had to in order to change an existing situation to a preferred one via the designing process.

The revelation that everyone designs comes as a surprise for most people because the designing process is generally unknown or, worse, is perceived as a form of black magic or other obscure activity imbued with mystery. Ask people how most of their everyday things came to be and the word 'designing' will most likely not be uttered. The situation is not unlike the one in which a child asked where milk comes from responds, "From the Safeway store." Clearly, the cow is no longer part of the production process.

Designing generally occurs in a process that is inclusive, comprehensive, and, more often than not, transparent. Yet, designing is not a formula. It is not an equation, with known variables and with the promise of consistent results and success. It is a human activity that includes with it all manner of variables and foibles that are typical of human activities.

With The Designing Triad, we have the basis for a better understanding of the designing process. We have the three active participants—the Designer, the Maker, and the User; we also have the Artifact, which is the end result of the Designer/Maker/User interaction; and we know that the interaction always occurs in Context in a process that is fueled by human needs and wants. By observing and analyzing the interaction of these components, we can develop a clearer image of this human activity, which may be universal in scope but which is also misunderstood and sometimes not even acknowledged.

Further Reading

Basalla, George. *The Evolution of Technology.*
Giard, Jacques. *Design FAQs.*
Rybczynski, Witold. *Home.*
Simon, Herbert. *The Sciences of the Artificial.*

Endnotes

[i] Basalla, *The Evolution of Technology.*

[ii] The stone tool may be the first designed everyday thing but whether it was deliberately designed remains an unanswered question. Some experts have suggested that the designer of the first stone tool did not yet have the mental capacity to do it with deliberate intent.

[iii] The Gossamer Albatross, a human-powered, heavier-than-air craft, was one of few successful planes of this type. In 1979, it made its way across the English Channel.

[iv] Simon, Herbert, *The Sciences of the Artificial.*

[v] In principle, animals do not design, although some activities, such as the use of straws by chimpanzees to collect ants, come quite close, at least in practice.

CHAPTER 2

How We Come to Know Everyday Things

Intellectually understanding interfaces in a diagram such as The Designing Triad is one thing; understanding how anyone manages to integrate the complexities of society into their lives is something quite different. At first glance, it is nothing less than amazing. After all, societies are enormously complex systems with equally complex sub-systems such as culture, language, social norms, belief systems, value sets, and laws, to name but a few. Fortunately, most of us never consciously ponder the challenge. The integration is natural and seamless, to a point that we are never really aware of it.

We only realize that the integration is challenging when we find ourselves in a foreign country for the first time. How, we ask ourselves, can people communicate using such a strange language? Or, how do these people manage to drive on the other side of the road without having any accidents? Or, how in the world can people eat with chopsticks? In every case, the answers are quite obvious. They, like us, have learned their social system from birth and over time. As a result, it is familiar, logical, correct, and serves its purpose. We, of course, perceive it as strange, illogical, wrong, and complex because we had to absorb it almost instantaneously whereas they did gradually over time.

Yet despite these formidable hurdles, people routinely address, navigate, reject, accept, and deal with an almost infinite list of issues every day. It would not be considered unusual, for example, for a person to face tasks ranging from turning off an alarm clock, preparing breakfast, showering, and getting dressed, then driving to the airport to catch a flight for a cross-country trip before starting another series of unrelated tasks upon arrival. Most people are not fazed by such challenges and confront them on a regular basis, sometimes daily. We deal with these and other complexities in a habitual way because, from birth, we have gradually become adept at it and have learned how to integrate these tasks into our lives. Driving a car, for example, is an extremely complex task. Understanding the act of driving—the hand-eye coordination required, the mechanics of the vehicle, how it functions—is daunting, to say the least. And then there are the rules of the road, including the infinite number of situations that can occur when driving. Given this complexity, it is quite remarkable that so many people learn to drive and learn as easily as they do. What we have come to realize is that everyone is born with the capacity to do many things but no one can do them at birth. In the case of driving, we must learn how to do it and to integrate the complexity of driving into our lives.

Driving is only one of many skills that we learn as we attempt to integrate ourselves into the world. There are many other skills, of course, such as reading, writing, and designing. The capacities for these skills have evolved over millions of years as humanity created an Artificial World within a natural one. Everything begins with the Natural World, but our existence and evolution is very much predicated on the Artificial World that we design. Central to this integration are three significant tools that make the integration process possible: learning, communication, and, as a sub-set of communication, the visual language. Each is dealt with in separate sections in this chapter.

Learning
There aren't enough pages in this book to uncover the mysteries of human learning let alone the knowledge that underpins the learning process. We already know a great deal about learning—through the works of J. Piaget, B. F. Skinner, and J. Dewey, to name but three significant pioneers, as well as the schools of learning

known as the behavioral/objectivist approach and the constructivist/cognitive approach. And the future holds promises for further developments especially as the result of research in neuroscience. Consequently, our goal at this point will be to focus on those aspects of learning and cognition that help to demystify design.

Three particular styles of learning are relevant to the task at hand: visual learning, or learning by seeing; auditory learning, or learning by hearing; and kinesthetic learning, or learning by doing. No one learns exclusively through one style; we all learn by combining these and other learning styles in our own individual way.

Visual learning occurs through images of one kind or another that provide information and ideas. The adage "A picture is worth a thousand words" is an acknowledgment of the power implicit in visual learning.

Auditory learning is learning by way of what is heard, such as the spoken word. This is how we learn when someone provides us verbal instructions or when we attend a lecture.

The kinesthetic learning style is familiar to all of us because it is how we all learned to swim, ride a bicycle, sew, play an instrument, and hundreds of other things we know how to do. No one learns how to ride a bike by being shown videos of people doing it or by listening to lectures on the topic. We learned by having our parents prop us up, coach us on how to keep pedaling, and then let go. We fell, got up again, and fell again. We did this several dozen times and eventually got the hang of it.

This kind of learning, which regularly happens throughout our lives, is learning by doing. Studio education in design schools, for example, is essentially kinesthetic learning.

Most scientists and psychologists are in agreement that different thinking functions reside in the two different hemispheres of the brain. Generally speaking, the left hemisphere deals with tasks that are rational, logical, and sequential. It is the part of the brain that provides an analytical function and that brings objectivity to our world. When we perceive the world via the left hemisphere, parts appear to be more important than the whole. The right hemisphere is just the opposite. Its capacity is to deal with randomness and issues that are more intuitive and subjective. Consequently, the right hemisphere is good at synthesizing and perceiving the whole rather than the parts.

The right hemisphere/left hemisphere phenomenon lends credence to the combination of intuitive and logical thinking exhibited by most people. Our right hemisphere is more involved in the intuitive thinking that we often associate with creative people such as artists and designers, whereas the left hemisphere is dominant for engineers, scientists, and others whose forte is logical thinking. Fortunately, most people are neither exclusively intuitive nor exclusively logical in their thinking style but combine the two, although they tend to lean toward one or the other.

Edward de Bono, the renowned expert on thinking, offered an insightful explanation of how we learn.[i] He compared the accumulation of learning experiences in the brain—especially how we deal with recurring stimuli—to something like the action of a small stream of hot water on a mass of gelatin. As each one of us undergoes an experience or is affected by a stimulus of one kind or another, the stream of hot water creates a channel in the gelatin. The first time a channel is created, it is very shallow. But repetition of the same experience or stimulus makes the channel progressively deeper. Completely new experiences create new channels, and experiences that share a combination of experiences create cross channels. Over time, the brain becomes striated with these channels, partially explaining why we tend to act and think in ways that have been conditioned by the past.

In the end, we integrate the existing world, both natural and artificial, into our lives and do so by various means of learning, some understood but others not quite so. More importantly, however, we learn to interact with the Natural and Artificial Worlds, thereby not only surviving but also evolving—as individuals as well as a society.

Communication

The desire to understand learning almost logically leads to the need to understand communication because a great deal of what we learn we do by way of communication. After all, communication—certainly verbal communication—has been part of human history going back some 200,000 years. Visual communication came quite a bit later, first with symbols and then with writing.

Evidence of symbols dates back 30,000 years whereas writing occurred about 5,500 years ago. The essential difference between the two—that is, verbal and visual communication—is the longevity of the message. Verbal communication depends a great deal on human memory, which is not always reliable over time. Visual communication is different. It provides a record that is much more permanent. Petroglyphs, which are signs etched in stone, are very permanent, and remain in place for many generations. As for writing, this became the most accurate and definitive form of communication if we consider its longevity. There are books, such as the Bible, that go back thousands of years. Based on this evidence alone, it is quite obvious that learning and communication are closely intertwined.

So, what is communication? In its most basic form, communication is signal transmission, that is, it is a signal that is created, sent, received, and responded to. The world is, of course, full of signals and each one of us has learned to react to them. Those signals that we know are easy to deal with and we react accordingly. Those that we don't know we learn and add to our repertoire. For example, no one is born with the knowledge that a red traffic light means that we must come to a stop. In fact, we do not even know what a traffic light is. We act appropriately in the presence of both the light and the color because we have learned what is meant by the combination of traffic light and red. Television signals are also examples of communication, in this case, telecommunication. A television signal is created, then transmitted, received, and becomes a program that we choose to watch or not to watch on a television set.

Described as such, the communication process appears simple enough. However, there are pitfalls. For example,

communication can fail because the transmission fails or is not received as sent or is not understood as created. The latter, what is called the response, is particularly critical in the communication process because it reflects the level of effectiveness. And to be effective, a communication signal must be understood by its User in the same way that it was meant by its Designer, but this is not always the case. Many things can occur to make the communication process less than successful, not the least of which may be the Designer's inability to communicate the message in the first place. This is especially the case with visual communication. It's one thing for the average User to be visually challenged; it is quite another for a Designer to be incapable of communicating effectively via the visual language. (Communication and the visual language will be discussed later in this chapter.)

Everyday things are also media of communication. They, too, are a form of signal transmission. However, this fact may not be immediately apparent, primarily because the prime intent of their design was not communication per se. Generally, we have learned how to read the signals in everyday things by what is called accretion. We certainly did not learn to read the signals theoretically. As a result, we understand the meaning of these everyday things and do not give them a second thought. For example, people rarely confuse a pick-up truck with a church. (See Figure 2.1.) We see both and immediately know which is which. Why is that? In part, it is because both are so visually different. They just don't look the same and we recognize that visual difference. The truck moves but the church doesn't. The truck is smaller than the church. The church has a steeple but the truck has wheels. In fact, we can even differentiate between the two by merely looking at photographs or pictograms of each. We never have to see an actual pick-up truck or church to tell the difference. Only in our wildest dreams would we confuse one for the other. The difference is visual and discernible, which is why we can tell the difference not only between pick-up trucks and the churches but also between all kinds of other everyday things.

The visual identity found in all everyday things has communicative properties. It is how we distinguish one everyday thing from another and also how we recognize one person from another. Admittedly, everyone has two eyes, a nose, and a mouth. But those features alone do not help us to tell one person from another. What does help are specific visual qualities that these features possess—blue eyes or a button nose or full lips or any imaginable permutation. These are the features that make each one of us look different. Even very young babies recognize their parents strictly by visual cues and at a very early age. This innate capacity has made it possible for human beings to develop an uncanny ability to learn subtle visual differences, an aptitude that is not only useful for survival but also powerful for human evolution. Imagine, for one moment, the variety of different visual stimuli encountered by the average person in a day, let alone in a year or in a lifetime. It numbers in the thousands if not the millions. Clearly, the pervasiveness and potency of visual communication should never be underestimated.

It's at this point that we realize how skillful people have become at interpreting correctly one image from another

amidst this visual onslaught. And it takes so little to interpret correctly one visual image from another. Look at one of the many out-of-focus photos on a Web site, some badly pixilated and others with inaccurate colors. Despite this technically erroneous information, most of us are able to quickly and easily recognize Queen Latifah from Queen Elizabeth. How is this achieved? The process is a highly complex psycho-neurological one that involves vision, the brain, and perception. For our purpose, however, the psycho-neurological details are not essential. What is more important is knowing how we learn the visual differences in everyday things and how we make sense of them as part of our survival skills.

The process of learning to detect visual differences is a very gradual one. It begins not long after we open our eyes for the first time as newborns and continues until we close them for the last time. Two features of this process are noteworthy. First, we learn to see our worlds even though we have vision at birth. That is, our ability to recognize among infinite visual differences is learned. That may not seem obvious at first but think of it. Can a baby recognize the visual differences between the pick-up truck and the church mentioned earlier? No chance! Over time, the baby will have to learn the visual difference in order to distinguish between the various makes of pick-up trucks and the various denominations of churches.

The second feature is how we learn to see. No child receives regular lessons in the many ways to see things, either at home or at school. As already mentioned, the ability to see occurs in a less structured way and more by what is called accretion learning—that is, a type of learning that is gradual, at times conscious but often not, and for which we are usually unaware. As a side note, accretion learning can account for up to 70% of what we know, which begs the question "Why aren't we teaching the art of seeing in schools?" (Vision and seeing are both discussed further in the section on visual literacy.)

Communications Theory

Several communication theories are based on four principal components or variables: a message; an output or transmission; an input or reception; and a response. Furthermore, the four components tend to operate in a linear fashion—that is, a message is created, transmitted, received, and responded to, in that order. The communication is deemed to be successful when the response matches the message. The closer the match, the better the communication; the opposite, however, is deemed to be a failure in communication.

The four variables of the communication process can produce various scenarios. Four are particularly significant for Designers and in understanding the designing process. (See Figure 2.2.)

Scenario One: The message is sent and means the same thing to receiver and sender. This is a case of successful communication and occurs when the User understands the everyday thing as it was intended. The response matches the message.

Scenario Two: The message is sent but not received; for some reason, there has been a breakdown in

communication. In designing, this scenario can occur when an everyday thing is designed but subsequently canceled or not made.

Scenario Three: The message is sent and received but means nothing to the User. This is particularly common in cases in which designs express the ideals and beliefs of the Designers in their language rather than in the language of the Users. If the Designer persists in using a totally unfamiliar visual language, such as was the case with visual elements found in Postmodernism, then the breakdown in communications is more apparent.[ii] For example, some designs of the Postmodernist genre purposely avoided the generic look that people had come to associate with many everyday things. To the average User, Gaetano Pesce's sofa, *Sunset in New York*, did not immediately appear to be a sofa, or at least not what Users had learned to expect was a sofa. (See Figure 2.3.) It had neither an obvious place to sit nor an obvious back for support. Rather, it was a collection of four fabric-covered geometrical volumes that vaguely looked like a child's drawing of buildings and something that could be interpreted as a setting sun. In very few ways does Pesce's piece of furniture visually communicate the essence of a sofa. This does not mean, however, that Pesce's design is useless or without purpose or that it cannot be appreciated. But as a communication device—and design is, after all, a form of communication—the average User can easily misunderstand his design.

Scenario Four: This scenario is a variation of Scenario Three but instead of meaning nothing to the User, the message is interpreted in a way that is contrary to the

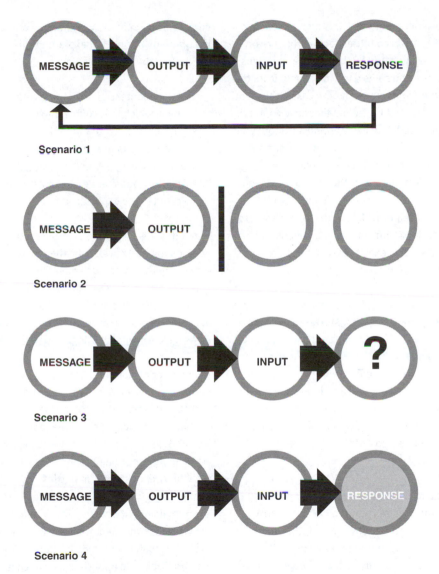

Figure 2.2: Simple Communication Process and Four Scenarios.

meaning the Designer intended. For example, building codes in many European countries require that fire or emergency exits be indicated by the use of green signs; in the United States, the signs used to communicate the same message are red or green. In both cases, the identical message is being sent but colors that have contradictory meanings are used. Red generally means stop; green means go. (See Figure 2.4.) An equally hazardous situation can arise when the color yellow accompanies a graphic image of a lemon on a bottle of lemon-scented bleach. There have been cases of people accidentally sipping the liquid. Their error was in the logical association of the color yellow with lemons and lemons with lemonade. These are two examples of serious breakdowns in design communication.

In the end, visual communications of one kind or another assail us every day. For Designers, Makers, and Users alike, there should be only one matter of concern: how effective is the communication? This concern was most likely the motivation behind early petroglyphs and remains the motivation behind today's high-tech communication methods. What has changed over time is the variety and complexity of visual communication and, consequently, the increased potential for error or miscommunication.

Communication and Context

Although the principles of communications theory could appear to be contextually neutral, this is not the case. Edward T. Hall, the American cultural anthropologist, discussed the nature of context in communication. His theory of high- and low-context communication deals with implicit and explicit codes in communication. Hall explained this contextual variable in the following way:

> A high-context (HC) communication or message is one in which most of the information is either in the physical context or internalized in the person, while very little is in the coded, explicit, transmitted part of the message. A low-context (LC) communication is just the opposite; i.e., the mass of the information is vested in the explicit code.[iii]

Defined in this rather academic way, Hall's theory appears to be removed from the practice of design and consequently not of much direct benefit to Designers. This is not the case. Certain public monuments clearly illustrate the phenomenon of HC and LC communication in design, and provide yet another example of implicit messages in everyday things.

When American architect Maya Lin designed the Vietnam Veterans Memorial wall in Washington, D.C. in 1982, she created an HC message. (See Figure 2.5.) Nothing in her design concept—a buried black granite wall and discreet inscriptions—explicitly expressed the visual images normally associated with war, especially the violence, destruction, patriotism, heroism, and human tragedy of war. Implicitly, however, these meanings remained but occurred in the minds and hearts of the visitors to the memorial. The meanings did not have to be the result of overt visual statements. This is exactly what Hall calls the implicit code, which is indicative of HC communication.

The adjoining memorial erected several years later is quite a different story. It is very explicit in its message. Its true-to-life depiction of three soldiers leaves very little to the viewer's imagination. It replicates many well-known images of war—guns, bullets, and uniforms. For Hall, this monument is an example of LC communication. The message resides explicitly in the design of the statue.

It is not necessary to ask if these same phenomena of HC and LC communication are present in everyday things. They are, most definitely. In fact, everyday things can easily be considered a form of complex visual language. The term language is used because of the multitude of visual signals and codes found in everyday things. By using design elements and principles—color, shape, form, space, emphasis, variety, and other design attributes—simple or complex messages can be communicated, albeit sometimes in discreet and subtle ways. Furthermore, visual signals are also analogous to language because they are capable of manipulation—much like words in a sentence and sentences in a paragraph. Considered in such linguistic terms, the Designer composes (or designs) a message (or everyday things); in turn, the Maker publishes (or manufactures) the text (or everyday thing); and the User reads (or selects) and understands (or uses) the everyday things.

Over the last few decades, there has been some development in visual communication theory focused on the adaptation of devices in written language to design, including the application of semiotics, semantics, and rhetoric to everyday things. These developments have provided a better comprehension of the visual language and have enhanced our understanding of visual literacy. The pictogram, a simplified two-dimensional image with a very specific meaning, is an excellent example of a visual language that plays a role similar to that of the written language. Pictograms provide a visual solution in situations where there is no guarantee that everyone understands the same written language. The countries of Europe were among the first to recognize the logic of the modern pictographic system. Given their dozen or so different national languages, it made sense to develop a highway signage system, for example, based on a shared and mutually understood visual language. This commonsense approach has since found favor in international airports, train stations, bus stations, and sports arenas the world over. All of these venues must deal with the challenge of communicating basic information to Users coming from many different language groups. Misunderstood signs could create all kinds of problems, from social embarrassment to outright physical danger.

Of course, the pictogram can provide effective communication only if the viewer knows the meaning. For example, the silhouette of a man or woman normally signifies a toilet, the letter P denotes parking, and so on. Over time, people have learned the meaning of these pictograms in their native country and know the meaning when they see them in a different country. It was for such a reason that the International Olympic Committee approved a set of pictograms for the 1972 Olympic Games in Munich and for all subsequent

Olympic events. The idea was to develop one visual language and make it standard at all Olympic games in order to create a common basis for effective communication. This approach made sense because only one visual language needed to be learned by participants and officials coming from scores of countries. Unfortunately, the pictograms were abandoned a few decades after their inception. Host countries were once again allowed to create pictograms unique to one Olympic event. The change more or less defeated the fundamental logic of pictograms as a common visual language understood by everyone, as originally envisaged.

Overall, pictograms have proven to be an effective way of communicating a specific message when the use of normal written languages is neither appropriate nor effective. To use Hall's terminology, pictograms become an explicit code and a form of LC communication in which personal interpretation is ideally nonexistent. Amusingly, certain pictograms can become outdated when changes, such as technology, evolve faster than the appropriateness of the visual language itself. In Europe, for example, railway crossings and other rail functions are often signified by the use of a graphic image representing steam-powered locomotives irrespective of the fact that such vehicles have not been in service for decades. However, people have learned the meaning of the pictogram and react accordingly, whether they have ever seen a steam locomotive or not.

Like two-dimensional designs, three-dimensional designs can also be a form of HC and LC communication. Such is the case with many Modernist everyday things, which are often excellent examples of LC communication. After all, one of the principal tenets of Modernism was the clear demonstration of function, as professed in such proverbs as "form follows function" or "less is more." The Designers who adhered to these principles produced so-called logical, or rational, solutions that allowed the uninitiated User to understand immediately the everyday thing in question—its function, its use, its operation, even its servicing. For many Modernists, anything less than this unambiguous message was considered a failure. Moreover, the understanding was supposed to be universal—at least that was what was implied by the moniker of the so-called International Style. Its very title suggests a movement whose designs would possess qualities that would transcend local boundaries and conditions. In retrospect, the assumption of *internationalism*—that is, a visual language both recognizable and meaningful internationally—was naïve, presumptuous, and perhaps pretentious. It failed to understand and respect other different yet valid cultures and value systems. For instance, people in the West may have difficulties in appreciating Islamic art, not because Islamic art is inferior to Western art but principally because Westerners do not know it well. And much the same can be said about the International Style. At best, it was a Northern European style, and not international at all. Its ethos was very much a reflection of northern European values. (See Figure 2.6.)

At the other extreme, most Postmodernist designs do not readily communicate the function of everyday things or even their typology. For a variety of valid reasons, they are often examples of HC communication. The chairs of Gaetano Pesce, the aforementioned Italian Designer, fit into this category very well. (See Figure 2.3.) Earlier, Pesce's sofa as a caricature of a setting sun on the New York skyline was offered as an example of an everyday thing that does not effectively communicate the essence of what we consider a sofa, at least not in traditional terms. Many of Pesce's other chairs are not always immediately recognized for what they are. However, that was never Pesce's intention. As such, his designs are more akin to HC communication and, like abstract art, the exact message of the communication is left to viewers to interpret as they wish. Pesce never intended to use LC communication in his designs. If many ways, his chairs are artistic expressions, for which, as we all know, beauty is in the eyes of the beholder.

Much the same can be said about HC and LC communication and the examples of the pick-up truck and church provided earlier in this chapter. The pick-up truck is a mixture of explicit and implicit communication. Two pick-up trucks may each have a V-8 engine, two doors, and four wheels but implicitly they can afford very different interpretations. General Motors makes the Chevrolet Colorado/GMC Canyon, a stereotypical mid-size pick-up truck with all the requisite visual attributes typical for such a vehicle. Place an intimidating paramilitary costume on the same frame, V-8 engine, four doors, and four wheels and you have the H3 Hummer, a vehicle that implicitly signals something very different from the agricultural image in the Colorado or Canyon. (See Figure 2.7.) And the church, with its steeple and the cross, provides an explicit signal. It communicates that this building is a

place of worship. However, there is also an implicit message, with a greater and more complex meaning. Among other things, it alludes to belief in one deity or another, adherence to certain rules, and codes of behavior. We immediately know or at least make assumptions about people when we learn which church they go to, and very little of that information is found in the explicit code of a building with a steeple on top.

In this same vein, there is probably no finer example of a sign having a combination of both HC and LC communication than the swastika. For many people in the West, especially those with vivid recollections of Adolf Hitler and the Third Reich, the swastika stood for some of the worst atrocities the world has ever seen. The swastika appeared on the flags, the buildings, and the military equipment of a regime that used brutal force to achieve its ends. Consequently, many of us may find it bizarre to see the swastika on a Buddhist temple, for example. (See Figure 2.8.) But the swastika originated with eastern religions. It's not at all unusual to see the symbol used in southeast Asia in religious texts, on wedding invitations, and as a decorative motif.

At this juncture, it may appear that HC and LC communication are somewhat similar to perception. They are, and principally because HC/LC communication and perception are two sides of the same coin. Perception is explored later in this chapter.

The Visual Language
Learning and communication can be studied and understood as independent yet complementary human

attributes. The previous two sections have described both, and have made connections between them and the Artificial World of design. In the section that follows, the visual language takes center stage. Like design, it is everywhere and yet not well understood. We react to a plethora of visual signals every day, but unlike the written language, the visual language has few rules. Therefore, our reaction to it is based much more on our kinesthetic knowledge rather than our theoretical knowledge of the visual language.

The visual language exists everywhere we look. It is what allows us to distinguish between the aforementioned pick-up truck and church, and, for that matter, everything else that has perceptible visual features. In other words, the visual language allows us to read everyday things. Combinations of discrete visual elements such as lines, shapes, form, color, and texture create a visual message that we perceive as a house, a car, an airplane, or any number of everyday things.

Learning and communication are certainly intertwined in the visual language but the effectiveness of the visual language—and there is no doubt that the visual language can be an immensely effective tool— depends on an interdependent relationship, or synergy, among all three. And this synergy is an integral part of designing.

In order to communicate, designing relies on the visual language. As briefly discussed earlier, the visual language is in many ways analogous to the written language. And like the written language, the visual language has a quasi vocabulary and grammar called the elements and principles of design, respectively. When appropriately used, the elements and principles can compose very effective messages—ones understood by a broad community of Users. That said, this analogy is not without certain conditions and reservations. In no way are design elements as well defined or as well understood as words and, in a similar way, neither are design principles exactly the same as the explicit rules of grammar and syntax.

The Elements of Design

The elements of design constitute a kind of visual vocabulary. They are the words, so to speak, that form the basic building blocks that allow Designers to communicate a visual message. Generally speaking, there are six elements in designing: line, color, shape, form, space, and texture.[iv]

Line. A line is a path traced by a moving point. Within this broad definition, lines can be straight, curved, geometric, organic, thin, bold, or almost any imaginable description. Furthermore, each type of line can carry with it some very specific meanings. A straight, precisely drawn line will most likely be interpreted as definitive and decisive unlike a hesitantly drawn, squiggly line, which could mean something quite different.

Color. As pigment, color is what we perceive in response to the different qualities in reflected light. It is described by three qualities: *hue,* which distinguishes what is loosely called the actual color or the different wavelengths perceived; *chroma*, or *saturation,* which is the degree of color strength as expressed in pure or grayed colors; and *value,* or *brightness,* which is the degree of lightness or darkness of color.

There are primary colors (red, yellow, and blue), from which all other colors originate, secondary colors (orange, green, and purple), and tertiary colors. Colors have other properties important to Designers. They can be warm, such as colors that are closer to red, or cool, such as colors that are closer to blue. Colors can also create sensations of expansion or contraction because light colors expand while dark ones contract.

Colors can also signify things. Red signifies the act of stopping, due to its use for stop signs and traffic lights. White symbolizes purity and is used for weddings in Western cultures; however, it is used for funerals in many Eastern cultures. Moreover, colors can have measurable psychological impact. Bright colors, for example, can actually raise a person's blood pressure, as can the white coats worn by physicians, something colloquially called "the white-coat syndrome."

Shape. A shape is an outline or a contour. It generally has a two-dimensional quality and should not be confused with form, which has a three-dimensional quality. Like lines, shapes can occur in many configurations, such as geometric, curvilinear, simple, complex, or any number of combinations. Also like lines, shapes allow Designers to convey an almost limitless range of visual messages with an equally limitless range of meanings. The cross is such an example: It has an obvious religious connotation, at least for Christians, but has found service in non-religious contexts such as medical care and humanitarian support,

with the red cross depicted on ambulances and other emergency vehicles, uniforms, and hospitals.[v] A white cross is a national symbol for both Switzerland and Denmark, appearing on their respective flags. For the Swiss, the white cross has also become a symbol of their national corporate identity. Both the Swiss army knife and the Swatch watch make use of the white cross as part of their brand identity. (See Figure 2.9.)

Form. A form is a three-dimensional shape or structure. Like shapes, forms can be extremely varied and help to create the presence and identity of a design or Artifact. Forms, even with well-defined limitations, can provide a basis for classification. Shoes are a good example. Human feet are quite similar—ankles, heels, arches, and toes. Yet, shoes are available in countless designs, and we can readily recognize the purpose of the shoe by its form. Flip-flops, tennis shoes, pumps, and hiking boots may all fit the feet of the same person but each shoe is formally very different.

Space. Space is a defined blank or empty area. Space occurs in a multitude of ways, such as wide-open space versus closed space or bright space versus dark space. One fascinating dimension of space is the positive/ negative attributes that it can possess. Objects in space occupy a positive volume. Imagine chairs in a room; they occupy a certain amount of space. However, these same chairs go on to create a negative space within the same room—spaces through which we can walk, for example. Of course, we in the West rarely consider this negative aspect of space, but some other cultures do. The Japanese, for example, consider negative space when doing floral arrangements, an art form called ikebana. The void created by the spaces between juxtaposed flowers or plants is just as important as the space occupied by the flowers themselves. The same phenomenon of positive and negative space also occurs in music. Musicians are well aware of the importance of the silence between notes, which is as important as the notes themselves.

Texture. Texture is the appearance or feel of a surface. It does not carry the same visual impact as the other five elements and normally only becomes relevant in everyday things that are in closer physical contact to the User. This is certainly the case with fabrics that we wear or chairs that we sit on or even pens that we hold. In all three instances, the User becomes quickly aware of the quality of the texture—even more so if it is annoying.

The Principles of Design

The principles of design serve as a kind of grammar in the visual language. They provide Designers with the tools to visually articulate messages using design elements. Generally speaking, there are six principles in design: unity, variety, balance, emphasis, rhythm, and scale.[vi]

Unity. Unity occurs when elements are used to create visual cohesion. By using similar elements, for example, Designers can create a design that has visual unity. Arne Jacobsen, the celebrated Danish architect and Designer, certainly applied the principle of unity when he designed the Cylinda line of products. Every object in that product line is based on a variation of the cylinder theme. It is the cylinder that creates the unity between and among all the different pieces.

Variety. Variety occurs when there are continual changes in elements. These changes in similar elements can create visual dynamics that can provide a certain energy or excitement about a design. The Cylinda objects not only shared a unified design, they also provided variety by being available in different sizes—tall and narrow or short and wide.

Balance. Balance is the distribution of elements. Two important aspects of balance are symmetry, or something in balance, and asymmetry, or something out of balance. The former is generally calming whereas the latter is not. Many everyday things are designed to be symmetrical. A dining room chair is a good case in point. When looking at it face on, the left side of the chair is identical to the right side. Much the same can be said about cars, boats, and airplanes, for example. When a known everyday thing suddenly appears in an asymmetrical version, we react—sometimes mildly and at other times in horror. Our expectation for something in balance is not met. Many Postmodernist Designers took advantage of this phenomenon of User expectation, purposefully building shock value into their designs.

Emphasis. Emphasis occurs when elements are used as centers of attention. The astute use of elements such as color, line, and form—individually or in combination—can create an emphasis, on such things as speed, stability, or lightness. Certain sport utility vehicles (SUVs), for example, emphasize their all-terrain character by using forms that are bold and aggressive. The H3 Hummer, for example, emphasizes a kind of paramilitary image by way of its styling, such as its box-like form, both overall and in detail.

Rhythm. Rhythm is the regularity of elements—that is, the coordinated placements of similar elements to imply visual rhythm. Rhythm was certainly evident with the rows of columns found in many Grecian temples of the past and continues in contemporary works of architecture, such as in airports where devices such as columns and windows, outside as well as inside, can play a rhythmic role in the visual language of the building.

Scale. Scale is the relative size of elements. Scale provides a sense of presence and relativity to a design, such as small-scale details at one end and large-scale components at the other. Scale is often relative to the physical size of people, leading us to talk about human scale. For instance, it is often said that Old World cities, such as London, Rome, and Paris, are more human in scale because their buildings are not overwhelmingly tall and people can walk about more easily in them, whereas cities like New York, Chicago, and Los Angeles overwhelm people and are therefore not considered human scale. But scale can have an impact on designs smaller than a city. Some easy chairs can swallow their Users because they are oversized, and calculators built in to wristwatches are often too small to be operable given the size of the human finger and the very small controls.

The Visual Language and Gestalt Psychology

The visual language operates within certain human boundaries of perception. German scholars and researchers in the early twentieth century explored an area of human perception called *Gestalt* psychology. One of its fundamental premises was the notion that in the perception of everyday things people tended to first see the whole rather than the bits and pieces that make up the whole. In other words, people first see a building as a large mass and only then begin to focus on some of the details such as doors and windows. (Some of these concepts of perception found their way soon thereafter to the Bauhaus,[vii] a revolutionary school of art, architecture, and design in Germany, that would take the lead in understanding and applying the principles of visual perception to design education.) If nothing else, the integration of findings in the social sciences such as *Gestalt* psychology would add to the rational thinking that was beginning to permeate design and the visual language.

For Designers, the important facets of *Gestalt* psychology reside in five basic areas of visual perception: proximity, similarity, continuity, closure, and simplicity. (See Figure 2.10.) All five impact our ability to read and understand the visual language.

- **Proximity.** Proximity deals with the relationships between and among visual elements. Simply stated, the closer two or more visual elements are, the greater the probability that they will be seen as a group or pattern. The grouping of controls inside a typical car is a good example of proximity. First, there is a general separation between and among different sets of control. The controls for the radio/CD player, for example, are

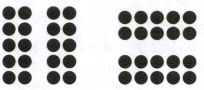

Proximity: The group of circles on the left is perceived as two columns whereas the one on the right is perceived as two rows.

Continuity: The tendency is to see two intersecting lines (left) rather than four quarter circles (right).

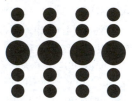

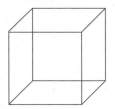

Similarity: Although all the shapes are circles, the larger ones in the middle row appear as a group.

Closure: The mind fills in the missing parts of the triangle.

Simplicity: Do we see a cube in perspective or many different shapes?

Figure 2.10: Gestalt Principles of Perception and the Visual Language.

grouped together and placed in a different place from the controls for the heater/air conditioner, which are also in a different location from controls for cruise control. Second, the spacing and location of the individual controls in these groups is also based on aspects of proximity. Consequently, drivers quickly learn to locate the necessary control by knowing the general location first and the specific location next. In other words, if the car is too warm there is no reason to look in the area where the cruise control is located. (See Figure 2.11.)

- *Similarity.* Similarity deals with a human propensity to place similar things into the same group, that is, visual elements that are similar, in shape, size, and color, for example, tend to be seen as related. Returning to the example of controls inside a car in Figure 2.11, it is not unusual to find that the climate control knobs tend to be more similar than different both in shape and in color. Even more demonstrative of this principle are sets of dishes. In fact, we call them sets because everything—color, shape, form, and size— constitutes a set of similarities.

- **Continuity.** Continuity is the tendency of people to perceive things as simply as possible with a continuous pattern rather than with a complex, broken up pattern. The cross that appears in the church in Figure 2.9 is perceived as two lines that cross and not four short lines that meet at one point.

- **Closure.** Closure is the tendency to perceive figures that are incomplete as complete. For example, the dots, or pixels, that make up an image on a screen will be perceived as a whole, identifiable image, not as a bunch of dots. Curved lines placed in a circular pattern will be perceived as a circle, because the brain fills in the gaps to imagine the circle. The circle in the Pepsi sign in Figure 2.12 is incomplete but we still see it as a circle.

- **Simplicity.** The remaining principle is simplicity. It occurs when complex visual elements are perceived as the simplest recognizable shapes and not individual parts. For example, we tend to use the word *house* to describe any architectural structure that remotely looks like a house irrespective of its features—size, windows, doors, gables, roof styles, etc. Somehow, we have a visual representation of a stereotypical house in our minds and use it to interpret more visually complex versions of a house. Children exhibit this tendency when they draw a house, which more often than not is a simple square with a triangle as a roof and smaller squares or rectangles as doors and windows.

As mentioned earlier, literary devices such as semantics have been previously applied to the visual language by astute use of both design elements and principles. The critical question was quite to the point: Could the application of semantic theory as found in language provide an enhanced level of understanding if applied to the visual language of everyday things? In this context, the Designers' ultimate goal was to have Users intuitively read or understand the function of an everyday thing by way of its visual language rather than have to learn it. In other words, a printer should look different from a paper shredder because their functions are very different. The printer produces documents while the shredder destroys them. This functional difference can be communicated via the visual language. This is an approach quite different from Modernism, or "form follows function," which focused more on the individual details related to the operation of the machine as a tool and not so much on its overall raison d'être.

Visual Languages As Universal Standards

Over time, humankind has developed a variety of standards that help to establish order or uniformity. Some of these have attained a level of near-universal acceptance such as the metric system. It has become the preferred method of physical measurement and is used in almost every country in the world. So, for that matter, has the system of musical notation. Through time and regular usage, both of these systems have lost most, if not all, their cultural attachments to the place of origin. In other words, they have become objective or value-neutral.

With the visual language, we have witnessed a similar tendency, especially in those cases in which the goal is a more universal acceptance of one image or another. The golden arches of McDonald's is one such image. The origin of such images as well as their social relevance may be of academic interest to social scientists. To a child, however, the golden arches signal one thing: instant gratification for their fast-food addiction. Be it in downtown Phoenix or an arrondissement of Paris, this visual signal seems to elicit the same Pavlovian reactions the world over. Much the same can be said for the logos of Starbucks, Nike, and Pepsi. Even when the product name appears in a different language or script, the fundamental form and color of the logo make it readable to most non-natives. (See Figure 2.12.)

The universality of design as a language can go well beyond the obvious logos of multinationals. The tricolor traffic signal, for example, is now an accepted controlling device the world over. As a result, its universality allows people from one country to effectively drive in an unfamiliar country even if they cannot read the local language. Similarly, the red brake-light at the rear of automobiles is standard, as are most of the driver controls in automobiles—turn signal, horn, and headlight control. They have become more and more similar over the last twenty years and not only from one model year to the next for the same manufacturer but even among different manufacturers from different countries. Gone are the days—or so it seems—when Designers were mandated to create yet another unique and novel set of gauges or controls, a strategy that forced Users to adapt to a new working environment from one year to the next in a machine capable of serious destruction of both human lives and property. In hindsight, we now wonder why design

was so frivolous in its treatment of such a critical piece of equipment.

As practical as these examples may seem to be, they are only the tip of the iceberg, especially for those Designers conditioned to seek originality in their design solutions. In the opinion of many of these individuals, the last thing needed is the blandness implied by universality—that is, everything being more similar than different. Yet, the standardization of form is already occurring with or without the contribution of Designers. The so-called global products—those everyday things designed and manufactured for the same lifestyle market regardless of culture—are perfect examples of this uniformity of product form. Many of today's small portable appliances are nothing more than a variation of the so-called Euro-style theme in which white is the only acceptable color and soft-rounded corners the only acceptable form. Similarly, the resurgence of aerodynamic considerations in certain categories of automobiles—both real and stylistic aerodynamics—has resulted in visual forms that are difficult to distinguish one from the other. This direction may be justifiable in technical terms, but what it has created is a marketplace where one law reigns supreme: the survival of the least visually offensive. For any market niche, it appears that no Maker wishes to be significantly different from the competition and therefore provides the market with a visual identity that is more similar than different.

Visual Literacy
Creating a visual message using design elements and principles is challenging; understanding a visual message is perhaps different but can be equally challenging.

Henry Ford, the American industrialist, recognized this fact nearly a century ago when he wrote that *"a piece of machinery, or anything that is made, is like a book, if you can read it."* [viii] Ford hit the nail on the head. Visual messages are successful for two reasons: our ability to create them and our ability to read them. The two acts are two sides of the same coin, and herein resides the challenge with visual messages. Generally speaking, we are taught neither to create visual messages nor to read them. Consequently, it could be said that most of us are visually illiterate.

In order to understand the challenge let alone resolve it, we need to delve into three interrelated components that are the constituent parts of visual literacy. There is vision, or the human capacity to receive visual stimuli; there is seeing, or the human capacity to interpret the visual stimuli once received, which is closely allied to perception; and there is designing, or the ability to create a visual message. Along with visual literacy, all three facets are discussed in further detail below.

Literacy is generally defined as the ability to use language to read, write, listen, and speak. By being literate, a person is capable of creating, communicating, understanding, and sharing ideas and concepts with other people. Much the same can be said about numeracy—that is, the understanding of numbers and numerical concepts. For people weak in numeracy, financial statements, like those published by large corporations, are almost meaningless, whereas for numerate people, such as accountants and tax lawyers, they provide a wealth of useful information. Visual literacy follows in these same general principles. It

is the ability that allows a person to comprehend and communicate using the visual language.

Visual literacy shares many of the qualities that we associate with literacy and numeracy. All three are human constructs and, therefore, are taught and learned much like we learn to read, write, and do arithmetic. One major difference, however, is that literacy and numeracy are normally provided as part of a person's general education whereas visual literacy is not. Indeed, this omission is unfortunate given how important the visual language is in daily existence. After all, a great deal of what we do every day is predicated on our ability to understand and react to various aspects of the visual language.

In a radio interview several years ago, Betty Edwards, the author of *Drawing on the Right Side of Your Brain*, talked about a visual literacy test she once administered to city officials in a small California town. This particular group of people was chosen because their responsibilities as elected officials included decisions that had considerable impact on all levels of town life, including zoning, garbage removal, law enforcement, and new construction. As is the case in most towns and cities in North America, these elected officials were local citizens with various professional backgrounds such as law, engineering, and accounting. Edwards found that no matter how well versed these people were in matters of literacy and numeracy, their visual literacy was roughly equal to that of a seven-year-old child. Yet, these same people would regularly make decisions on important visual issues such as a sculpture for the town square or architectural renovations. Except for their personal likes and dislikes, most of these councilors were totally unqualified to render credible, visual judgments. It was as though people who could neither read nor write were running the library. Such appointments would be considered ludicrous and outright irresponsible. Nevertheless, we allow people who are visually illiterate to act as if they are. Edward T. Hall was certainly of that opinion when he stated,

> "Man is used to the fact that there are languages which he does not at first understand and which must be learned, but because art is primarily visual he expects that he should get the message immediately and is apt to be affronted if he doesn't."[ix]

The examples cited above clearly demonstrate the paradox of our visual world: it totally surrounds us yet few people can adequately read it. Fortunately, the very nature of visual literacy provides part of the solution to this paradox. Visual literacy is a learned aptitude and therefore, like reading and writing, it can be taught.

Vision and Seeing

Becoming visually literate begins with a general understanding of the interrelationship between vision and seeing, because vision and seeing are not the same thing. As mentioned earlier, vision is a birthright. Most of us are born with what we call vision. However, seeing is very different. It is learned. We measure vision by way of standards in optometry and use scales such as 20/20 to gauge it. But seeing cannot be measured in this same quantitative way. Seeing is the ability to discern and differentiate between and among different visual shapes, forms, textures, and color. More importantly, it is a learned skill but not one that is regularly taught. When was the last time a class in seeing appeared in a school curriculum? The closest to this would probably be an art class, but most public school systems persist in classifying art as a pastime or hobby. Rarely is it a mandatory part of the general education of the average student.

The dominance of vision and its self-acquisition provides a partial explanation for this omission in teaching visual literacy. We tend to take vision for granted except perhaps on those rare occasions when we dare to imagine what life would be like if we could not see. As the physical ability in our sense of vision develops from infancy to adolescence, we absorb and assimilate visual stimuli in an ad-hoc way. Rarely, however, do we ever question the phenomenon of seeing itself. It is a natural part of who we are and we do not give it a second thought.

The dominance of vision can lead us to easily make two false assumptions. The first is the belief that what is seen is the same for everyone, which is not necessarily true. The second assumption is that all persons bring the same seeing ability or visual literacy to the situation at hand. This, too, can never be assumed. As already stated, visual literacy is learned and some people have learned it better than others, much like some people have a refined palate for food and others a trained ear for music.

These two assumptions also find their place with other senses, such as hearing, touch, taste, and smell. For example, it is not unusual to find that a blind person has developed a sense of touch to a level not found in people with sight. This heightened level of touch is a form of adaptation to or compensation for their blindness. Their sense of touch has become highly developed allowing for, among other things, the differentiation between nearly identical tactile surfaces, such as a dime and a penny, or the reading of Braille instructions in an elevator. Without specific training, most sighted people are incapable of doing either.

Returning to our original consideration—vision as opposed to seeing—a simple analysis allows us to comprehend this somewhat perplexing proposition. At birth, an infant is given the physiological capacity to receive the visual stimuli in the surrounding world—that is, the eyes, brain, and nerves are interconnected in such a way as to receive and process visual stimuli. However, only time will allow the same infant to comprehend the daily dose of visual stimuli and to differentiate, for example, between the facial features of the parents and those of a stranger. Instinctively, the baby confirms the former with a smile of joy but often responds to the latter with a cry of fear. Irrespective of either, the baby is learning to see. Over time—a lifetime, in fact—the brain will accumulate an almost infinite number of visual stimuli, sort and filter them, and provide the person with meanings based on past experience. If this process sounds similar to perception, it is because it is essentially the same.

Although the logic of the vision/seeing argument just presented is self-evident to most people, one well-known experience in psychology has provided proof to substantiate the claim that we learn to see. The evidence came as the result of people who, blind at birth, were subsequently given sight later in life, usually as a result of surgery. Two results from this experience are of particular interest. Both help us to further understand the role that vision and seeing play in the world of everyday things.

The first revelation was the seeming inability of newly sighted people to differentiate visually between and among simple graphical shapes such as circles and squares. The persons were entirely capable of distinguishing between the shapes, both by touch and by describing the differences; however, they found them the two shapes indistinguishable when looking at them. For most of us, this realization is difficult to comprehend and to accept, at least initially. After all, circles and squares are so logically and geometrically different. Moreover, the circle and the square are often cited as examples of exact opposites. However, certain situations in everyday life help to explain this behavior further and show it to be the rule rather than the exception. For example, the first attempts by a child to draw a circle or a square do not immediately show an appreciation for the opposite visual nature of either shape. These attempts usually produce oblong rectangles or squares, a kind of hybrid circle-square. It is only after appropriate corrections have been made that the child learns to see the difference.

The second discovery from the experience was the difficulty encountered by the newly sighted because of the almost instantaneous introduction of visual stimuli never before seen. They had great difficulties coping with this sudden influx of things that were totally unknown. The effect was overwhelming, and the impact was overpowering. It was like trying to sip water from a fire hose. Prior to their surgery, crossing a busy street had been an everyday activity for these blind people. They had learned to negotiate the task by relying on a highly adapted level of hearing and sense of touch. With the addition of sight, the task should have logically become easier. But it didn't. If anything, it had become more daunting. Why? Because the sight of vehicular traffic was unknown to them. It totally overwhelmed their sensory system. Now, the barrage of new but unknown visual images, such as speeding cars and charging buses, disoriented them. They had not learned to see these things and incorporate them into the reading and understanding of a situation. As an unfortunate footnote, many of these patients reverted to a way of life with which they were more familiar: dark glasses and white canes.

Perception

Imagine, for a moment, a beautifully clear and crisp autumn day. Spurred by some romantic urge, you and a friend decide to go to the countryside for a picnic. As you drive through the hills toward your destination, you cannot help but notice the splendor in the color of the leaves—red, scarlet, orange, yellow—and the contrast created with the deep blue sky and the occasional dark green pine or spruce. You arrive at a secluded spot, a small meadow now turned to warm gold, near a small lake. Nothing could be more visually beautiful. Just before you are ready to unpack the picnic gear, you

observe an unusual pallet of colors on the other side of the lake, a combination of hues and tones you have never seen before. Too beautiful to miss, you wander down the path toward this newly found treasure. As you near the spot, you momentarily lose sight of this beautiful landscape while negotiating a small ridge. Panting your way to the top, your anticipated joy is immediately shattered when you discover that the exciting colors that you perceived at a distance are nothing more than the colors of discarded candy wrappers, cereal boxes, aluminum cans, and soda bottles. In other words, a garbage dump! The scene is suddenly ugly. Why?

Rhetoric aside, the above anecdote clearly shows that there are two very distinct components in perception: the visual stimulus, or what we see, and our previous experiences, or how we evaluate or compare what we see to what we already know. Both components—the stimulus and our past experiences—work hand in hand. Together, they provide us with a definition of perception, which is what exists and what is known to exist. Along with learning, communication, and the visual language, perception adds yet another element to the human process that allows people to integrate both the Natural and the Artificial worlds into their lives.

It is almost impossible to imagine an existence in which everything is forever experienced for the first time. Comparison, which is a natural human trait, would be unknown and unnecessary. The concept of past experience would not exist. De Bono, in the explanation of learning previously presented, alluded to past experience when he described the analogy of deepening rivulets created by the repeated passage of hot water on the gelatin that is the brain. Perception works in much the same way, constantly comparing new stimuli to previous ones. Over a lifetime, of course, the underpinning process of perception evolves differently. When we were children, almost every experience was new; there were few possibilities for comparisons. As we grew older, however, we accumulated countless experiences and these influenced our reactions to new ones. This is why babies do not fear putting almost anything into their mouths, whereas adults have learned from experience what to ingest and what not to.

Quite obviously, perception is a critical element in design because design relies heavily on past experiences. How else, for example, can we speak of good design without reference to other designs we have known? Modernism in furniture and furnishings may fill the typical IKEA store today but that would not have been the case when the first manifestations of Modernism appeared in Europe at the turn of the twentieth century. We do not give it a second thought, for example, when we see a chair made of polished chrome steel tubing or undecorated stainless steel flatware. The design of these everyday things is commonplace today but was revolutionary one hundred years ago. The average person would have most likely rejected the bent-tube chair or undecorated flatware then. Today, these same styles are bestsellers. We perceived them differently because of what we have experienced of them.

When combined with visual literacy, perception moves well beyond the mere act of seeing one visual stimulus or panother. More importantly, perception incorporates a level of meaning that we have learned and our reaction to that meaning. For example, color can be described as a specific wavelength; shape can be described using principles of geometry. Once received by the eye and transmitted to the brain, however, the visual signal is compared and evaluated to past visual signals, similar or different. Because of perception, our reaction will be based on previous signals of similar or different nature. And it is these reactions that form the basis of our values. If we have received the signal before and the results have been pleasant ones, we give it a positive evaluation; however, if the previous signal produced an unpleasant experience, then there is a strong likelihood that we would once again judge it as negative. When the signal is unknown, it is normally compared to past signals and, if found not to match, becomes new experience for future reference.

There is one additional layer to perception stemming from what has just been stated, one that is important in understanding designing. The British art critic and author Eric Newton explored it in his book *The Meaning of Beauty*.[x] In it, Newton explored the concept of beauty—that is, why we like certain things and not others and how we attribute different levels of aesthetic value to these same things. On that very topic, he expressed two important points of view, both connected to perception. First, Newton elaborated on certain aspects of beauty and, more particularly, in nature.

In the eyes of most people, Newton stated, the horse is considered a beautiful animal whereas the pig is not. Why would that be so? Most observers use descriptors such as elegant, stately, and refined when referring to the horse but words such as fat, lazy, and dirty for the pig. Upon closer examination, the physical attributes that the horse possesses, such as its elegant long legs, are no more or less practical than the pig's short legs. In each case, the legs are appropriate to the task. It is we, the viewers, who project a sense of beauty onto them. And the same conclusion can be drawn about the beauty of a sunset or the loveliness of a rose. Nothing is inherently beautiful in itself; we only perceive it as beautiful and learn to call it that.

It is this projected sense of beauty that leads to the second point. Newton concluded that it's not that we know what we like but that we like what we know. In other words, familiarity is the essential force that most often makes people like things. Should we therefore be surprised with the power of branding in today's marketplace? Certainly not, because branding is predicated on the astute application of the knowing-is-liking principle. The sight of the polo pony on a shirt or the swoosh on running shoes or the golden arches on a building automatically triggers the reaction—we know it, therefore there is a good chance that we will like it.

Summary

We seem to have come full circle. Chapter 2 began with learning and how the human capacity for learning allows each one of us to integrate into a world—both Natural and Artificial—that is highly complex. In other words, no one is born with any pre-acquired knowledge that assists in the deciphering of these two very different worlds. Rather, we learned how to do it in several ways and over time. It also became clear that communication was at the core of this learning process. That is, all of us read the ever-present visual signals in the Natural and Artificial worlds and respond to them accordingly. Moreover, the reading of the signals—for that is exactly what it is—occurs through the visual language, which is an immensely powerful tool in communication. Many of the signals in the visual language we have learned; many others we have not. Regardless, we almost always react to them in ways that are known and predictable, as if they were a written language.

In the end, a picture is truly worth a thousand words, perhaps even more, if we can effectively read it. And we can read the visual language if we learn it.

Further Reading

De Bono, Edward. *Mechanism of Mind.*
Hall, Edward. *The Silent Language.*
Newton, Eric. *The Meaning of Beauty.*
Sparke, Penny. *An Introduction to Design & Culture in the Twentieth Century.*

Endnotes

[i] De Bono, Edward. *Mechanism of Mind.*

[ii] Postmodernism began around 1975. As a movement in design and architecture, it questioned the fundamental premises of Modernism, ones that were based on logic and rational thinking.

[iii] Hall, Edward T. *The Hidden Dimension.*

[iv] Not all sources agree on these particular six elements of design. There can be more than six and they can include elements other than the six listed above. That said, the premise for a set of fundamental elements as a basis for visual design remains.

 As universal as the red cross may first appear to be in the context of emergency medical aid and humanitarian support, Islamic countries actually use the red crescent instead. In order to find a more universal solution, the International Committee of the Red Cross adopted a third logotype in 2005, this one in the shape of a red crystal. This move was predicated by the challenges faced in those places where the religious differences make the cross or the crescent problematic.

[vi] Once again and similar to the elements of design, there is no absolute number of design principles. There can be more than six, and they can include principles other than the six listed above. That said, the premise for a set of fundamental principles as a basis for visual design remains.

[vii] The word *gestalt* is present in the name of design schools in Germany even to this day—e.g., Hochschule fur Gestaltung.

[viii] Sparke, Penny. *An Introduction to Design & Culture in the Twentieth Century.*

[ix] Hall, Edward. *The Hidden Dimension.*

[x] Newton, Eric. *The Meaning of Beauty.*

CHAPTER 3

Everyday Things: Tools, Structures, and Signs

The fundamental principles of the designing process have not changed dramatically over time. Designing exists today much as it did at the time of the earliest stone tools. Simply stated, the ingenuity of a person is applied to an existing situation in order to change it to a preferred one. This human intervention—at least in its most basic form—generally occurs in one of two ways. It can be reactive, that is, designing can occur because of the recognition of a misfit, or it can be proactive, that is, change for the sake of change.

Reactive designing occurs when something needs to be changed because there is no other choice—a certain material is no longer available or changes in the climatic conditions force a change in human behavior.[i] Designs from native cultures were often of this type and remain so in many parts of the world. For example, native huts in certain parts of central Africa have become measurably smaller over time not because the people who inhabit them wish them to be smaller but because the large tree branches previously used to span the roofs are no longer readily available. Consequently, the people are forced to use smaller branches, resulting in homes that are smaller in diameter. And the survival of the Sinagua people, mentioned earlier, was determined in a reactive way based on the availability—or not—of water. Today, modern civilization is facing situations that will most likely demand reactive designing as a response to the effects of climate change and other environmental challenges.

Designing can also be proactive. That is, design can occur as the direct and deliberate intervention by people irrespective of an external need to change or of a recognition of a misfit, as described above. Most passenger cars, for example, do not undergo a yearly model change because there is an external need for a change or a recognizable misfit. A one-year-old car does not become obsolete twelve months after it has left the showroom; it has at least ten more years of life, if not more. Yet, automobile manufacturers make model changes annually as if some external factor had created a need for them. Changes are made only for the sake of

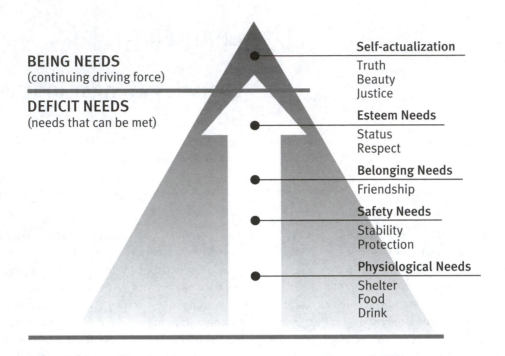

BEING NEEDS
(continuing driving force)

DEFICIT NEEDS
(needs that can be met)

Self-actualization
Truth
Beauty
Justice

Esteem Needs
Status
Respect

Belonging Needs
Friendship

Safety Needs
Stability
Protection

Physiological Needs
Shelter
Food
Drink

Figure 3.1: Maslow's Hierarchy of Needs.

change. Raymond Loewy, the acclaimed American Designer, certainly expressed that sentiment in his book *Never Leave Well Enough Alone*.[ii] Most designs in the developed world tend to fit into this category. Fashion and furniture are among the best examples, as they go through regular changes with little more than superficial improvements.

What really drives both reactive and proactive designing are the needs and wants of Users. Without needs and wants, there is no requisite rationale for designing. To

move forward in demystifying designing, we need to acquire a better grasp of human needs and wants. Useful insights into human motivation can be found in the work of Abraham Maslow, the American psychologist. Maslow was at the forefront of research and studies in human needs and provided us with an exceptionally good paradigm for understanding them. Maslow spoke of a Hierarchy of Needs. (See Figure 3.1.) According to his theory, humans have two types of needs: deficit needs and being needs. Deficit needs included physiological needs such as food and drink; safety needs such as security and psychological safety; belongingness needs such as affiliation, affection, and acceptance; and esteem needs such as competence and approval. Being needs are qualitatively different from deficit needs; they are essentially about self-actualization, such as the desire to fulfill potentials including concepts of truth, beauty, justice, and finding oneself. The identification of various needs is important; equally important is the interrelationship among the various levels of needs.

In simplistic terms, Maslow believed that the first requirement for human survival is satisfying the need to eat and drink; everything else is secondary. Once the need for nourishment is fulfilled, humans proceed to try to satisfy needs such as safety, clothing, and shelter. Once those needs are taken care of, the need to belong takes precedence, and with it the establishment of bonds of friendship and membership in social groups. Only then do people begin to consider the being needs, first in terms of shared values such as beauty, goodness and justice, and, finally, self-actualization. It is important to note that the hierarchical nature of the pyramid does not assume that all needs at one level need to be satisfied before the individual moves on to the next. For example, when the Taliban regime fell in Afghanistan and chaos ruled, ". . . men lined up at barbershops to have their beards shaved off. Women painted their nails with once forbidden polish."[iii] For these men and women, esteem needs (in this case, the need to be well-groomed) were more important than physiological needs, or so it appeared. Clearly, there is no inviolate rule to Maslow's hierarchy.

Does such a simplistic paradigm provide a plausible explanation as to why we design? In principle, it does, as long as we understand that to every rule there is most likely an exception or two. Looking at Maslow's Hierarchy of Needs in the context of developed countries such as the United States, many of us are not acutely aware of the lower levels of needs. For example, first-level needs such as eating are rarely a daily concern. Few of us struggle for food from dawn to dusk; rather, we go to the supermarket or to the restaurant and easily get our fill. Neither do we question the availability of clothing and shelter; the department stores and our apartments easily provide both.

However, one need only look at people living in poverty in the inner cities or at victims of a natural disaster in order to see the model's value. Studies have clearly shown that children from financially deprived families, for example, are less likely to derive the full benefits of public education than are children from more affluent families. It appears that the ability of these underprivileged children to succeed has been jeopardized for two reasons. First, undernourishment deprives them of the required physical well-being necessary to learn. Second, their minds are focused on where their next meal will come from rather than on some seemingly meaningless lesson in class. The need to eat—a physiological need—supersedes the supposedly higher need for scholastic competence—an esteem need.

In a similar vein, the clothing we wear has much more to do with a need for affiliation than with mere protection from the elements. By adhering to the appropriate dress code—and thereby gaining a kind of seal of approval—we clearly demonstrate to others that we belong to a specific group or culture.

Of course, there are exceptions to the rule that meeting basic physical needs takes precedence over the need for higher level needs. An example is the poet or artist who foregoes food in order to be able to afford pens or paints with which to express her creativity. The being need of self-expression, or self-actualization, seems to be in the forefront of her existence. However, the overall premise of Maslow's hierarchy is not invalidated because of such exceptions. In general, the theory provides a model that both clarifies and gives substance to the complex motivational imperatives in people, their behavior, and values as they relate to the everyday things that pervade their lives.

Wants Versus Needs

As Maslow showed, deficit and being needs are universal. However, the manner in which people satisfy them is not. For example, we may need to eat, but what we eat is not the same the world over. A variety of variables—some unique to the individual, others more global in nature—play their role in this equation. Inuit hunters of Alaska and Arctic Canada savor the taste of raw liver from a freshly killed seal whereas many Americans consider a Big Mac a culinary treat. Each group needs to eat, but what each wants can be very different. And much the same can be said about our need for safety, shelter, and belongingness. Needs are part of a biological common base among all people, whereas wants reflect the value systems of different people and different cultures.

The same principle applies to everyday things. A quick historical survey would reveal that everyday things originally satisfied a very definite need and, more importantly, that the link between the need and the everyday thing was quite obvious. To our early ancestors, clothing was a form of protection from the elements; fashion was not an issue. Over time, however, the connection between needs and everyday things became less obvious, to the point that it now often appears to be nonexistent. Today, few people wear clothes for protection only. How else do we explain film stars wearing fur at a Hollywood gala on a warm evening! Over time, the obvious connection between fur and protection from the elements has been totally lost. The universal physical need for shelter has manifested itself as a local want related to style, fashion, or fad. Other universal needs have created with it the cornucopia of everyday things that we have in the developed world. This phenomenon merely adds to what appears to be a disconnect between basic needs and our want for everyday things. Our world has become much more visually diverse—and complex.

In the above Context, the respective meanings of the words *needs* and *wants* provide us with a clearer picture of why we design the way we do. However, many people continue to misuse the words. Regardless, Designers should not make the same error. More importantly, they should understand that no one truly needs this or that particular everyday thing. When hunger strikes, no one really needs KFC chicken; nor do people need an iPod for listening pleasure; nor do they need a Porsche for personal transportation. In the end, needs and wants explain why people design because both are directly connected to human survival and evolution.

Returning to the central topic of this chapter, three everyday things from material culture—tools, structures, and signs—will serve as the metaphoric vehicles in the demystification journey that we are about to undertake. Together, the three object types are fitting examples that will serve to illustrate human qualities that not only define the human species as unique but that do so over both time and place. Tools, the first of these three artifacts, are obviously associated with the concept of the everyday things. For our purpose, tools will be those things that are mobile—from small-scale objects such as the first stone-cutting tools to larger scale everyday things such as a chair, which is a *tool* for sitting. Structures constitute the second object type. They are also everyday things but are different from tools because they are immobile and therefore more closely associated with a locale or place. Various examples of structures will illustrate how humanity has found ways to create a sense of place, whether to seek protection from the elements or enemies or for myriad other reasons. Lastly, visual signs will be explored. This is the third object type with a focus primarily on signs as visual communication such as we find in early petroglyphs, letterforms, and, more recently, digital visualization.

Tools

The word *tools* may not be the most appropriate word for this category of everyday things, at least at first reading. We do not use the word *tool*, for example, when talking about automobiles or powerboats. Other words more quickly come to mind, such as vehicles or modes of transportation. Perhaps *device* is a better word but it has its limitations too. Tool becomes an adequate and acceptable word only if we include everyday things that go beyond the typical meaning of the word to one that describes those everyday things that are physical extensions of mankind. This meaning for tools is much more inclusive and will be the one used hereinafter.

Edward T. Hall regularly referred to extensions of mankind in his many studies of material culture. He was of the opinion that mankind evolved as much as it did, if not more so, because of extensions such as the wheel.[iv] Marshall McLuhan, the Canadian communication theorist, also perceived certain everyday things as extensions of mankind. His subject was media, which he explored at length in his book, *Understanding Media: The Extensions of Man*. McLuhan coined the phrase "The medium is the message," meaning that the way in which information is provided is often more important than the information itself. McLuhan's comment bolsters the idea that extensions of mankind are, indeed, extremely significant.

What do we actually mean by extensions of mankind? For our purpose, we will discuss extensions to human capabilities that become the basis for some kind of everyday thing. In this Context, the wheel, when used on, say, a bicycle, is an extension of the human leg and of a person's capacity to walk. Based on this simple definition, the number of human extensions is almost infinite because of the human capacity to design. Moreover, as we will see later in the discussion, most of these human extensions can be neatly classified into one of three general categories, each based on a particular human capacity.

The first of the three categories are extensions derived from the muscular capacity in humans. (See Figure 3.2.)

As we all know, muscles provide us with the potential to do a range of activities, from writing by using the muscles of our fingers to lifting and moving heavy objects with the muscles of our arms and legs. Our muscles also allow us to walk, run, and swim.

A quick look at our Artificial World quickly shows the extent to which muscular capacity in humans has influenced the design of everyday things. The automobile has already been mentioned, but there are many others, such as tools that use the principle of the lever. Cranes and lifting devices fall into this category. Somewhat more complex but still an extension to the human muscles are tools that use pneumatic or hydraulic power, such as we find in the pneumatic power tools in garages or the hydraulic brakes in our cars. These tools are based essentially on the amplification of human muscle power—pneumatic tools make our arms more powerful much in the same way that hydraulic brakes make our legs more powerful.

A second category of extensions is one that groups tools that extend our human senses, especially sight, hearing, smell, and touch. (See Figure 3.3.) Our senses have been central to the survival and evolution of mankind even though, generally speaking, human sensory capability is rather limited when compared to that of many animals. In reality, it was our cerebral capacity, not our senses, that allowed us to evolve differently from animals. Despite these limitations, our senses provide the foundation for a range of extensions allowing people to increase their natural capacities. Vision is a good case in point. Of all our senses, it is by far the one that most impacts our lives. Yet, our vision is rather limited—at least when

compared to that of certain animals. Birds of prey, such as hawks and owls, can see distant things that we cannot detect at all; cats can see much better at night than we can. Over time we have compensated for these and other vision challenges with a range of everyday things, from microscopes to see very tiny things to telescopes to see very distant things, and from X-rays to see through human tissue to radar to see through fog and in the dark.

The ability to hear has also served as a source for the design of artificial extensions. Like vision, hearing in humans is rather limited. So is the range of audible sounds that a human can hear. Yet these limitations have not prevented people from designing useful extensions. Physicians, for example, use the stethoscope as a tool to listen to organs in the body because the unaided human ear is not capable of doing so. Similarly, the telephone extended the range of natural voice transmission and allowed us to hear anyone from anywhere in the world. Interestingly, it is perhaps not a coincidence that the inventor of the modern telephone, Alexander Graham Bell, was first and foremost a speech therapist. He understood the basic capacity of human speech and hearing, and extended that knowledge to the concept of the telephone. Today's ubiquitous cell phone—with its ease of mobility and extensive range—owes everything to the human capacity to hear and to the ingenuity of Alexander Graham Bell.

Important developments have also occurred with everyday things as extensions of our capacity to smell. Like our other senses, our olfactory sense—smell and taste—are not that well developed. Dogs or sharks, for example, have much better olfactory systems. They can react to the smallest smell stimulus, an amount that we as humans could never detect. Perhaps for this reason, certain everyday things have been designed to compensate for our inability to sense certain odors, especially those coming from sources that could harm us. The smoke detector is an excellent example. It can warn us when there is smoke in the environment when we are unable to discern the odor from the surrounding air. Smoke detectors are found in offices, homes, and in the lavatories of airplanes, the latter to detect people who are unlawfully smoking on a flight. However, there are occasions when natural olfactory systems are superior to the ones we have designed. For example, law enforcers use dogs to sniff out drugs because these animals are capable of identifying the odors of certain drugs, whereas human beings have been unable to design detectors that can do the job.

Touch is no different from our other senses; it too is not well developed in humans. There are exceptions, of course. Most blind people have compensated for their loss of sight by developing an extremely refined sense of touch, which is what enables the blind to read Braille. Next time you find yourself in an elevator, test the Braille signs for yourself and see to what level your sense of touch is refined. You will discover that reading Braille is not that easy. The sense of touch also plays a role in determining the weight of smaller everyday things such as pens and, by inference, a perception of their quality and status. For example, many people appreciate the heft of a good pen such as a Mount Blanc to that of a mediocre one such as a Bic. By weight alone, they find

the former to be a quality pen whereas the latter is not. When it comes to determining exact weight, however, the sense of touch is not as refined as scales—everyday things that have been designed to overcome our inability to accurately determine the weight of something. We find these in our bathrooms, grocery stores, laboratories, airport check-ins, and at highway weigh stations.

As a side note, it is probably the healthcare and medical sectors that have most benefited from technology that has extended human sensory capability. The X-ray and stethoscope have already been mentioned, but there are many other such tools, such as magnetic resonance imaging (MRI), the electro-cardiogram (ECG), computed tomography (CAT scan), and the angiogram, a test that provides an image of blood flow in the human heart. These tools allow us to see what no human eye can see. And what about the information that physicians can derive from the laboratory analysis of a mere drop of blood? It is nothing less than astonishing. Technology, functioning as an extension of our senses, allows us to detect things that our actual senses cannot.

The third and last category involves extensions of the human brain, or the capacity to think. While our muscular and sensory capacities are often deficient when compared to those of other species—horses are stronger than us, birds have better eyesight than we do, and dogs can detect smells that we can't—the human cerebral capacity is phenomenal. It is clearly what distinguishes us within the animal kingdom. It is not that animals cannot think—they do. But animals have not evolved to a point where they have created a language system, for example, like humans have. Neither have animals designed the plethora of everyday things that societies have. Only a very few animals have created tools, and these are extremely basic, such as sticks used by chimpanzees to capture ants or rocks used by sea otters to crush shellfish.[v] In contrast, our capacity to think has allowed humankind to make unbelievable technological leaps. In the space of one lifetime, for example, we have witnessed the first tenuous developments in powered flight of around 200 feet by the Wright brothers in 1903 to Neil Armstrong's walk on the moon, 240,000 miles away in 1969. And much the same kind of progress has occurred in medicine, telecommunication, and computer technology because of our cerebral capacity.

Not surprisingly, our capacity to think has been replicated in tools that mimic, at least in part, the thinking process. Early adding machines certainly achieved that end by enhancing our capacity to deal with numbers. But adding machines are crude when compared to today's hand-held calculators with their many mathematical, algebraic, and engineering functions. Moreover, today's calculators are very small when compared to their predecessors, which now appear as behemoths. It is the computer, however, that best exemplifies the concept of human thinking as an extension. It has provided a level of artificial cerebral power never seen before except in the human brain. Moreover, the computer is not only becoming smaller it is also becoming faster and more powerful.

To return to the defining qualities of a tool for the purpose of our analysis, one condition remains essential. A tool must be mobile. Generally speaking, most everyday things are either mobile or immobile—that is, they either have been designed with the capacity to be moved or they have not. By design, a pocketknife is a mobile everyday thing but a building is not. Size alone does not determine whether an everyday thing is mobile; what is more meaningful is the intent behind the design. Therefore, a cruise ship is an example of a mobile everyday thing even though it is larger than the average home, which is an immobile everyday thing. More information will be provided on immobile everyday things in the section on structures.

In summary, tools are all manner of everyday things—big or small—that are mobile and that are extensions of human capacities, especially muscular, sensory, and cerebral, in the context of addressing human needs and wants.

Structures

Like tools, we need a working definition for structures—one that may also require some boundaries. For our purpose, structures will include everyday things that are immobile. In fact, there is an insightful linguistic connection between the words *immobile* and *building*. Beginning in the Middle Ages, it was not unusual for the nobility to have several residences or homes but furnishings for only one of these. As a result, people would pack up everything—furniture, tapestries, and household belongings—and take them all with them whenever they decided to go live in another one of their homes. It was not unusual, for example, for the French nobility to move furniture and belongings from their Paris homes to their chateaux in the Loire Valley and then back again. (See Figure 3.4.) Not surprisingly, the word for furniture in French is *meuble* and the word for building is *immeuble,* and those same two words are the source for mobile and immobile.[vi] To be considered a structure, therefore, an everyday thing will have to be immobile. Logically, examples of structures include buildings, but bridges, dams, and power transmission lines are also structures.

The examples in structures will span several human cultures and technological eras. Furthermore, structures will include various types, such as dwellings, places of worship, and public buildings. Individually or in combination, the qualities imbedded in the various structures will allow us to understand better the design process that created them—especially contextual conditions such as environment, culture, and socio-political developments.

Signs

Signs are only one facet of human communication, but they are central to understanding the designing process. However, the term is used guardedly because of the many meanings for signs that reside in areas of study, such as communication, anthropology, and linguistics. In the context of designing, signs are the visual elements that form the basis of our visual language and the phenomenon we call visual communication. Although other facets of communication, such as oral communication, written communication, and nonverbal communication, share many of the underlying principles of communication, they are not as critical to understanding designing as signs are. Consequently, the focus of the third category of everyday things will be on signs and the role that they play in the visual language and in designing.

Signs are neither tangible objects that you can hold, like tools, nor are they things that you can enter, like structures. Yet, signs surround us and are everywhere. Most everyday things, for example, have a visual quality or visual personality about them. Consequently, they signify something. That is why we can immediately tell the difference between a television remote control and a carving knife—even without touching them—merely by looking at them. TV remotes and knives look very different; their visual configurations appear as different signs. In design, signs are a type of visual communication and provide us with an explicit message as well as an implicit one. At one level, signs assist in differentiating between the TV remote and the carving knife; this is an explicit message. At another level, the same signs that provide this visual differentiation between a TV remote and a carving knife do not constitute a deliberate form of communication such as a written language, with its collection of signs with very specific meanings. The latter is an implicit form of communication. An expensive car does not need to have the word *status* painted on its door In order to trumpet its status; it does so by the many signs implicit in the style, material, and features that define the design of the car.

The interplay between explicit and implicit visual communication is perhaps best explained by way of signs and symbols—that is, visual communication can occur as either a sign or a symbol or a combination of both. The red octagonal stop sign, for example, is understood to signify one thing and one thing only: a driver must come to a full stop at an intersection where the sign is posted. (See Figure 3.5.) We learn this explicit message very early in our driving careers, even in our childhood as young cyclists. Moreover, we go on to associate the color red with other critical situations such as emergency exits in public buildings. As clear as the explicit message of the stop sign may be, it also has symbolic value. The stop sign is an implicit mirror of certain societal qualities, such as a sense of order, control, and respect for the law.

The Starbucks logotype—readily recognized by millions—is also a sign but is very different from the stop sign. It acts more like a symbol than a sign. Indeed, the logotype does signify that the location is an official outlet of the well known purveyor of coffee. More importantly, however, the logotype is a powerful symbol, one that symbolizes, at least for Starbucks Users, a lifestyle—a promise for certain experiential qualities. As we know, few people frequent Starbucks simply because they need a cup of coffee; they go there for many other reasons.

As mentioned above, the phenomenon of signs and symbols as found in an everyday thing can also be understood as visual communication that, at the same time, can be both explicit and implicit. This is because all tangible everyday things have the potential to be deciphered like a visual code. The composition of lines, shapes, forms, and colors found in everyday things become visual signals, and visual signals are a form of communication. Users look at these visual signals and respond accordingly. But they do so because of the combination of explicit and implicit visual communication imbedded in the visual signals. The aforementioned Starbucks example made the point. Explicitly, the logotype does two things: it identifies

the Starbucks location and sets the company apart from the competition; implicitly, the logotype promises to fulfill an experience associated with Starbucks.

Three kinds of signs will be explored in *Designing: A Journey Through Time*. The first will be the signs that first appeared as the earliest form of human visual communication—that is, petroglyphs. Although it remains unclear what these signs actually meant, there is a general agreement that they represented various aspects of daily life, both material and spiritual. Some petroglyphs, for example, depict recognizable animal species, such as elk and turtles, while others, such as spirals and jagged lines, appear to be more symbolic.

The second type of sign or visual communication is much more explicit. This is the kind that we associate with letterforms or typography. These are abstract signs with very specific meanings. Letterforms and typography have a long history in most cultures and are the basis for alphabets and other writing systems throughout the world. As a form of explicit visual communication, their meanings are precise and unequivocal. Their goal is to avoid ambiguity whenever possible.

The third type of sign is even more abstract. It is the world of visual communication that has been created via endless strings of ones and zeros. This is the digital world—a world in which the utter mathematical simplicity of digitization seems to hold few promises. Yet, exactly because of this mathematical simplicity, there is an ethereal capacity that is boundless and that is just beginning to manifest itself. Clearly, signs have taken the first steps into a virtual world—one that will not replace the real world but will complement it.

Summary

The mission of *Designing: A Journey Though Time* is to understand designing by tracing the evolution of everyday things as the result of major changes in the participants of The Designing Triad. For that reason, examples and case studies will be invaluable. But not just any examples and case studies. Those selected must both inform and support the mission, which is exactly what examples of tools, structures, and signs will do. All three categories provide the necessary breadth to inform the reader about the evolution of many everyday things as well as impart a deeper understanding of any one of these everyday things. After all, everyday things are mirrors of culture. They reflect our values, both explicit and implicit.

Chapters 1, 2, and 3 have prepared us for the pending exploration. We are now better informed about designing via learning, communication and the visual language as well as the three categories of artifacts: tools, strutures, and signs.

Let the journey begin.

Further Reading

Giard, Jacques. *Design FAQs.*

Hall, Edward T. *The Silent Language.*

_____. *The Hidden Dimension.*

_____. *Beyond Culture.*

_____. *The Dance of Life.*

McLuhan, Marshall. *Understanding Media: The Extensions of Man.*

Rybczynski, Witold. *Home.*

Endnotes

[i] In his book *Notes on the Synthesis of Form,* Christopher Alexander explored the phenomenon of design in self-conscious and unselfconscious cultures. In self-conscious cultures, design was strongly self-referential whereas design in unselfconscious cultures was generally the recognition of misfits. A more detailed explanation of this phenomenon appears in Lesson 4 in chapter 7.

[ii] Loewy, Raymond. *Never Leave Well Enough Alone.*

[iii] Postrel, Virginia. *The Substance of Style.*

[iv] Hall, Edward T. *Beyond Culture.*

[v] A distinction needs to be made between the deliberate design of a tool such as the chimpanzee's use of a stick to gather ants and the building of a nest by a bird or the making of a dam by a beaver. The latter two examples are the result of an instinctive behavior and not of deliberate design intent.

[vi] Rybczynski, Witold. *Home.*

Part II

The Journey

CHAPTER 4

The Age of Needs

The second section of *Designing: A Journey Through Time* is a metaphorical journey that provides a chronological description of the evolution of designing and everyday things. It does so by way of a general overview of the times with a description of place, people, and process—the 3Ps of designing—as well as two methodological devices. The first of these is The Designing Triad, which serves to illustrate how designing began as an activity in which the Designer, the Maker, and the User were the same person and how it evolved to the situation that we have today, with the three participants more often than not functioning as separate entities. The second methodological device is the study of everyday things themselves—specifically, tools, structures, and signs—as examples or case studies to illustrate and help us understand the direct effects of the designing process on the Artificial World.

Place, People, and Process

We begin the journey in the Stone Age—also known as the Paleolithic Age—between 3.4 million and 10,000 years ago. Humans began designing in the so-called era of hunter-gatherers, when people were essentially nomads. As a result, everyday things were portable, permanent buildings were exceptions, and signs served as rudimentary notice boards.

What was different then compared to now, especially in the developed world, is that individual communities were by necessity completely self-reliant. The functions of the Designer, the Maker, and the User resided in most persons. Today, this is not the case at all for most of us. We may be Users of everyday things but few of us are their Designers or Makers. For example, few people design or make their own furniture, appliances, clothes, or houses. We may use all of these everyday things, but we have essentially become a small cog in a very large wheel of designing and making. Clearly, that was not the case for our early ancestors. Tools, structures, and signs were generally the result of designing by one and the same person acting as the Designer/Maker/User.

For our earliest ancestors, life was a constant struggle for survival. Conveniences that we take for granted—grocery stores, hotels, and clothing boutiques—were totally unknown, of course. Satisfying the basic physiological needs of food and shelter—the physiological needs in Maslow's Hierarchy of Needs—was the primary goal. Furthermore, people were essentially nomadic and constantly moved about, at times over great distances, in order to be wherever the animals had migrated or where fruits were ripe. For these reasons, people had few possessions, and the few they did have, such as everyday tools—knives, spears, and axes—had to be transportable. According to all evidence at hand, the period of the hunter-gatherers was bleak—at least from the perspective of any legacy passed on to future generations and societies. There was no written language or great architecture or splendid art.

Yet, it was in this unpromising Context that designing began. It did so rather inauspiciously by way of a stone or rock being chipped to reveal a cutting edge. This modified stone was nothing less than the earliest knife. More than that, this stone tool became the first designed everyday thing for which we have evidence. As important as this first act of designing may have been, there is little to show that designing was undertaken with the same deliberate and mindful intent that we readily associate with designing today—certainly not designing with clear intent as done by most companies in the industrialized world, for example. Quite obviously, hunter-gatherers did not design by first developing a business strategy, nor were there ethnographic research, market studies, or design ideation. Nevertheless, the designing of the first

stone tool had all of the qualities that we find in designing today. Humankind was finding the means, as Herbert Simon described it "to change an existing situation into a preferred one." This first stone tool was the very first product of what we now know to be one of the most significant human capacities: designing. And designing would drive human evolution from that day forward.

The first stone tools date back some 3.4 million years, appearing in what is known as the Paleolithic Era. These first nomadic humans populated parts of Africa. Over time, some would migrate to Southeast Asia, then Europe, and eventually North and South America. These early ancestors survived by foraging for plants and hunting animals found in their immediate environment. There was no domestication of either plants or animals. It would be another two to three million years before humans would settle down into villages and practice basic agriculture, sometime at the end of the Mesolithic period, in various parts of the world such as the Middle East and Asia. Moreover, the pace of evolution was not the same in every place. For example, many Native Americans and Australian Aboriginals continued to live as hunter-gatherers well after inhabitants in parts of Europe and Asia were already mass-producing bronze tools.[i]

Except for rudimentary stone tools, the earliest humans did not leave any artifacts of any consequence, such as art or even bone tools. It was not until about 50,000 years ago that more sophisticated tools of stone or bone and other artifacts such as jewelry appeared, first in East Africa and, and later, in the Near East and southeastern Europe. This is also the time of the first statues and cave paintings. Later, around 35,000 years ago, people developed the first watercrafts and began to colonize the islands and archipelago around what is now New Guinea. It was around this same time period—35,000 to 14,000 years ago—that a great deal of the earth was going through an Ice Age, which allowed people to cross the Bering Sea and enter North America for the first time. The earliest evidence of habitation is around 12,000 BCE in Alaska, yet, in less than one thousand years, people would populate parts of South America.[ii]

Quite obviously, the period of the hunter-gatherers was the Age of Needs. It was a time of subsistence when survival was based on satisfying basic needs and, in order to do so, people moved from place to place. In terms of The Designing Triad, the Designer, the Maker, and the User were one person; the immediate Context, or environment, was critical to survival; and Artifacts, or everyday things, were mobile because of the nomadic lifestyle. Permanent structures or shelters were essentially non-existent, and signs, via cave paintings, began to make their appearance but not yet written language.

Tools

The first evidence of human adaptation to the Natural World were simple, basic tools—instruments that made survival just a little bit easier. These very early everyday things were principally meant for cutting and were nothing more than stones that were chipped in order to create sharp edges. Later, wooden handles would be attached to the stones. This design created a so-called compound tool and gave the User a distinct advantage: additional force because of the extension provided by the handle.

This simple tool—as exemplified by the axe of the Salado people of Arizona—became the antecedent to many of today's designed objects. The modern hammer and axe, for example, are nothing more than more evolved versions of these early tools. Similarly, many of the grinding tools that we use for food preparation, both in industry and in the home, have their origins with simple stone tools. The Salado people developed such tools in order to grind beans and corn into flour of one kind or another by using one movable stone as the pestle and a larger, stationary stone as the mortar. (See Figure 4.1.)

The North American Birch-Bark Canoe

As we have already seen, stone was essential to the evolution of humanity, and its resistance to natural deterioration has provided us with an abundance of very early artifacts. Wood, which deteriorates quickly, was as important as stone. It was used not only in the design of tools but also in the construction of shelters of one kind or another. The native people of North America, especially the Algonquin and Ojibway tribes, became exceptionally clever in using locally found wood, including the bark and the roots of trees, and their talent is apparent in the design of the birch-bark canoe. As a tool, the birch-bark canoe evolved as a contextually appropriate solution for travel over the lakes and rivers of North America. It was made of found materials, using simple hand tools such as the axe and the knife. Moreover, the birch-bark canoe was environmentally sustainable; when it reached a point where it could no longer be used, nature took it back through natural decomposition. On a very limited scale, the birch-bark canoe continues to be made in a few native communities, but it is no longer used as it was even one hundred years ago. (See Figure 4.2.)

In North America, the birch-bark canoe originated generally in the northeast where birch trees are abundant. As a tree, the birch is unique in that its bark is like paper and can be peeled off the tree. This is especially so with the American white birch, a species that grows from Alaska in the west to Newfoundland in the east, and as far south as Colorado.

The building of a birch-bark canoe begins by first finding and cutting down a large white birch tree, minimally 18 to 24 inches in diameter—the larger the better. The cutting normally takes place in late spring when the sap in the trees is running, making the tree's bark more flexible. Once the tree is on the ground, a short-bladed knife—called a crooked knife—is used to make a longitudinal cut about 1/4 of an inch deep along the length of the trunk, perhaps 10 to 12 feet in length. A similar cut is also made around the circumference of the trunk at each end of the longitudinal cut. With care, the birch bark is peeled away from the tree as one large piece that easily measures 50 square feet. It is rolled up and taken to the village where the canoe will be built. The birch wood that remains after the peeling of the bark is not wasted; for example, some of it may be used to make the paddles and the thwarts for the canoe.

To build the canoe, the roll of birch bark is laid flat on the ground and kept flat with the use of several large stones. A frame-like template made of wood is placed on top of the flat birch-bark. This template determines the overall shape of the canoe but does not become part of the canoe itself. The template is elliptical and made of timber about one inch square with spreaders at its widest sections. Next, the ends of the flat birch-bark roll are brought together and temporarily held in place with wooden pegs. Hot water is sometimes poured on the bark to soften it in order to bring the ends together. The general canoe shape then begins to take form. The template is removed in preparation for the next step—the installation of the floorboards and ribs.

The floorboards and ribs of the canoe are made of cedar wood. Cedar is used because of its availability, inherent flexibility, and ease of use. White cedar boards—approximately 2 x 30 inches—are left to soak in water for some time and then carefully split into thin sheets, about 1/16 of an inch thick and 30 inches long. These sheets will eventually become the floorboards for the canoe. Other slightly thicker boards, about 1/8 x 1 x 36 inches, are also soaked. These are bent in the shape of a U and in different sizes. They become the ribs of the canoe. The floorboards are selected, carefully trimmed, and set into place on the bottom of the birch-bark. They serve to reinforce and protect the birch-bark. The installation of the ribs comes last; they go on top of the floorboards at about every six inches from bow to stern; they keep the floorboards in place and provide structural integrity to the canoe.

At this point, the canoe has an overall form, but there is still a great deal of detail work to be done. There are many other materials that need to be gathered and prepared. For example, the canoe will need a gunwale, which is the wooden rib that circumscribes the outer edge of the birch bark around the open part of the canoe.

It will also need thwarts; these are the cross pieces in the canoe. The gunwales and the thwarts all need to be lashed onto the birch bark and the ribs. For this type of detail, various materials are used including roots and tree gum. Roots from spruce trees are first pulled from the ground and then soaked in very hot water. They have a property similar to strong string or twine and are used to lash the ribs and the birch bark together as well as the bark at the bow and stern of the canoe. The last step is sealing—that is, making the canoe water-tight in the many seams where the bark has been stitched. To do this, gum gathered from spruce trees is heated and then mixed with animal fat to create a tar-like mixture. This mixture is liberally applied to the seams and let to dry and set. The paddles are carved from locally found wood such as pine or birch; these paddles make the canoe practicable by providing both power and steering.

As simple as the construction of a birch-bark canoe may first appear to be, its design is rather magical. From material found in their immediate natural environment and without either an instruction manual or formal instruction, one generation of native people after another has constructed this magnificent craft. No one knows who invented the canoe. The knowledge and skills to make it are passed down from father to son. The birch-bark canoe is the perfect example of an everyday thing from an unselfconscious culture. Moreover, it is an everyday thing for which the Designer, the Maker, and the User are one and the same person.

The obvious suitability of the birch-bark canoe to its environment did not go unnoticed by non-native people in the United States and Canada, especially in Maine, New Hampshire, New Brunswick, Québec, and Ontario. During the late nineteenth and early twentieth centuries, many companies began making canoes using industrial technology. Few if any of these companies used birch-bark. The process was considered too labor-intensive and could not be done efficiently by machine. The companies adopted the same general shape and features for their canoes but used materials better suited to factory production. Two materials became standard: cedar and canvas. They chose to use cedar for the same reasons native peoples did: it was readily available, resistant to water and rot, and easy to cut and shape. Canvas was used in place of birch bark and served to cover the cedar structure of the canoe. In combination, these two materials were used to create what became known as the cedar canvas canoe.

If we fast-forward to today, we see that materials other than cedar and canvas are now regularly used to make canoes. Aluminum canoes are popular, as are canoes made from various plastics, especially glass-reinforced polyester (commonly called fiberglass), plastics reinforced with carbon fibers such as Kevlar, and flexible plastics such as ABS (Acrylonitrile Butadiene Styrene). Regardless of the materials used in its construction, one thing has remained the same: the shape of the canoe. Generally, speaking, it has changed very little over time.

It is worthy to note that one significant feature exists in the white man's canoe that doesn't exist in the native birch-bark canoe: the seat. Native canoes do not have seats. When native people paddle, they squat. As uncomfortable as that position may be for many of us, it is not for those people who squat on a more regular basis. In almost all canoes made by and for non-natives, a seat is *de rigueur*. Perhaps it is because most of us would have difficulty squatting for long periods of time or because seats are common in most watercraft. Nevertheless, seats are found fore and aft in almost all non-native canoes. Seasoned paddlers, however, squat when negotiating white water or whenever stability on the water is required.

Structures

For hunter-gathers, there was no such thing as permanent structures or shelters. Protection, whether from the elements, beasts of prey, or enemies, came via whatever was found locally or constructed temporarily. Permanent structures would come much later. Until quite recently, for example, the Inuit people of Alaska, Northern Canada, and Greenland, continued to have tent circles. As nomads, they followed game such as caribou or run of fish such as the Arctic char. To make these long treks less arduous, the Inuit carried only the skins for their tents and not the rocks that weighed them down. These were left at various hunting or fishing sites and used on each visit.

Basic structures or shelters followed an evolution similar to that of tools. The first shelters were probably caves. Then, early civilizations began to use whatever was at their disposal to create permanent structures as protection from the elements, animals, and marauding tribes. In many parts of the world, people used wood, mud, and other materials to build shelters that, like all human artifacts, were a reflection of place, time, and culture. The cliff dwellings of the Sinagua Indians in Arizona, built about six hundred years ago at Montezuma Castle, are particularly interesting as they are cave-like in one respect but also demonstrate the creative ability of people to design according to needs.

Coincidentally, most of these structures were also environmentally appropriate; Mother Nature easily reclaims wood and mud. Other civilizations, especially the nomadic ones, created temporary structures such as teepees and igloos. The latter is perhaps the finest example of a temporary structure or shelter and one that is totally appropriate to its Context. It is made of a found material, easily constructed, and is unbelievably effective in keeping its residents warm. It too, like the birch-bark canoe, can be easily and quickly reclaimed by nature.

Much like the tools described in the previous section, early structures, including cliff dwellings, had all the qualities of Artifacts created by a combined Designer/Maker/User in Context. Unlike today, people then did not create clear demarcations among the three roles. For our purpose, the Context will be the American southwest, where these early cliff dwellings remind us of how the early inhabitants designed structures for protection and did so reflecting the Age of Needs.

The Cliff Dwellings of the American Southwest
The American Southwest—more specifically Arizona, New Mexico, Utah, and Colorado—is the geographical

area where many of the first native North American tribes traveled and eventually settled. The earliest evidence of their presence dates back to around 9,000 BCE in the area known as Clovis, New Mexico, where spear points and knife blades were found in close proximity to bones of a now-extinct species of elephant. Clearly, this was still the period of hunter-gatherers. Later, at around 7,000 BCE, the first settlers arrived in the same general area in what is now western Arizona. Over time, people drifted eastward into New Mexico. Over the next several millennia and in various locations, the early inhabitants of the American southwest would develop the first permanent settlements.[iii] Three of these are discussed below.

The White House at Canyon de Chelly. Canyon de Chelly is located in northeast Arizona and has been inhabited on and off for nearly five thousand years, which is longer than any other locale in the Colorado Plateau. The first visitors, sometimes called the Anasazi or ancient people in Navajo, did not permanently settle in the canyon but came periodically to hunt and gather. Later, between 200 BCE and 750 BC, the pattern of the visitors changed from hunting and gathering to farming. Known as the Basketmakers, these people remained in the canyon and were the first to begin permanent settlements here, although in dispersed dwellings. Over time, they became more sedentary, starting communities, and with this change built structures such as granaries.

It would be the Pueblo people—between 750 CE and 1300 CE—who would eventually build the cliff dwellings at Canyon de Chelly. For unknown reasons—perhaps for defense or for more efficient farming, the Pueblo people left their scattered dwellings and began to create villages that included formidable structures such as cliff dwellings. The White House at Canyon de Chelly is one of the more magnificent of these southwest cliff dwellings. (See Figure 4.3.) The White House faces south in order to receive sun in the winter. It uses the cave as part of its architecture—both for structure, as the cave provides the floor, the roof, and the rear wall, and for protection from the elements and possible enemies. Quite obviously, the walls and other architectural elements are built using local stone and wood. The reason for building high up in the cliffs is not known exactly, however. There is speculation that it was for defense, but it could also have been for protection from flooding in the canyon or for allowing the land to be used for agriculture rather than as a building site.[iv]

Simon Ortiz is an Acoma Pueblo. His poem, Canyon de Chelly, captures several points of view important to Native Americans such as being one with nature and of timelessness. Combined with the visual impact that a visit to Canyon de Chelly has on an individual, his words resonate with the spirit of this place.

> Lie on your back on stone
> the stone carved to fit
> the shape of yourself.
> Who made it like this,
> knowing that I would be along
> in a million years and look
> at the sky being blue forever?

My son is near me. He sits
and turns on his butt
and crawls over the stones,
picks one up and holds it,
and then puts it in his mouth.
The taste of stone.
What is it but stone,
the earth in your mouth.
You, son, are tasting forever.

We walk to the edge of a cliff
and look down into the canyon.
On this side, we cannot see
the bottom cliffedge but looking
further out, we see fields,
sand furrows, cottonwoods.
In winter, they are softly gray,
The cliff's shadows are distant,
hundreds of feet below;
we cannot see our own shadows,
The wind moves softly into us,
My son laughs with the wind;
he gasps and laughs.

We find gray root, old wood,
so old, with curious twists
in it, curving back into curves,
juniper, pinon, or something
with hard, red berries in spring.
You taste them, and they are sweet
and bitter, the berries a delicacy
for bluejays. The plant rooted
fragilely in a sandy place

by a canyon wall, the sun bathing
shiny, pointed leaves.
My son touches the root carefully,
aware of its ancient quality.[v]

Tonto: Upper and Lower Cliff Dwellings. The Tonto cliff dwellings are set in the Tonto Basin in southern Arizona overlooking the Rio Salado, or Salt River. (See Figure 4.3.) There are two dwellings, a lower one and an upper one. Nomadic people traveled throughout this verdant valley as far back as seven thousand years ago, but the first people to inhabit the area permanently came much later, sometime around 100 to 600 CE. These early people took advantage of the bounty found in the river valley—small game, rich soil, and native plants—all of which provided an ideal setting for a permanent community and settlement.

The original Tonto settlement was abandoned around 1,400 years ago and, for unknown reasons, did not have any other residents for some 150 years. This is when the Hohokam people began to populate the valley and reestablish a community here. They not only lived in the Rio Salado area but also extended their range as far as the Gila River and present-day Phoenix. By 1150, the residents of the cliff dwellings had again changed, or at least the culture had changed, such that the people who resided there were no longer considered to be Hohokam but what we now call the Salado people. They lived in the valley and in these dwellings for some three hundred years and then again, for unknown reasons, left sometime between 1400 and 1450.

Walnut Canyon. Climate and natural resources play a central role when people decide to settle in one place instead of another. This would have certainly been the case for the Sinagua people some eight hundred years ago when they decided to inhabit Walnut Canyon. (See Figure 4.3.) The Sinagua were essentially hunter-gatherers but did do some trading with other tribes. In an area that tended to be arid and without much water, Walnut Canyon must have been a lush kingdom for them. Earlier people had previously visited the canyon, but no one before the Sinagua had ever permanently resided there.

Walnut Canyon is in northern Arizona, east of what is now the town of Flagstaff. The canyon provide the Sinagua people with not only wild game and useful plants but also shelter of a particular type. By their very nature, canyons can provide shelter; in some cases, they can also provide a microclimate in which certain plants can grow and certain animals can thrive. In the case of Walnut Canyon, however, it provided one thing more: a unique geological formation in the canyon walls that permitted the construction of shelters. Throughout Walnut Canyon, deep indentations in the canyon's limestone walls created ideal locations for permanent cliff dwellings. All that was needed were walls because the floor, rear wall, and roof already existed.

The Sinagua people occupied the cliff dwellings of Walnut Canyon for a relatively short period of time—a little over a hundred years—from around 1125 to 1250 CE. Like other cliff dwellers, they too moved to other parts of Arizona for unknown reasons. Some experts believe that the Sinagua were eventually assimilated into Hopi culture.

Arcosanti. Today, few if any contemporary structures are conceived with the same intentions that existed for the inhabitants of cliff dwellings. There is really no need to anymore. But there are exceptions. One of these structures supports a lifestyle pattern similar to the one set by the early cliff dwellers of the southwest United States albeit one thousand years later. Arcosanti is the structure. It is the life's work of Paulo Soleri, the Italian architect and former student of Frank Lloyd Wright, who, in many ways, replicates some of the same fundamental principles that underpinned the way of life for the Anasazi, Hohokam, Sinagua, Salado, and other Native Americans for about a thousand years. (See Figure 4.4.)

Arcosanti began in the 1960s and is based on a concept called arcology—a fusion of architecture and ecology initiated by Soleri. Even back in the 1960s, Soleri was keenly aware of the impact that people could have on the environment as they intervened with it in their quest to create an Artificial World within a Natural World. He was also equally aware that this intervention had consequences, especially as the scale of the intervention grew.

> In nature, as an organism evolves it increases in complexity and it also becomes a more compact or miniaturized system. Similarly a city should function as a living system. Arcology, architecture and ecology as one integral process, is capable of demonstrating positive response to the many problems of urban civilization, population, pollution, energy and natural resource depletion, food scarcity and quality of life. Arcology recognizes the necessity of the

radical reorganization of the sprawling urban landscape into dense, integrated, three-dimensional cities in order to support the complex activities that sustain human culture. The city is the necessary instrument for the evolution of humankind.[vi]

To visit Arcosanti today is to catch glimpses of how some Native Americans must have lived. Although the land on which Arcosanti sits is vast, the sector designated for human habitation is small and concentrated in one area. Most of the land is left untouched for environmental reasons. The people who live at Arcosanti do so in a communal way, which includes the sharing of facilities as well as the work required to make the community subsist. Residents are involved in the building of additions to the structures, for example, as well as the making of everyday things such as the famous Soleri bells. Fruit and vegetables are grown on the land. To a large extent, Arcosanti is a self-sustaining community, much like the cliff-dwelling communities were centuries ago.

Signs

Communication at the time of the hunter-gatherers was oral. Primitive forms of signs or visual communication came much later and in Africa, sometime around 200,000 years ago. Most of these earliest signs occurred as either pictographs or petroglyphs. A pictograph is an image painted on stone usually using charcoal for black and red and yellow oxides for the ochre tones.[vii] What may be some of the earliest known examples of pictographs were discovered in Italy and may have been created anywhere between 32,000 to 36,000 years ago.

Similar evidence of early pictographs also exist in southern France at the Grotte Chauvet, dating back about 32,000 years, and at the famous Lascaux caves dating to 15,000 to 10,000 BCE.

Petroglyphs are also a visual representation but are different from pictographs. They are images carved into a rock (*petro* means rock; *glyph* means carving). Because they are etched and not painted, petroglyphs generally stand up better to the elements and therefore tend to last longer. Petroglyphs are usually of three types: anthropomorphs, or human-like figures such as stick figures; zoomorphs, or figures in the shape of animals such as snakes, turtles, and deer; and geometric figures of one sort or another such as parallel lines, spirals, and arrows. They are found throughout the world, especially in Africa and North America. (Figure 4.5 shows several petroglyphs found on three different sites in Arizona.)

There is a temptation to perceive and understand both pictographs and petroglyphs in the context of today's mindset about visual representations. Consequently, some people consider the magnificent cave paintings at Lascaux early examples of fine art. It is an error to do so because the societal values and mores of the earliest hunter-gatherers were dramatically different from those of today. These cave paintings and other pictographs and petroglyphs were not examples of fine art—not unless we consider fine art as being anything to which we attach the name. If anything, the drawings in Lascaux were the earliest form of visual communication and told a story. They most likely served a utilitarian or ritualistic function.[viii] In the same vein, these pictographs and petroglyphs were not writing per se but would be the foundation of what would become written languages much later. (Written languages are discussed in greater detail in chapter 5.) Signs remain as important today as they were hundreds of thousands of years ago. We see their contemporary version every day and everywhere—in the wayfinding systems found at airports, on washroom walls in public buildings, on highway signs as we drive to and from work, and on our computer screens as icons—for icons are nothing more than a virtual version of the cave dwellers' pictograph.

Signs in the American Southwest

The petroglyphs found throughout the southwest United States may not be among the oldest signs created by human civilization but they do offer a varied collection of styles and, like all petroglyphs, are extremely revealing. They date from as early as 650 CE to around 1425 CE. Some of the better groupings are in various parts of Arizona, especially in the Sedona area.

The petroglyphs located on the V Bar V Ranch near Sedona are among the best anywhere in the American southwest. (See Figure 4.5.) There are some one thousand individual petroglyphs etched in a sandstone wall no more than 40 feet wide. The oldest of these most likely dates back to 1150; most of them, however, were executed later, probably between 1300 and 1400. All three types of petroglyphs can be found at the V Bar V Ranch site.[ix] One geometric petroglyph is particularly interesting. It appears to be a crude calendar meant for agricultural purposes. It is composed of a series of lines and, because of its location on the wall and a crack in an adjoining rock, a shadow is cast over the lines. The location of the shadow of the rock made it possible for people to predict the start of a season.

The petroglyphs at Palatki Ruins, also near Sedona, are equally interesting. (See Figure 4.5.) They are located near the cliff dwellings at the same general site but are not connected to the people who inhabited the dwellings. The petroglyphs predate them by several thousand years. Like the petroglyphs at the V Bar V Ranch, the earliest ones were created by the Sinagua, the earliest people in the area and thereafter by the Yavapi and the Apache. The petroglyphs at Palatki Ruins are a collection of signs representing both anthropomorphs and zoomorphs as well as geometric figures, and include human figures, bears, deer, snakes, and circles.

The petroglyphs at both the V Bar V Ranch and Palatki Ruins have been extensively studied. Consequently, a great deal is known about them. However, not as much is known about the petroglyphs found at Baird Ranch in Winslow, Arizona. (See Figure 4.5.) They are numerous—easily over one thousand on both sides of the canyon walls—and, once again, probably date back four to five thousand years. There are certainly some indications of Hopi influence in some of the later petroglyphs, as can be seen in the figure of the woman giving birth. Her hair is arranged in buns on each side of her head, which is a tradition in Hopi culture.

Summary

Most of our earliest ancestors were Designers/Makers/Users all rolled into one. Moreover, there was little choice in the matter. Driven by their daily need for survival, people had to design everything that they needed—tools, structures, and signs. There were no "expert" Designers to create novel solutions to everyday problems as we have today nor was there a plethora of Makers to produce these everyday things. The White House at Canyon de Chelly is a good example of this scenario. It most likely did not have either a designated architect or a designated general contractor—at least not in the way that we understand these roles today. However, the White House certainly had Users, and as with all everyday things of the era, Users were equally Designers and Makers.

This inclusive relationship among the Designer/Maker/User would not change for thousands of years. With survival as the only driving force—the physiological needs as described in Maslow's Hierarchy of Needs—designing would evolve extremely slowly. It would be the Age of Surplus that would set the stage for the first significant change in The Designing Triad. The User would become an independent entity for the first time and exist as something different from the Designer/Maker. This is the topic for the next chapter.

Further Reading

Bryant, Kathleen M. *Stories in Stone*, in *Arizona Highways*.

Carr, Geoffrey. *The Story of Man: The Proper Study of Mankind*.

Diamond, Jared. *Gun, Germs, and Steel: The Fates of Human Societies*.

Meggs, Phillip B. *A History of Graphic Design*.

www.arcosanti.org/theory/arcology/main.html; November 20, 2007.

Endnotes

[i] Diamond, Jared. *Guns, Germs, and Steel*.

[ii] Ibid.

[iii] Lister, Robert H. and Florence C. Lister. *Those Who Came Before*.

[iv] Thybony, Scott. *Canyon de Chelly National Monument*.

[v] Ortiz, Simon. *A Good Journey*.

[vi] www.arcosanti.org/theory/arcology/main.html

[vii] Meng, Philip B. *A History of Graphic Design*.

[viii] Ibid.

[ix] Bryant, Kathleen M. *Stories in Stone,* in Arizona Highways.

CHAPTER 5

The Age of Surplus

Place, People, and Process

In different places and at different times in human evolution, people became less nomadic and ceased to move about constantly in order to hunt for game and forage for food. The reasons for this change to a more sedentary lifestyle varied from culture to culture and from one geographical location to another. It also occurred sooner in certain parts of the world and later elsewhere, where things remained much the same for centuries.[i] Some Bedouin people of North Africa, for example, are still semi-nomadic, even today, as are some isolated tribes in Mongolia, Tibet, and Ethiopia. Nevertheless, the pattern of change was much the same throughout the world. People began to settle down in permanent locations, and, with this change, village life began to appear on most continents. This change marked the beginning of the Agrarian Age.

By settling down, our early ancestors forever altered designing in two significant ways. First, they created settlements or communities larger than the small tribal groups that had preceded them. With larger communities came

social dynamics and political systems that had not been present in small groups. Along with communities came the need for permanent shelter or buildings. We first saw a hint of this in chapter 4 with people who lived in cliff dwellings. Such primitive abodes would ultimately give way to more complex entities such as villages, towns, and cities—all of which occurred because of designing, including the tools associated with this social development.

The second change that altered designing was the existence of surplus. In the context of The Designing Triad, this was highly significant because it forever changed the relationship among the Designer, the Maker, and the User. No longer were they inseparable; their respective functions no longer needed to reside in one person as they did in the Age of Needs. This separation came as the result of the surplus of crops and other food products that often resulted from agriculture and animal husbandry. Farmers produced more food than their families could eat, and these surpluses became commodities that could be traded for goods, such as other kinds of food or everyday things. This meant that farmers, for example, could own and use everyday things that they themselves did not make. The User now existed as someone independent from the Designer/Maker. This scenario had never occurred previously.

The age of the Designer/Maker was the age of artisans—people who both designed and made everyday things. Artisans exercised their crafts in myriad ways, from useful wares such as tools and weapons to everyday things that were more artistic such as sculptures and applied decorations. The Etruscans, a pre-Roman civilization in Italy, exhibited some of the earliest works that we associate today with artisanship, or craftsmanship. They not only created architecture that inspired the Romans but also designed and made exquisite jewelry as well as magnificent bronze statues. The Etruscans may not have been the first society with a strong artisan culture, but they clearly established the model for what would become the role of the Designer/Maker in the Designing Triad and in society.[ii]

Returning to the agrarian shift in civilization, the first signs of village life and of farming occurred simultaneously around 8500 BCE in several parts of the Middle East and North Africa. These early efforts were limited to the cultivation of wild grains but eventually would include other crops as well as the domestication of dogs, goats, and sheep. Around 7000 BCE, wheat and other similar grains were regularly cultivated at the same time that pigs and cattle were domesticated. Evidence of pottery indicates that storage devices were needed in these cultures. Baskets, ceramic jars, and jugs were among the first everyday things, and these existed because of the need to store the surplus that was being created on a more regular basis. (See Figure 5.1.) Eventually, people learned to design things using various metals. The first everyday things made from copper show up around 6000 BCE, and then bronze, around 3000 BCE, in what would become known as the Bronze Age. Later came the Iron Age, with early examples of iron tools around 1200 BCE in parts of the Near and Middle East (what is now Iran) and India, and later in Europe at around 800 BCE in Central Europe and around 600 BCE in Northern Europe.

By about 3000 BCE, the Egyptians were beginning to establish a society that was significantly more complex than anything that had existed previously. Their civilization would last for over two thousand years, leaving behind social developments that we now take for granted, such as the model for a national government, fundamental concepts of mathematics, and the 365-day calendar. It also left a rich legacy of Artifacts and architecture, while its hieroglyphics provided one of the earliest examples of signs as a written language.

As an example of structures, the pyramids certainly rank as the most important visual expressions in Egyptian culture. The Egyptians constructed them as tombs for their rulers. The importance of the pyramid as an archetype is manifestly evident today, so much so that when the American architect I. M. Pei was commissioned to do an addition for the Louvre Museum in Paris in the mid-1980s, he based his design on the classic form of the Egyptian pyramid, some four thousand years after the Egyptians built the first ones. (See Figure 5.2.)

Other societies flourished in the Mediterranean area in this same era. Like Egypt, early Greek civilization—in the period between 2000 and 200 BCE—was also rich in Artifacts and architecture, as well as philosophy (Socrates, Aristotle, and Plato), mathematics, and early studies in the sciences. For Designers, the most significant and pervasive formal element bequeathed by the Greeks was the architectural column, of which there were three visually distinctive orders: Doric, Ionic, and Corinthian. Throughout many European capitals and modern American cities, the architectural column remains a visual symbol of prestige and authority. Most state capitol buildings, for example, are festooned with columns of one kind or another, as are the homes of many of the so-called rich and famous. Designers can also use columns in a way that is contemporary, such as was done by Gae Aulenti, the Italian architect and Designer, when she renovated one of Milan's main railway stations. She used an array of undecorated deep-red columns on the outside of the station's main entrance as a kind of visual break between the streetscape and the building itself. As people enter or leave the station, they transition from one environment to the other via this landscape of colorful columns. (See Figure 5.3.)

In much the same vein, Roman civilization (750 BCE to c. 500 CE) provided new directions in art and architecture that continue to influence design and the built environment today. The most important of these is probably the arch, an architectural device that permitted phenomenal feats of construction such as bridges and viaducts, some of which are still standing today. Beyond its appropriateness as a structural element, the arch also came to play a symbolic role in society. It was often constructed to commemorate an historical event. Probably the finest example of an arch—at 162 feet, it is, at least, the largest—is l'Arc de Triomphe in Paris, begun in 1806 and completed in 1836. Napoleon I commissioned it as a memorial to his armies and soldiers, long after the Roman Empire had used the concept for similar purposes. The arch's fundamental structure was to eventually lead to the dome, which is essentially an arch projected 360°. It would become yet another architectural device that would serve both a practical and a symbolic purpose. (See Figure 5.4.)

The period between the fall of the Roman Empire and the Gothic era is generally considered bleak and dark throughout Europe. The barbarian invasions brought destruction, and with it the end of any memorable evolution in art and architecture. It was not until the Gothic era (1100 to 1600 CE) that a slow but progressive development with strong religious overtones was to occur in architecture and everyday things. This was especially the case with the Gothic arch. The religious fervor that transfixed European societies affected people in many ways but probably none was more expressive as the pointed arch, symbolically pointing to the heavens. Structurally, it allowed the builders of Gothic churches to erect edifices that surpassed all others of the time. It was by far the most impressive architectural device and became a timeless formal element of the era. Pointed arches are not as common as they used to be, at least not in modern architecture, except perhaps for those used by McDonald's. The fast-food restaurant chain came to be known for its golden arches after adopting them as its signature marketing tool some six hundred years after the first arches appeared in Europe. (See Figure 5.5.)

By the time of the Renaissance (1300 to 1600 CE), or rebirth, European civilization had made phenomenal advances in the arts and sciences. The Renaissance borrowed heavily from the retrieved aesthetic ideals of Greece and Rome, but only in form; in scope, it would surpass both. Art and architecture became more refined and the scale more grandiose.

Renaissance architecture reached its pinnacle with Michelangelo's design of Saint Peter's Basilica in Rome. Two elements of the Basilica—Saint Peter's Square and the Dome—stand out as exemplars of the Renaissance as well as the Baroque style in the later additions to the Basilica. The square (Piazza di San Pietro designed by Gianlorenzo Bernini between 1656 and 1667) is the metaphorical motherly arms of the church, greeting and embracing you as you walk toward the basilica itself. The arms of the square are composed of two elliptical colonnades containing twin pairs of columns. In the center of the square stands an obelisk, which is over 25 meters tall (nearly 85 feet). The obelisk is originally from Egypt and dates back to the thirteenth century BCE. It was moved to Rome in AD 37.

As an architectural statement, the dome of the Basilica is as impressive as the square. However, the dome that now exists is not exactly faithful to Michelangelo's design. His original idea was for a spherical dome but at the time of his death in 1564 only the base of the dome had been completed. The dome on St. Peter's Basilica today was the work of Giacomo della Porta, who redesigned it as a vaulted structure. It is a double dome of brick construction (you can actually walk between the two layers) with an interior diameter of nearly 150 feet and which rises nearly 400 feet above the floor.

As impressive as the architecture and construction of Saint Peter's Basilica may be, it is the emotional and spiritual impact that resonates with visitors and forever changes them after their visit. It is not just the first visit that resonates—it is every visit afterwards. No text, photograph, or virtual tour could ever provide or replicate the overwhelming feelings one experiences when inside. The scale of both the square and basilica is certainly one factor. They are massive, yet not so much that people feel alien in the place. However, scale alone is not the only reason for the emotional and spiritual impact of Saint Peter's; larger buildings are constructed every day, but few of them elicit the same emotional and spiritual feelings. If scale is not the reason, then perhaps it is the superb details, which are almost infinite in number and found throughout St. Peter's. In combination, they create an environment that is not only visually integrated but also spiritually powerful. How can details alone, no matter how good, be so potent as to emotionally and spiritually move people as Saint Peter's does?

Perhaps it is the history of Saint Peter's that is its main asset. After all, history provides a sense of continuity and permanence. For most of us, anything that has survived the test of time—an idea, a philosophical concept, an ethical premise, a scientific theory, a classic design—is deemed to be superior to something that has been short-lived. Yet, a person can visit churches as old as St. Peter's and never leave with anything like the same feelings. In the end, there is no one element that adequately explains the impact of Saint Peter's. Scale, details, history, and other attributes all factor in to the physical nature of Saint Peter's, but it is the unexplainable synergy that results from their unique combination that makes it such a mystical place to experience.

The Renaissance was equally known for scientific and technological advances. The invention of movable metallic type was certainly among the most important of these. Although the Chinese and Koreans had developed a similar printing process using wood blocks or porcelain type, it was Johannes Gutenberg (ca. 1400–1468) who in the mid-1400s provided the means for a practical and efficient way of printing books, eliminating the need to tediously hand-write copies. At a more substantial level, printing would begin to democratize Europe because a broader segment of the population would become more literate, and with literacy came empowerment.

Perhaps more than any single person, it was Leonardo da Vinci (1452–1519) who exemplified the qualities implicit in the Renaissance. He was both an artist and an engineer, and became the model for what we today call the Renaissance man. His combination of intuitive and rational thinking was to become a model for modern-day Designers. A quick glance at only a few of his inventions aptly demonstrates the breadth and depth of his imagination. Many of his concepts were so clearly ahead of his time that the technology of the day was incapable of producing them. (See Figure 1.9.)

Today's Designers have a great deal to learn from the Renaissance period. The least obvious and yet most important may be the fact that history repeats itself. The revival of past ideas and styles and their reinterpretation—as undertaken by Renaissance artists and architects—would eventually become common and be referred to as pattern and pattern recognition. Isn't the new Volkswagen Beetle the revival of the original Beetle designed nearly seventy years ago? What about retro fashion? Isn't that retrieving from the past? Clearly, what is old can always become new again.

By the seventeenth and eighteenth centuries, art and architecture in Europe had become refined, sophisticated, and, in some respects, visually contrived. This was especially true with the Baroque and Rococo styles, both of which epitomized this refinement in visual expression. Three elements contributed to this change. First, there was a rejection of visual and aesthetic ideals of the Renaissance, a direction governed by restraint, control, and symmetry. Second, buildings and everyday things were almost always designed and meant for the royalty and nobility—the so-called elite of society—as an overt means of expressing their position and power. This was certainly the case in France with opulent chateaux like Versailles and the smaller yet no less opulent ones of the Loire Valley. (See Figure 3.4.) In their insatiable quest for beauty in every aspect of life, Europeans—led principally by the French—demanded and received extraordinary accomplishments from their artisans. These exceptional craftsmen transformed the most ordinary everyday things—furniture, cutlery, tableware—into true works of art and, in the process, forged themselves into consummate Designer/Makers.

If that wasn't enough, a religious revival swept Europe and along with it a desire to manifest this enthusiasm in the design of buildings, especially churches. Toward the end of the eighteenth century, when hints of the

Industrial Revolution began to appear, all ranks of artisans seemed to be driven by one compulsion: to demonstrate their stupendous skills to the world before technology would begin to make them superfluous.

One artisan of this period who remains current even today is Antonio Stradivari, the well-known Designer and Maker of the Stradivarius violins. Stradivari was born in Italy in 1644 into a family of Makers of violins and other string instruments. His early instruments were not particularly remarkable, but sometime after 1698 there was a noticeable change in quality. His violins became works of art, not only as Artifacts but also as tools that could produce sounds like no other. No one knows exactly how Stradivari achieved this level of quality. Was it the materials that he selected—spruce, poplar, and maple? Was it the treatment of the wood, which he did himself? Was it the finish that he applied, which has been analyzed but never replicated? Was it his craftsmanship and attention to detail? Most likely, it was all of these elements and more. Nevertheless, his violins continue to be coveted by musicians and prized by collectors. On May 16, 2006, a Stradivarius sold for $3,544,000 at a Christie's auction. As a point of interest, the tradition of fine instrument making continues in Cremona, Italy, the city where Stradivari worked. Violins and cellos are still being made by the craftsmen who have followed in his footsteps. The best of them can produce no more than four to seven instruments a year, which on average sell for $20,000 for a violin and $40,000 for a cello.[iii]

This situation—ornate everyday things masterfully executed mostly for the elite—was to radically change with the Industrial Revolution and the mechanization that

ensued. The Industrial Revolution was characterized by the unfolding of an enormously complicated series of events. In the seventeenth century, industrial techniques had become more elaborate. Many of the discoveries of the Scientific Revolution had entered the public domain, such as those of the English scientist and mathematician Sir Isaac Newton (1642–1727). After 1760, the date commonly used to mark the beginning of the Industrial Revolution, the rate of change—scientific, cultural, and economic—increased rapidly. In the remaining years of the eighteenth century, the number of patents for inventions granted in England, for example, increased ten times over, and hundreds of factories sprang up—many of them powered by James Watt's perfected steam engine. Many everyday things, such as books and furniture, began to be mass-produced and available to a greater number of people.

The Independent Maker

Designing was continuing to democratize society. The separation of the User from the Designer/Maker, which had first begun in the Agrarian Age, had been the first step in this process. However, this separation was now a fait accompli. What was now beginning to appear was a split between the Designer and the Maker. Industrialization facilitated this split because its potential, irrespective of the Designer, allowed the Maker to become an independent agent in the making process.

It was industrialization, especially in England, that became the thin edge of the wedge of this separation. But why England? One reason was the abundance of venture capital at low interest rates. An even more significant factor was the rise in the number of consumers. With better sanitation, including the introduction of the modern water closet in 1778, the availability of improved medical care, and the provision of cleaner water, the population of England and Wales jumped from roughly 6.5 million to 9 million in the last half of the eighteenth century.

Labor for the new factories came principally as the result of the mechanization in agriculture. Until about 1730, farming practices in the English countryside had remained unchanged from those of the Middle Ages. After 1730, however, the great landholders, who followed the lead of a few pioneers, became increasingly aware that farming could be immensely profitable if done scientifically. This change decreased the need for manual labor, thereby making workers available to the factories.

Despite the obvious social benefits that were created as the result of the Industrial Revolution, not even the most ardent admirer of the capitalistic system would paint this period in history as a golden age for human rights. The new manufacturers, free of legal restraints—and often of ethical ones too—moved with ruthless confidence in the midst of moral confusion. Uncertain whether it was wicked or good to hire children, they hired them. Able to provide men with regular work and regular pay, they seldom, if ever, raised wages and often required their workers to work fourteen, sixteen, and sometimes even eighteen hours per day. Workers had to conform to the most rigid discipline, and punishment for those who disobeyed the rules was often harsh and brutal.

There were at least three important social divisions that can be attributed to the Industrial Revolution. One was the division between skills, such as manual aptitude to make everyday things, and knowledge, which was the result of scientific discoveries.[iv] It created the concept of specialization that would become the trademark of the eighteenth century. Its impact on skills was especially evident as it gave rise to the trades, the unions, and the professions. It also had an impact on knowledge because physics, astronomy, mechanics, chemistry, and psychology gradually broke away from the all-inclusive natural philosophy of the seventeenth century and became individual fields of study.

This division of skills and knowledge led to another division: the division of labor. That is, manufacturing became more efficient and effective with the division of making into separate parts and functions. This was totally different from the Age of Needs, when one person was more often than not responsible for all of the making process.

The third social division was the aforementioned split between the artisans, or Designers, and the manufacturers, or Makers. This division seriously impacted designing then and still does now to various degrees. The role of artisans—the predecessors to the Designers as independent agents from the Makers—became both questionable and controversial. On the one hand, artisans had always been responsible for the formal appearance, or design, of everyday things prior to the Industrial Revolution; on the other hand, most manufacturers did not see the need to employ artisans. With machine production, copying was much easier. As a result, many everyday things mimicked the visual language of handmade Artifacts although they were produced in a radically different way. In the end, mass production won the day, and most artisans were systematically excluded from the designing and making process. Everyday things that had been previously handmade became nothing more than mass-produced copies. Moreover, the design of these new everyday things did not reflect the new manufacturing technology.[v] The exclusion of the Designer from the making process would remain a pattern in manufacturing and would only be challenged deliberately in the latter part of the eighteenth century with Art Nouveau.

An important development that resulted from the conflict between craftsmen and mass-producers was the notion of design for industry and for the masses, as opposed to design for crafts and the elite. Unfortunately, it was almost inevitable that the first mass-produced designs would formally mimic their handmade predecessors. Consequently, the overriding question of design ethics soon became *Should the designs created by the new technology don a new costume or should they continue to wear the fashions of the old?* The question was not fully answered then, and in many respects remains unanswered today.

Three individuals would prove to be noteworthy exceptions to the fissure between Designer and Maker that was becoming apparent. One was the master potter, inventor, industrialist, and retailer Josiah Wedgwood (1730–1795). He did not accept the concept that the artisan needed to be divorced from the manufacturing process. He established a "manufactory" at Stoke-on-Trent, England, where he put his beliefs into practice. Wedgwood employed artists and other artisans, but not for their specific artistic vocations. He was a shrewd judge of the marketplace and clearly saw

that a visual enhancement of his designs would serve to increase his sales. He also introduced the concept of division of labor, as well as the production of 'useful' wares, which was a precursor of the everyday thing.

William Morris (1834–1896), like Wedgwood, objected to mass production's elimination of the artisan as Designer and Maker. Unlike Wedgwood, however, Morris condemned industry and manufactured design, especially the ethical, moral, and social conditions created by the new technology. He advocated a return to the past and to the handmade objects of medieval times. With a group of other like-minded individuals, including the social critic John Ruskin, Morris founded the Arts and Crafts Movement. Its key goals included the revival of handcraftsmanship; improvement of the quality of life; artistic cooperation; collaborative design unifying the interior and exterior; and function and simplicity. Unfortunately, the ideas of Morris, as enlightened as they may have been, had minimal effect on British industry. In large part, industry generally continued to evolve without the input of artisans or Designers.

Michael Thonet (1796–1871) also made a unique contribution to the challenges posed by industrialization by taking advantage of the opportunities provided by the new industrial methods. (Thonet's contribution is discussed in greater depth in the section on tools later in this chapter.)

Wedgwood, Morris, and Thonet exemplified a recurring phenomenon in designing: changes in technology and in society can create new opportunities. Wedgwood took the opportunity to involve artisans because it made commercial sense; Morris responded to change by retrieving values from the past; and Thonet adapted to technological change by taking furniture design and manufacturing in a totally new direction. Because of their actions and that of others, everyday things began to enter the public domain at a faster pace and the designing process came to be more democratic. This was only the beginning. Over the next century, design would become less elitist and clearly more populist in character.

The philosophical discourse between the formal attributes of craftsmanship and mass production continued well into the nineteenth century. Everyday things were now being produced in ever-greater numbers, and the paradox between old styles and new means of production was becoming more apparent. While academic research and intellectual debate were directed at determining which historical form was most suitable for adoption as a contemporary national style, manufacturers pillaged the stylistic canons of past cultures in search of novelty. Consequently, the indiscriminate application of ornament resulted all too often in a gulf between style and function.

One of the first persons to address this gulf in an official manner was Henry Cole (1808–1882), a British civil servant who took the basic design and social concerns expressed by his predecessor, William Morris, and formulated them into a contemporary position. As sound as Morris's arguments may have been, they had not been adopted by a large audience. Cole proposed a different approach. He did not advocate a return to the values and lifestyles of a bygone era but was much more concerned about the contemporary scene and how art could serve industry. In 1849, Cole founded the *Journal of Design*, in which he promoted his ideals.

> Design has a twofold relation, having in the first place, a strict reference to utility in the thing designed; and, secondarily, to the beautifying or ornamenting of that utility. The word design, however, with the many has become identified rather with its secondary than its whole signification—with ornament, as apart from, and often even as opposed to, utility. From thus confounding that which is in itself but an addition, with that which is essential, has arisen many of those great errors in taste which are observable in the works of modern Designers.[vi]

Fortunately for Cole, Prince Albert—the husband of Queen Victoria—was a great ally of this new industrial direction and became the patron behind the Great Exhibition of 1851. Under the theme of "Progress," the exhibition was designed to display "the Works of Industry of All Nations," a kind of world showcase of contemporary everyday things. To house the exhibition, a specially designed building was commissioned, which, in retrospect, became more important in terms of design than the everyday things displayed within its walls. The Crystal Palace, as it was called, was in every way indicative of this new era of mass production without an obvious dependency on a visual aesthetic of the past. It provided a functional environment with open spaces and natural light; it did not advocate a particularly well known architectural style. If anything, it was an example of what would become industrialized fabrication.

The Crystal Palace covered nineteen acres in London's Hyde Park, with an overall floor space of nearly one million square feet. Everything from a block of coal weighing twenty-four tons to a thirty-one-ton Great Western locomotive were displayed under one roof. Given that there were more than 6,500 exhibitors from around the world, the Great Exhibition was a clear demonstration of industrial progress. While major exhibits were mounted by Belgium, France, Germany, and the United States, Britain stood out among all the other countries; half of the hall was dedicated to its designs.

The designing picture in the United States was quite different than it was in Europe during the same period. To begin with, America was not burdened with well-entrenched social norms and conditions such as those found in most of Europe. On the contrary, the United States was an experiment begun by Europeans fleeing from these very same social norms and conditions. Their desire was to create something new and better, something based on the principles of egalitarianism and meritocracy. Be that as it may, this idealism was not directly reflected in the formal qualities of early design. If anything, the first examples of design in early America were essentially extensions of designs found in Europe. American Designer and author Victor Papanek called this phenomenon "post-pioneer society," referring to a situation in which colonists bring with them what they already know, whether it is their literature, music, art, cuisine, or design. Of course, this was only natural. Cabinetmakers who had emigrated from England, for example, brought templates and models with them and proceeded to make replicas of the same furniture in America.

Consequently, early American design—furniture, tools, and architecture—was strongly influenced by the traditions in England and France.

Moreover, an American style would take some time to evolve because the concerns of the average citizen were more focused on the challenges of creating a country, which often included a struggle for physical survival. Additionally, the transfer of new ideas from Europe was exceptionally slow. Therefore, it comes as no surprise that design was not a preoccupation of early Americans. As one case in point, the United States of the late nineteenth century was a place where "the freedom of the pioneer soon came to mean freedom to make money, which is probably why America developed so differently in social terms than Europe."[vii]

History would go on to dramatically show that the success of the American democratic experiment was due in large part to the tenacity and resolve of Americans as expressed through their innovation but not necessarily their artistic exploration. What logically developed were mechanical contrivances rather than aesthetic or cultural statements. The socio-economic profiles of these cultures—Europe and the United States—provided two quite different scenarios, one with a long-established history in both artistic and scientific evolution, and the other revering a young, post-pioneering value system. As a consequence, the strong industrial movement already afoot in the United States did not have an artistic counterpart. The United States would continue to look to Europe for anything cultural. Designing—as a unique and original art form—would only begin to develop in the late nineteenth century.

The Centennial Exhibition in Philadelphia in 1876 provided some early but limited encouragement in terms of design and form development. Under the banner "Industrial Arts and Good Taste," the exhibit showcased achievements in both the arts and the sciences. Invitations were extended to all nations of the world to come and participate in the event under the theme of "the happy mean . . . which combines the utility that serves the body with the beauty that satisfies the mind." However, most of the everyday things displayed were no more than "ostentatious echoes of European eclecticism." To some design critics, these styles became known as "Late Halloween" or "Early Awful." The separation of function and aesthetics was evident in many of the exhibits. As the eminent American design scholar Arthur Pulos has noted, the very long tradition of the fine arts, which was a fait accompli in Europe and well integrated in everyday life there, was not part of the American cultural scenario.[viii]

Despite this artistic vacuum, the United States was becoming known as a nation of inventors, where mechanical devices were more valued than aesthetic ideals. In this respect, four individuals stand out and are exemplars of this American inventiveness in the fields of communication, technology, and transportation, respectively.

Alexander Graham Bell (1847–1922) is best known as the inventor of the telephone.[ix] Although not born in the United States, Bell researched and developed many of his ideas on American soil. In 1874, at the relatively young age of twenty-seven, he discovered the principles of electrical speech transmission. This was significant because speech had never been transmitted over a wire, although signals and music had been via the telegraph. In 1876, just two years after Bell's initial discovery, he was granted a patent for the telephone.

It is fascinating to note that Bell's personal interest in speech and speech transmission came from his vocation as a teacher of the deaf. It was said that he would have preferred to be remembered as a teacher rather than as the inventor of the telephone. His father, Alexander Melville Bell, and his grandfather, Alexander Bell, had also taught the deaf and specialized in speech education. Therefore, the inventor's curiosity about speech and his passion for the deaf were not at all surprising. In one of those rare and often mysterious moments of insight so common to inventors, Bell made the connection between speech and speech transmission. Today's ubiquitous cell phone owes everything to our capacity to hear and to Bell's ingenuity. All that we have done with the cell phone is to stretch the effective distance and mobility of Bell's invention.

Bell's inventiveness and curiosity, however, went well beyond the telephone. He is credited with the invention of the hydrofoil principle in naval architecture and played a significant role in the first powered flight in the British Commonwealth when he assisted John A. D. McCurdy, a Canadian engineering student, in a biplane that flew across Bras d'Or Lake in Nova Scotia, Canada.

Thomas Alva Edison (1847–1931) would become the epitome of the American inventor-genius. By any standard, he was one of the most prolific inventors of his or any other time. Moreover, many scientists and historians would consider that Edison's greatest contribution was not one invention or another but the concept of the first modern research laboratory. The process, it would seem, was as important as the findings. Among his many inventions, it would be difficult to select the most important. Was it his ideas for practical electrical lighting, the phonograph, or the light bulb? Perhaps it was his improvements and innovations to the telegraph, telephone, and motion pictures.

Edison embodied what we now consider to be the inveterate Designer. He was never satisfied with one solution to a problem but would develop multiple avenues of design exploration. Nor did Edison limit himself to a narrowness of perception when it came to using technology. He vigorously explored features from one technology and then adapted them to another. Moreover, he was exceptionally curious, working closely with his assistants to understand their areas of expertise such as mechanics, electricity, and chemistry.

In another respect, Edison had a talent possessed by few designers: he was an exceptionally good businessman. Not only did he amass a personal fortune for himself, but he was also among those responsible for positioning the United States as a world industrial leader and economic power. He obtained 1,093 American patents as well as thousands more from other countries. No other person has ever received that many patents from the U.S. Patent Office.

Few inventions have changed our lives as much as air transportation. What was initially perceived as an unimaginable feat—people actually lifting off the ground and flying like a bird—soon became an everyday activity, reducing traveling from days to hours. More than that, air transportation would eventually become accessible to almost everyone. We owe all of this to two people: Orville and Wilbur Wright, born in 1871 and 1867, respectively. They are generally regarded as the inventors and builders of the first controllable airplane—that is, the first powered and sustained heavier-than-air human flight with controls, which allowed a person to actually fly the airplane. Other inventors had built and flown experimental aircrafts, but it was the Wright brothers who made it possible for the pilot to control the flight by way of what was called a *three axis-control,* which would become a standard aeronautic principle in all fixed-wing airplanes.[x] This milestone in human invention occurred on December 17, 1903, in Kitty Hawk, North Carolina.

Like Bell and Edison, it is interesting to note that the Wright Brothers were involved in myriad activities, all of which most likely combined to provide the skills and knowledge necessary to make possible this phenomenal technological leap forward. For example, both brothers had extensive experience in their shop with printing presses, bicycles, motors, and other machinery. One can only imagine the synergy that would be derived from such an experience and how that same synergy would eventually allow for the breakthrough of controlled flight.

Bell's telephone was exhibited in the Centennial Exhibition in 1876, but so were many other ingenious inventions or, better stated, contraptions. They included a bed that could be transformed into a sofa and a washstand that became a writing desk. The creation of both of these products was justified on the grounds that a young couple furnishing their first home needed such adaptability for economic reasons. This attitude of function at the expense of form was noticed and commented upon by many observers: "The Anglo-American [nation]. . . seems [to be] the only nation in whom the love of ornament is not inherent. The Yankee whittles a stick but his cuttings never take a decorative form . . . an electric telegraph, but not an embroidery machine."[xi]

This penchant for function over form was applied not only to inventions but also to the manufacturing processes. At the same exhibit, the American Watch Company showed how a watch could be produced in large quantities using interchangeable parts. This process became known as the American System of Manufacture. It was precisely this notion of quantity that gave American design its particular flavor. Whereas certain European designs continued to be available generally to the upper classes, the American ideal was significantly different: make all designs available to all Americans. This direction was the direct result of an underlying political premise of egalitarianism, a concept that did not have much currency in the monarchies and other class-bound countries of Europe. The inventions of Alexander Graham Bell, Thomas Alva Edison, and the Wright brothers, much like the manufacturing innovations of Henry Ford, were focused much more on practicality for and availability to the User. No one ever truly expected that aesthetic qualities would also be considered.

Tools

If there was one feature most identified with the Age of Surplus, it was the increasing abundance and availability of everyday things. In this vein, the furniture of Michael Thonet and the early automobiles of Henry Ford are exemplars of this phenomenon. Admittedly, there were other Designer/Makers of the day who were also contributing to the cornucopia of everyday things, but Thonet and Ford stand out as innovators on two fronts. Both men had the User squarely in mind when designing and both developed appropriate technology for the making process.

Michael Thonet

The Thonet story begins in Germany at around 1819, when Michael Thonet (1796–1871) started to manufacture wooden furniture. A decade or so later, he began his first experiments with bentwood construction and produced the *Bopparder Schichtholzstuhl* (Boppard layerwood chair) in 1836. Thonet continued to experiment with bent wood and found that laminated wood rods, steamed and bent, would not crack, unlike straight-grained wood, if carved into the same shapes. This technical revelation became the basis for bentwood furniture and what would be the trademark of the Thonet company.

Thonet was probably the first Designer/Maker whose foresight was conditioned by an extremely progressive attitude toward manufacturing. Many of his early concepts, with their undecorated and undulating lines, predated the creations of his contemporaries by at least twenty years. (See Figure 5.6.) Yet, the forms Thonet chose were not based on artistic flamboyance but rather on the functional parameters imposed by a new manufacturing technique.

For one of the first times in history, the unique form of a design was the result of an astute application of new production processes. The cheap substitution for craftsmanship was no longer a mission for design.

The use of bent wood as a manufacturing technique was clearly innovative. However, this was not the only innovation that Thonet brought to furniture making. Two other aspects of his methods of production were also revolutionary. First, unskilled workers could produce chairs on an assembly line; second, Thonet shipped his chairs worldwide using the "knockdown" principle—that is, chairs were shipped in parts and assembled on site. Over time, Thonet managed to sell over 50 million copies of his No. 14 café chair before World War II. No other chair had ever sold in this quantity. This same chair continues to sell extremely well today, at around 50,000 per year.

By the turn of the nineteenth century, Thonet's manufacturing facilities and expertise were so advanced that his company had begun to manufacture furniture designed by some of the leading architects and Designers of the day, such as Otto Wagner, Joseph Hoffmann, and Marcel Breuer. In the period after World War I, Thonet continued to experiment with new technologies. His company was one of the first to use bent metal for chair production and did so in the manufacturing of the designs of Marcel Breuer (the Wassily chair), Ludwig Mies van der Rohe (chairs #533 and #534), and Le Corbusier's lounge chair.

Henry Ford

Chairs and automobiles are very different everyday things but not so the fundamental principles for designing and making them. From this perspective, Thonet's No. 14 café chair and Ford's Model T have a great deal in common. Like Thonet, Henry Ford (1863–1947) was fascinated with technology and its potential for the making of everyday things. Moreover, his technological interests were strongly conditioned by his social agenda, one that had a populist overtone. Ford's desire to make his car available to the population at large as well as offering a wage of five dollars per day to workers—very generous for the time—were both clear evidence of this agenda, one that placed people at the center of the designing/making process.

The industrial attitudes of Henry Ford reflected the egalitarian beliefs that had taken hold in America. In that spirit, Ford's goal was to produce automobiles on a scale that would make the vehicles affordable for all. In order to achieve this end, Ford perfected the moving production line in 1913 and, between 1908 and 1927, produced over 16 million Ford Model Ts. So effective was his method of production, which became known as *Fordism*, that it actually reduced the price of the car year after year. Ford's pay scale also played a part in his egalitarian goal. What first appeared to be a ridiculously generous wage, perhaps even foolish, proved to be nothing less than brilliant. Not only was he able to hire and retain the best workers available, the wages paid allowed the workers to buy the Model T car.

Ford may have also made another important contribution to designing when he paved the way for standardization as a principle in the making of everyday things, including even styling. Color was such a case in point. Anyone could purchase a Ford as long as it was black. The color black was standardized because it dried faster than any other color, thereby saving production time.

There are many similarities between the Thonet story and that of Ford. Both industrialists were Designers and Makers at the same time. For Thonet and Ford, these two roles were inseparable. Both were also fascinated by the potential offered by the application of appropriate technology. From their perspectives, technology was not an impediment to innovation; rather, it provided opportunities that didn't previously exist. Both Thonet and Ford perceived that the beneficiary of designing should be the User. Thonet's chairs and Ford's Model T car were both exemplars of everyday things designed with one goal in mind: availability to the greatest number of Users. Design as an instrument of elitism was never considered as an option.

Structures

Saltaire

Domestic structures or shelters—buildings such as houses, apartments, and condominiums—are not unusual in the developed world today. However, the same could not be said for England in the mid-nineteenth century, which is what made Saltaire unique. (See Figure 5.7.) Sir Titus Salt was a textile baron in northern England at a time when Great Britain was a leading world industrial power. The Industrial Revolution, which had begun some hundred years earlier, had made England a center of manufacturing in several important sectors including machinery and ceramics. Textile was also one of these industrial sectors, and Sir Titus was one of its industrial leaders.

Like Josiah Wedgwood, Sir Titus had great respect for the workers and the direct connection they had to the productivity of his mills. He was of the opinion that his company would benefit if the workers were provided with adequate housing, social services such as education and healthcare, and a strong sense of community. This he proceeded to achieve by creating and building the village of Saltaire next to his textile mills. The village bears his name as well as the name of the Aire River, which flows nearby. Saltaire was a self-contained village. Its citizens not only lived next to their place of work but the families had ready access to services that workers in other parts of England could only dream about, such as education for the children, health care for everyone, and shops all in close proximity.

Quite logically, the mill was the focal point of the town and was strategically built next to the local canal, which served as a major mode of inland transportation. Saltaire was planned on a simple grid pattern, with residences designed as row houses, and with services such as schools, stores, and town hall located in the town center. There was nothing particularly unique about the architectural style; it was typical of the brick construction found in many towns in Yorkshire at that period. What was unique, however, was the availability of housing within a well-planned community. Saltaire still exists today, but the mill is no longer in operation. Homes and shops are now privately owned. In December 2001, UNESCO designated Saltaire a World Heritage Site.

The Shakers

Shaker communities shared at least one thing with the community of Saltaire: although designing was central to the development of both communities, there was no design dogma in either one, at least not in the formal sense that we associate with architecture and design today. Moreover, designing for the Shakers was self-taught. Nevertheless, the Shakers produced a variety of useful and beautiful everyday things as well as some exceptionally functional buildings.

The Shakers' story begins in England in the late eighteenth century. Ann Lee, their founder, was known as a zealous advocate of her own brand of religion, an off-shoot of the Anglican Church. The group had become known as the 'Shaking Quakers' and, eventually, the Shakers.[xii] While in prison for religious incorrectness, Ann Lee had a vision that God wanted her to go to America. With a small entourage of devoted followers, she arrived in New York in 1774.

Although the first years in America were difficult, numerous Shaker colonies eventually were established, all dedicated to a deeply religious lifestyle, hard work, and celibacy. (See Figure 5.8.) Furthermore, Shaker communities were self-sufficient. They did not need access to the world outside of their communities for subsistence. In that spirit, Shaker communities designed and constructed their own buildings, manufactured their own furniture, made baskets, and even their own brooms. The work ethic adhered to by the Shakers was quite different from the work ethos that governed most Americans during the same era. Members of the Shaker community did not work for personal monetary gain but for the satisfaction of a job well done. Despite this obviously different incentive in a country where time was money, the communities were very productive.

Without wishing to purposely create a unique visual style—for that would have been contrary to their religious ethics—the ascetic visual qualities of Artifacts created by the Shakers eventually found great favor with the general population and design authorities alike. The book *Shaker: Life, Work and Art* captures the essence of these everyday things: "The humblest, most mundane objects—a coat hanger, a clothes brush, a wheelbarrow—[revealed] a concern for excellence and grace. Many Shaker products were distinguished by a subtle beauty, derived from the simplest of elements: thoughtful proportions, graceful lines; cheerful, bright colors."[xiii] Much like in nature, where everything exists because of function and in which we often find beauty, the everyday things of the Shakers have, over time, acquired a universal visual appeal. These everyday things—tools and buildings alike—functioned extremely well, made appropriate use of available material and processes, and were culturally and contextually correct. Few of our contemporary everyday things meet these same high standards.

The Crystal Palace

The living communities of Saltaire and of the Shakers may have been unusual because they were predicated on a User-driven model based on functional requirements without any special regard to form. In both cases, there was nothing original or exceptional about the visual style. It was traditional and certainly did not defy any known architectural conventions. Not so the Crystal Palace designed by Joseph Paxton. The Crystal Palace was the site of the Great Exhibition of 1851 in London and its design—especially its fabrication—was a clear departure from the conventional building of the day. It was light and airy, did not adhere to a style of the past, and, if anything, reflected the potential for the future. In a more sublime way, however, its design foretold the roles that the Designer, Maker, and User would eventually play as the Designing Triad would soon divide into three independent entities.

Joseph Paxton, a former gardener for the Duke of Devonshire, was the Designer of the Crystal Palace. The building resembled a gigantic greenhouse, and as coincidental as this may first appear to be it was the functionalist design that we associate with greenhouses that distinguished the Crystal Palace from the symbolist architecture of most other buildings. In many ways, the Crystal Palace was a precursor of Modernist design with its credo of form follows function. Like any good Modernist Designer, Paxton incorporated the latest technological developments in the building. This direction seemed obvious to him, although it was not the case for most architects of the time. Perhaps this freedom of exploration was because Paxton was not trained as an architect and did not feel the need to follow one dogma or another.

As a result, the Crystal Palace was designed not as a monolith but as a module. Components were produced in factories throughout England and delivered to the building site in London to be assembled. It had nearly 300,000 panes of glass and more than 5,000 columns and girders of iron. Size was not its principal distinguishing feature. What made the Crystal Palace remarkable was its method of construction or, more accurately, its prefabrication. Many of the building components were made in factories throughout England and brought to the site. For example, the glass panes—the largest ever made—were delivered already cut to size, and the columns and girders were manufactured in the factories of Birmingham and delivered by railroad. Less than twenty-four hours after delivery, many of the components were already set into place. Compared to the construction techniques commonly used at the time, the approach utilized by Paxton was radical and foreshadowed a new age of building construction. (We will see that with Levittown and Habitat '67 in the next chapter.) Lastly, the User was not a passive bystander in experiencing the Crystal Palace. The building would have certainly challenged the intellect of the User: large greenhouses were certainly not considered mainstream architecture and had little to do with the expectations, at least in formal terms, that Users had for public architecture, which was more often than not Gothic revival. At the same time, there was something comfortable about a known building type commonly associated with the values implicit in vernacular architecture.

Signs

The development of signs from the strictly pictorial communication embodied in pictographs and petroglyphs to signs with specific meanings in letterforms did not evolve in the same chronological timeframe as did tools or structures. However, there is a connection among all three. There is evidence to show that the earliest visible language was in Mesopotamia at around 3000 BCE. The reason for such a visible language was that our agrarian ancestors needed a way to record information related to surplus from agricultural production. How much food was being produced? Was there enough until the next planting season? When was the best time to plant? How would farmers be taxed in the form of crops?

This information needed to be written down and kept for future reference. For example, Sumerian pictographic tablets dating back to 3100 BCE show the earliest evidence of what could be called letterforms, with distinct vertical and horizontal lines as we find in today's letterform including the use of columns.[xiv] By 2800 BCE, the layout of writing evolved further and we began to see the first appearance of left-to-right rows and top-to-bottom columns. About three hundred years later, a change in the writing instrument dramatically altered letterform. Previously, a sharp stylus had been dragged across the clay to create the pictographs; now, a wedge-shaped stylus was pushed into the clay, greatly increasing the speed of writing and creating a more abstract writing form called cuneiform. Not only did the graphic style of writing change but its content did as well. For example, what had been symbolic signs in the past, such as the sun, began to take on meanings other than the obvious—meanings such as day or night.[xv] However, it would take some time before signs of one type or another would depict the nuances of the spoken language.

Writing had many other impacts on early village culture. People who could write became empowered; those who couldn't were not. It is in this era that we begin to see, for example, the early development of those professions dependent on literacy. Writing as an integral part of societies also led to the creation of rules, laws, and a greater sense of order. It also led to the keeping of historical records and literature in general. Inevitably, writing led to the concept of libraries—that is, a place to keep written records of one kind or another. Life in the village also imposed a need to identify property and creations. Farmers needed to identify their cattle, a need that led to branding. Artisans began to identify their creations, a first form of intellectual property.[xvi]

Writing in Egypt was not that dissimilar to writing in Mesopotamia, as pictographs were the basis for what is known as hieroglyphs. The first appearance of Egyptian hieroglyphs dates back to around 3100 BCE, and their last recorded use was around 394 CE, a time span that more or less coincides with that of the civilization in Mesopotamia. Whereas the writing style evolved in Mesopotamia to the cuneiform style, no such change occurred with Egyptian hieroglyphs. It wasn't until the early nineteenth century, in fact, that Egyptian hieroglyphs were deciphered.

During this same general period, around 1800 BCE, Chinese society was also developing a form of visible language and contributing to signs as communication devices. However, Chinese calligraphy—much like that of many of the Asian visible languages—was not based on the principle of an alphabet. It is a true visual language, in that each pictographic symbol is composed of lines within an imaginary square and, in combination, has a specific meaning in much the same way that words have specific meanings.

It is important to note that it was the Chinese who invented printing—albeit a very rudimentary form of it—with all the basic principles that we associate with it: a raised pattern carved from a hard material on which ink is applied and then pressed onto paper. The Chinese had already invented paper around 100 CE.[xvii]

All three writing forms discussed—cuneiform, hieroglyphs, and calligraphy—were undoubtedly useful in their respective societies, but all three suffered from the same difficulty: they were not easy to learn and therefore limited the number of people who could write. Consequently, literacy was a luxury for a few people. It was the invention of the alphabet that would provide a major shift, both in the general use of this particular visible language and in the subsequent rise in literacy. No one has yet determined where the alphabet originated. However, the source is most likely the Mediterranean area. Evidence of early alphabet systems has been found in Crete, for example, dating around 2800 BCE. It is the Latin alphabet, however, that has probably most affected the evolution of literacy in the Western world. This is the alphabet that most of us know well and that we use every day. It came to Rome via Greece, and had only twenty-one letters. Over time, other letters such as J, U, Y, and Z were added because of the need to include certain vocal sounds not found in the original alphabet, which explains the twenty-six letters in many of today's modern alphabets.[xviii]

Although this section has dealt principally with signs of one kind or another, it is the purpose of the signs that is important. In and of themselves, signs are merely a form of human visual scribbling. When these same signs are attached to a specific meaning, however, they take on a very different presence. More significantly, they can have a formidable impact. As visible language, signs provided people with the ability to record, to transmit, to communicate, to share, to think, and to create. The visible language and the accompanying state of literacy are nothing less than empowering. Canadian historian Gwynn Dyer

has gone so far as to state that there appears to be a direct correlation between the literacy rate of a country and the rise of democracy in that country. In his words, a society governed by an autocratic government will most likely become democratic two or three generations after the literacy rate reaches 50% or better.

Mexico serves as a good example. For decades, it was under the same political regime. Only recently did its citizens feel that they could elect a different political party. Mexico may not have had a dictatorship, but one-party rule was close enough. As long as the literacy rate was low, the reigning party had every expectation of remaining in power. As literacy rose, however, the electorate became more informed and people became empowered. Not surprisingly, the sitting political party was soon voted out of office.

China has gone through and is still going through a similar process. The first part of the contemporary Chinese story begins with Mao, who supported the development of a more simplified version of Chinese written characters—not for some altruistic reason but rather to keep the Chinese from being able to read ancient texts or anything else prior to Mao's rise to power. Many scholars believe that access to such information could have created difficulties for Mao. Mao's need to control access to information is not that different from the challenge facing Chinese leaders today. As literacy continues to increase in the Chinese populace, so does the desire to access the Internet, for example. Chinese political officials are, of course, keenly aware of this situation and are doing their best to control and censor the Internet. The battle, however, is ultimately futile. Literacy and democracy will eventually find their place in Chinese society.

Summary

The Age of Surplus provided the impetus for several important interrelated shifts that would alter the dynamics of the Designing Triad. The first of these was the democratization of designing. The introduction of the alphabet and other visible languages had begun to empower people, and more everyday things were becoming available. The phenomenon of surplus was especially evident in tools, buildings, and signs as each became increasingly abundant. Everyday things such as tools were no longer restricted to the nobility and upper classes. Thonet and Ford were undoubtedly role models in this respect. Buildings also evolved albeit in more modest ways. Exceptionally, examples such as Saltaire in England and Shaker communities in America demonstrated how communities could be planned if the User was at the center of the designing/making process. Signs as alphabets—especially when printed in books—had increased the rate of literacy in most societies. Clearly, the Age of Surplus had created an irreversible separation in the Designing Triad, one that saw the User split from the Designer/Maker. This would be the second important shift in the Designing Triad. No longer did someone have to play the three roles of Designer, Maker, and User in order to have everyday things. Designer/Makers were now creating and producing everyday things and Users were acquiring them.

Perhaps more significantly, industrialization created another separation—the one between function and form. The rapid and constant developments in the sciences, technology, and engineering provided an ever stronger platform and justification for the functional and pragmatic attributes in everyday things. Function and form were being considered as separate elements of the same everyday things. This division would come to a climax with structures such as the Eiffel Tower, which in the eyes of many artists and architects of the day was nothing more than an expression of mechanistic values with little consideration given to form. In the centuries leading to industrialization, the Designer/Maker had been bound together in one individual—the artisan. Consequently, function and form were seamlessly integrated. The separation of the two combined with the pervasive presence of technological developments left the artisan or early Designer totally out of the picture. As a process, designing still existed but it was not the Designer as an independent agent who was charged with it. Self-referential designing and formal expression as something independent from functional parameters would not occur until Designers created a unique position for themselves. This would become the third shift in the Designing Triad, and the topic of the next chapter.

Further Reading

Banham, Reyner. *Theory and Design of the First Machine Age.*

Birdsall, Derek, and Carlo M. Cipolla. *The Technology of Man.*

Ferebee, Ann. *A History of Design from the Victorian Era to the Present.*

Giard, Jacques. *Design FAQs.*

Gideon, Siegfried. *Mechanization Takes Command.*

Heskett, John. *Industrial Design.*

Kubler, George. *The Shape of Time: Remarks on the History of Things*.

Mang, Karl. *The History of Modern Furniture*.

Meggs, Phillip B. *A History of Graphic Design*.

Pevsner, Nikolaus. *The Sources of Modern Architecture and Design*.

Pulos, Arthur J. *American Design Ethic*.

Sprigg, June and David Sprigg. *Shaker Life, Work, and Art*.

Wilk, Christopher. *Thonet: 150 Years of Furniture*.

Endnotes

[i] Diamond, Jared. *Guns, Germs, and Steel*.

[ii] We continue to make reference to the artisan today. For example, we talk of artisan-made bread or beer brewed in the artisanal fashion. In these cases as well as others, the word is used to denote a greater care taken by the artisan in the designing and making of certain everyday things. At Arcosanti in Arizona, Soleri bells are still hand-cast in the artisanal way.

[iii] *Con Brio* in The Economist, January 19-25, 2008

[iv] Few people would consider barbers and surgeons to be members of the same professional association. Yet, that was the case in England in the Middle Ages. Over time, the two professions separated as surgeons began to acquire more medical knowledge whereas barbers continued to rely on manual skills.

[v] Manufacturing processes cannot be separated from the materials being processed. As efficient as a metal press is, it cannot process wood. In principle and by practice, artisans generally know their materials extremely well. Consequently, a glass object would have a specific shape because of how glass could be manipulated by the artisan. However, manufacturers sometimes do not consider the potential of the machine when making a similar glass object but use the machine to copy the artisan's design. Thonet was an exception to this rule.

[vi] Heskett, John. *Industrial Design*.

[vii] Mang, Karl. *History of Modern Furniture*.

[viii] Pulos, Arthur J. *American Design Ethic*.

[ix] Credit for inventing a new technology and being the first person to come up with the idea are not necessarily the same thing. Italian immigrant Antonio Meucci could not afford a patent for a telephone device similar to that of Alexander Graham Bell although he had invented it years earlier; Edouard-Léon Scott de Martinville invented the phonautograph, a device to record the human voice and did so seventeen years before Thomas Alva Edison received a patent for the phonograph; and many people were involved in the development of early flying machines but it was the Wright brothers who earned the patent. (Matt Richtel, Edison. . . Wasn't He the Guy Who Invented Everything?, in the New York Times, March 30, 2008)

[x] The three-axis control refers to the three principal attitudes of flight: pitch (vertical relationship between the nose and horizon); roll (how much the nose "tilts" to the left or right); and yaw (the direction in which the nose of the aircraft is pointing).

[xi] Mang, Karl. *History of Modern Furniture*.

[xii] Sprigg. Shaker Life, Work, and Art.

[xiii] Ibid

[xiv] Meggs, Philip B. *A History of Graphic Design*.

[xv] Ibid

[xvi] Ibid

[xvii] Ibid

[xviii] Ibid

CHAPTER 6

The Age of Self

The complete separation of the Designer, the Maker, and the User in the Designing Triad would not begin to become obvious, especially in Europe, until the middle of the eighteenth century. Early on in the Age of Surplus, the User separated from the Designer/Maker; by the nineteenth century, with industrialization, the split between the Maker and the Designer became evident. In the period that followed, Designers began to assert their presence in the designing process. When they became recognized by name, the split was complete, and thus began the Age of Self.

Place, People, and Process

Everyday things that resulted from a clear division among designing, making, and using had existed prior to the Age of Self, but there were only a few different types. Two are particularly noteworthy: building bricks and cast or molded Artifacts such as bowls and appliqués. Both of these early everyday things serve as good examples of Artifacts made by one individual, the Maker, to be used by another, the Designer, in order to serve a third, the User.

Building bricks come in many types, shapes, and sizes. Historically, they date back to between 7500 and 10,000 BCE, with the earliest found in what is now the Middle East. These bricks were made from sun-dried river mud mixed with straw. Evidence of this type of brick was found as far back as 4000 BCE in the ancient city of Ur in Iraq. The oven-fired brick came later, around 3000 BCE, also in the Middle East. Its design was much better suited to inclement weather such as rain. Buildings constructed from oven-fired bricks tended to be more permanent than those built with the earlier mud or sun-dried bricks. By 1200 CE, the making and the use of oven-fired bricks had spread throughout Europe, especially to Italy and Germany, and to parts of Asia.

Of particular interest is the cathedral in Roskilde, Denmark, which dates back to the twelfth and thirteenth centuries. (See Figure 6.1.) Unlike the many Gothic churches in Europe that were made of stone blocks, the church at Roskilde was built of bricks and helped to develop the so-called Brick Gothic style in northern Europe. Looking back, one wonders if the pervasiveness of bricks as a construction material in Denmark had any influence on the invention of Lego bricks, the Danish building toy known all over the world.

Early cast bowls and molded appliqués also foretold of the eventual separation of the Designer, the Maker, and the User. Cast bowls made of glass have been found both in Greece and Rome dating from the first century BCE to later examples in Rome as late as the seventh century BCE and even to early Byzantium. Molds were also used to produce small everyday things made of metal that could serve, for example, as decorative pieces on furniture. By their very concept, molds permitted the making of many copies of the same everyday thing. The investment of time and resources to create one mold allowed the Maker to produce many copies, that is, a surplus. The previous chapter dealt at length with the impact of surplus on the Designing Triad.

These two examples aside, it was during the Industrial Revolution that the strain between the Designer and the Maker would begin to manifest itself. The User had become a discrete entity in the Designing Triad but not so the Designer/Maker. These two players continued to generally act as one.[i] But with the split between the formal qualities in an everyday thing and its functional properties, as well as the growing self-referential direction in painting and sculpture, the independence of the Designer from the Maker was becoming inevitable. In more recent history we actually can attribute the design of an everyday thing or building to an individual, but that was not always the case. By convention, we normally refer to early periods in the history of art, design, and architecture by

the empire (Egyptian, Greek, or Roman); somewhat later, reference is made to an era (Byzantium, Gothic, or Renaissance); and then a reigning monarch (such as Louis XIV or Victorian). Names of individuals only appeared now and again starting around 2630 BCE, when it is known that Imhotep designed the stepped pyramid for Djoser in Saqqara, Egypt.[ii] Gradually, names of individual artists, architects, and Designers become more the rule than the exception, with people such as Michelangelo, da Vinci, and Bernini to modern-day individuals such as Le Corbusier, Charles Eames, and Frank Gehry.

The Proto-Modernist Era of Designing

In a relatively short period, from around 1760 to 1850, technology began to assume a greater presence in people's lives. Not only did this presence have a utilitarian quality but it also provided a particular visual quality—one that was becoming very mechanistic and industrial in style. Not surprisingly, certain individuals began to react against the tendency, which is often the case with certain artistic directions or movements. This was certainly the case with the community of artists and Designers who were part of the movement known as Art Nouveau. Its exponents were against the void of formal language in the new technology as exemplified by designs such as the Eiffel Tower erected in 1889 or by the wholesale borrowing of past styles. Encouraged by the sermons of William Morris, many artists gave up their careers as painters to become what later would be called Designers, as we will see below. As a group, many of them welcomed machine technology and mass production, knowing very well that they would enable them to create well-designed everyday things for a greater number of people.

Three important aspects of Art Nouveau should be noted. First, it offered a radically new visual language to everyday things. Second, Art Nouveau adopted a symbolist aesthetic of form and pattern using peacocks, lilies, swans, plants—a kind of visual antidote to the reigning mechanistic style. And lastly, Art Nouveau considered the relation of the form to the Artifact, which, to some extent, foreshadowed the Modernist movement that was soon to come. Form was, indeed, beginning to follow function.

Even though the name Art Nouveau is French, the roots of Art Nouveau were English. The Celtic manuscripts and a revival of Irish and Scottish culture inspired Designers toward a new rectilinear mode of expression. This group was led by Charles Rennie Mackintosh (1868–1928), Peter Behrens (1869–1940), and Joseph Hoffmann (1870–1956), and became known as Rectilinear Art Nouveau.

Art Nouveau also had a biomorphic counterpart that contrasted sharply with Rectilinear Art Nouveau. This direction became known as Curvilinear Art Nouveau and was led by Designers from France, Spain, and Belgium, including architects such as Hector Guimard (1867–1957), Antonio Gaudi (1852–1926), Victor Horta (1861–1947), and Henri van de Velde (1863–1957). (See Figure 6.2.)

America also experienced an Art Nouveau movement, although it was not as prolific as the European one. One person particularly important in this movement was Louis Comfort Tiffany (1848–1933). Born into a family that had already founded a famous jewelry business, Tiffany's initial career in the arts was as a painter. Soon, however, it was the decorative arts, especially stained glass, that piqued his interest, as is evidenced by the many lamps that bear his name. But his design involvement went beyond stained glass and lamps. In 1880, Tiffany received a patent for iridescent glass. He went on to design and produce his vases and plates in this type of glass, something that became a kind of trademark for Tiffany. Like many other Art Nouveau Designers of his time, Tiffany relied on amorphous shapes and forms derived from nature, which served as an antidote to the reigning mechanistic style. Tiffany's legacy lives on with the chain of exclusive retail stores that bear the family name and that continue the reputation of fine glassware.

The Early Modernist Era of Designing

The era known as Modernism, which began in the late nineteenth and early twentieth centuries, was governed by an overwhelmingly functionalist ideology toward design. Even in the fine arts, most works were the result of reasoned and rational thinking, indicative of a more objective approach. Several art movements helped shape this functionalist dogma, three of which had a particularly important impact on designing. They were Cubism, de Stijl, and Functionalism. All appeared before World War I and, although each one of these movements was quite different, they shared many fundamental ideas and formal characteristics.

A catalyst partially responsible for this dramatic directional change in fine arts was without doubt the invention of photography in 1837 by Louis J. M. Daguerre, a French stage Designer and painter. His invention had the unwitting effect of challenging the underlying premise of fine art—especially of the pictorial arts such as painting.

Until then, one of the fundamental roles of the artist had been to represent the everyday world by way of realistic landscapes or portraits. But photography changed the need to paint such true-to-life representations. Artists were suddenly out of a job, or so it appeared. What was to evolve, of course, would be quite different. Photography became a catalyst for change, as artists began to explore dimensions beyond the world of reality. They delved into more fundamental issues such as composition and emotion. Cubism, de Stijl, Impressionism, and Expressionism all became different modes of this kind of visual exploration that went well beyond the photography of the period.

Cubism flourished in France between 1907 and 1914. As probably the most influential movement in the history of modern art, it sought to bring visual perception and composition back to basics—that is, back to simple geometric shapes and forms. It reversed what had been the Victorian emphasis on content to one of form. Advocates of Cubism, such as Pablo Picasso and Georges Braque, urged artists to concentrate on cones, cubes, cylinders, and spheres. The search for pictorial fidelity was replaced by a kind of reductionism, where everything natural was reconstructed using simple geometric shapes.

De Stijl, or the Style, was a Dutch art movement that began in 1917. It explored the primary or basic colors and focused attention upon simple abstract geometry. In some respects, de Stijl went beyond Cubism and removed any visual connections to form and volume such as shade, shadow, depth, and perspective. It was the painter Piet Mondrian who was the inspirational leader of de Stijl. Gerrit Rietveld (1888–1964) explored a somewhat different direction and gave de Stijl a third dimension by designing buildings such as the Schröder House and furniture such as the Red-and-Blue chair.

Of all of these almost-concurrent developments, Functionalism—with its roots in logic—was the movement that most influenced design in the first half of the twentieth century. Functionalism is "a particular way of design thinking," one closely associated with the concept "form follows function" as advocated by the American architect Louis Sullivan. And it was in Germany that Functionalism gained its first footing, especially with the Bauhaus and, to some extent, the Deutscher Werkbund.[iii]

Hints of a radical departure in the visual language of architecture and design were beginning to surface in the late nineteenth century with the Vienna Secession in Austria. But the clearest indication of a break with the overly decorated buildings and everyday things of the époque came with Adolf Loos (1870–1933). Working in Vienna in the early twentieth century, Loos wrote what was to become a seminal treatise on modern design and architecture, *Ornament and Crime*. In it, he stated,

> Ornamentation is wasted effort and therefore a waste of health. It has always been so. But today it means a waste of material as well, and the two things together mean a waste of capital.

But for Loos, words were not enough. He put his beliefs into practice, and the Steiner House in Vienna, built in 1910, demonstrates his passion for useful form over useless decoration, at a time when useless decoration was the rule. Loos's house was a stark box with a few judiciously placed windows—nothing more.

Viennese Designers were not the only ones who considered design a visual language for modernity. In 1907, German industrialists, businessmen, artists, and architects joined to form the Deutscher Werkbund. Its task, as formulated by its statute was "the ennoblement of industrial labor through the collaboration of art, industry and crafts in education, propaganda and a united approach to relevant questions." As expounded by its founder, Hermann Muthesius, the thrust of the Werkbund's manifesto was to protest against the ugliness of the built environment and to revive artistic, moral, and social ethics, with an overall bias toward standardization. The founders of the Werkbund acknowledged the potential division between technology and design but also recognized the opportunity for a Modernist vision. Their ideology, as expressed in 1907 by Ernst Schumacher, stated as much:

> In the wake of an economical and technical development which can no longer be checked, a great danger has appeared, the danger of estrangement between the accomplishing and the inventing spirit. This danger cannot be concealed, neither can it be banished from the world again so long as industry exists. We must therefore try to bridge the gap that has occurred. This is the great aim of our association.[iv]

The manifesto's audience included such design leaders as Ludwig Mies van der Rohe (1886–1969), Walter Gropius (1883–1969), and Le Corbusier (1887–1965), people who would eventually shape the design and architecture of post-war Germany and Europe.

While art movements such as Cubism and de Stijl were largely experimental and visionary, the essence of the Bauhaus ideology was based on a more practical application of art and design theory, having as its goal the education of a new and very different generation of artists, Designers, and architects. Design and design imagery were to be the result of functional parameters as well as artistic imperatives. Siegfried Giedion, the noted design historian, clearly expressed the spirit of the Bauhaus when he wrote:

> The Bauhaus was not an institution with a clear program—it was an idea, and [Walter] Gropius formulated this idea with great precision . . . The fact that it was an idea, I think, is the cause of this enormous influence the Bauhaus had on every progressive school around the globe. You cannot do that with organizations, you cannot do that with propaganda. Only an idea spreads so far . . .[v]

The Bauhaus began as the integration of a school of arts and crafts and an academy, a kind of marriage between the hands and the mind, or practice and theory. At a time when there was a very clear division between manual training and academia, this direction in higher education was nothing short of revolutionary. Not surprisingly, these two basic yet diverse educational elements did not enjoy equal status in the early years at the Bauhaus. In fact, there was a kind of anti-academic feeling at the institution: its program leaned heavily toward training in the practical portion of the curriculum. In the years that followed, this initial tendency gave way to the acceptance of theory, an approach that was more in tune with *educating* people than with *training* them.

Over its relatively short history, the Bauhaus was situated in three different cities. The first was Weimar in 1919. However, the radical zeal exhibited by the school proved to be too much for the city fathers, and Walter Gropius, the founder and first director, was pressured to move. In 1925, the Bauhaus was resettled in Dessau. New facilities—designed by Gropius—were built. Later, Ludwig Mies van der Rohe became director. Once again, political pressures were brought to bear and, in 1933, the Bauhaus was forced to relocate to Berlin.[vi] But by then the spirit of the Bauhaus had been broken and, six months after the move, the school closed. Certainmembers of the Bauhaus left Germany before World War II to establish themselves in the United States. Some of these people went on to later establish the New Bauhaus in Chicago, which eventually became the Institute of Design at the Illinois Institute of Technology.

The Bauhaus was the leading and most influential school of architecture and design of the first half of the twentieth century. As such, it had the greatest impact on both design education and design practice of any movement in the modern era. Within its framework of activities and interventions, the Bauhaus dealt with everyday things, including architecture, furniture, graphics, and textiles.

What made the Bauhaus pedagogically unique was both its focus on design as a distinct matter for study and its approach to teaching it. For example, there was less distinction made between the teachers, or masters, and the students. An environment was purposely created to encourage interaction between the two groups. It is worthwhile to note that the studio environment of today's schools of architecture and design is partially a result of this Bauhaus experiment. Furthermore, Gropius insisted that students explore the nature and the potential of various materials by learning the crafts associated with each one of them. He felt that it was only after students had a true understanding of a material that they could contemplate how to use it to design for machine production. Lastly, the incorporation of theory into the program's curriculum was novel and actively encouraged. At the Bauhaus, design was perceived as being more than the application of a known style in a kind of monkey-see, monkey-do fashion. The theme proposed by the Bauhaus was an intellectual one in which Designers were expected to explore design concepts based on rational and logical thinking. Consequently, form and function were perceived as interdependent in what became known as *gestalt* thinking. Form could no more be separated from function than function could be separated from form. And if that premise alone wasn't enough, the integration of new materials and manufacturing processes was paramount. Such an approach led to chairs that were revolutionary, such as the ones designed by Marcel Breuer using bent metal tubes and the manufacturing technology associated with bicycle making. (See the Wassily chair in Figure 6.6.) The approach also redefined the functional and formal qualities of architecture, graphic design, and product design. Today, we do not give a second look at a bent-metal chair or a Modernist house but that would not have been the case in the 1920s.

Various explanations abound as to why the Bauhaus was so influential. Some design historians claim that it was the powerful influence exerted by the Bauhaus leaders—especially Gropius and Mies van der Rohe. Others believe it was the reputation of the teaching masters—especially the painters—that contributed to the importance of the Bauhaus. Still other experts feel that the strength of the school lay with its innovative pedagogy; students and masters were learners and teachers at the same time. All of these factors played a role in creating a distinct identity for the Bauhaus. And it was the synergy that resulted from these qualities that created the idea behind the institution. This was probably best stated in the Manifesto of 1919, which called for "the unity of all creative arts under the primacy of architecture and for a reconsideration of all artists."[vii] This unity became the goal of the revised Manifesto of 1923, under the thesis Art and Technology—a New Unity. It was a deliberate attempt on the part of the Bauhaus to reconcile the split that had occurred earlier between artisanship and industry.

Much like the Modernists in northern Europe, America had its own design revolutionaries. The most important of these was undoubtedly Frank Lloyd Wright (1867–1959), who brought an American interpretation to the practice of architecture. Wright's interpretation was based on the particularities of the American Context. Up until his time, American architecture—especially of public buildings—imitated or at least borrowed heavily from the visual styles of Europe. It was not unusual to see, for example, neo-Gothic architecture such as in Saint Patrick's Cathedral in New York City or Renaissance architecture such as the U.S. Capitol Building in Washington, D.C. From Wright's point of view, these styles reflected or mimicked European values and history, and had no place in America.

Few American architects have had the influence both on the architectural profession and the general public that Wright has had. Not only was his career a long one—it spanned almost seventy years—it was also extremely productive. He worked on projects of varied scales, from private homes to large public buildings, many of them quite exceptional. It is important to note that Wright was generally self-taught and became an architect as the result of several apprenticeships in his early years, a learning process that is not all that unusual in architecture. It was while working for Louis Sullivan that he developed sensitivity for form as a reflection of function. Sullivan was an advocate of some of the early ideological pillars of Modernism. Wright also became known for his speeches and writing.

Over time, his persona fed an appetite for a cult-like following of architects and fans alike. Studying at the feet of the master or owning a Wright house had cachet, and Taliesin and Taliesin West were extensions of his persona. Both provided a locale where young aspiring architects could study under the spiritual guidance of Wright.

Once in his own practice, Wright began to exhibit what has become known as the Prairie Style of architecture, a first attempt to create a style that was a reflection of the American

Context and not that of Europe. Prairie Style architecture was a blend of outdoors and indoors, with an accent on horizontal forms in which buildings seemed to grow out of the ground. An excellent example of this style is the Robie House (1909–10) in Chicago. The house appears to be a series of horizontal layers floating above the ground.

Of the public buildings designed by Wright, the Guggenheim Museum in New York City (completed in 1960) stands out as one of the most imaginative solutions to a recurring architectural challenge: the museum. Few architects have matched the ingenious yet simple concept that Wright developed for the Guggenheim—that of a downward spiral. Visitors take an elevator to access the highest point in the museum and then, at their own pace, walk down the spiral to the ground floor.

Equally significant, especially in the context of appropriateness to site, is Taliesin West in Arizona. Wright was very cognizant that the landscape of the desert was not the urbanscape of New York City. And neither was the climate of Arizona the climate of New York. True to his belief, he designed Taliesin in the same appropriate way that he designed the Guggenheim Museum—two very different designs for two very different buildings for two very different places. (See Figure 6.3.)

However, the pattern of borrowing from Europe did not immediately stop because of Wright. It continued, for example, with Art Deco, which had its origins with the Exposition Internationale des Arts Décoratifs et Industriels Modernes in Paris in 1925. As a design expression, Art Deco attempted to bring art and industry together as complementary forces, thus allowing manufactured everyday things to display a new stylistic direction. Suddenly, furniture, jewelry, pottery, and textiles as well as buildings were visually redefined by way of geometric shapes and smooth lines. Many everyday things also incorporated chrome and a new material called plastic. And just as suddenly, America fell in love with Art Deco.

Some of the formal language of Art Deco showed clear influences derived from Cubism and from the art of ancient America. Architecture was also affected by the influences of Art Deco, with the finest example being the Chrysler Building in New York City. Its soaring tower with its arches of stainless steel expresses Art Deco in the most dramatic way, especially when the arches turn to a golden color in the setting sun.

Art Deco's success aside, design—where form and function are interwoven—had yet to become a mainstream activity in America even as late as the 1920s. Invention and utility still dominated the manufacturing and making ethos. For example, furniture by Frank Lloyd Wright was not truly mass-produced, and glass objects by Louis Comfort Tiffany were expensive and not accessible to many people. We must jump to the Great Depression and its aftermath before we begin to see visible signs of design as an influence on the American scene.

It was the crash of the stock market in 1929 that precipitated the Great Depression—a devastating economic slowdown whose repercussions touched everyone. The scope and the suddenness of the devaluation of stocks caused many manufacturers to become leery of any form of industrial expansion. Simplistically put, this apprehension led to layoffs, which led to a sharp reduction in consumer purchases, which then led to a reduction in the production of manufactured goods, which then led to more layoffs. The whole process became self-perpetuating and self-accelerating. In a very short time, companies went bankrupt and unemployment soared.

Design found a niche during the darkest moments of this era. The few manufacturers that had not gone bankrupt believed that the cyclical nature of depression could be broken by stimulating the consumer to buy. And this stimulation was to be created by visually enhancing products in order to persuade the consumer to purchase them. Therefore, design became a tool of sales promotion, one that focused on product styling and packaging. Design's principal role was to encourage sales in order to invigorate the economy. This strategy had clear repercussions. At best, design introduced innovative solutions to product areas that had gone unchallenged and unchanged for decades; at worst, it was a highly superficial exercise in which form often had little to do with function.

Two important elements formed the underlying basis of American design during these years. The first was the fact that the pioneers of this new profession often came from a background other than engineering or architecture. For example, Henry Dreyfuss had an education in theater-set design and Raymond Loewy was a fashion illustrator. Given that both set design and fashion deal more with visual perception than with technical performance, it is not surprising that design developed almost exclusively in terms that were strong visually rather than merely functional.

The second important element that profoundly influenced attitudes of the times was the role played by the aircraft and, in its wake, air travel. This mode of transportation strongly appealed to the American psyche. It was an excellent example of Yankee ingenuity and was ideally suited to the national character. Air travel promised quick and efficient transportation along with a glimpse of the future. The visual language that emanated from this particular product, specifically the aerodynamic form, was to have a great influence on everyday things. Streamlining—a term that came from the scientific study of aerodynamics—gave its name to this very American design phenomenon.

Probably more than any other Designer of his day, Raymond Loewy utilized the sweeping curves and teardrop look on the everyday things that he designed, such as the highly streamlined locomotives. Unfortunately, streamlining began to be used as a commercially acceptable visual crutch and was often inappropriately used on objects such as children's tricycles and pencil sharpeners. In these instances, perceived rather than actual aerodynamics had become paramount.

The Modernist Era of Designing

By 1939, World War II had erupted and several European and Asian countries normally associated with design— Great Britain, Germany, Italy, and Japan—were embroiled in mortal combat. It wasn't until the early 1950s that European, Asian, and American societies and industries fully returned to a peacetime environment and that design, in the form of Modernism, surfaced once again. The first countries to return to prewar design and industrial activities were the Scandinavian countries, followed soon thereafter by Great Britain and Germany. Italy arrived somewhat later, as did the United States and Japan. The Asian Tigers—Hong Kong, Taiwan, Singapore, and South Korea—are more recent design phenomena.

Scandinavian Modern

Although perceived by many people as one cultural group, Scandinavia comprises five countries: Denmark, Sweden, Finland, Norway, and Iceland. However, the movement that came to be known as Scandinavian Modern emanated principally from Denmark, Sweden, and Finland. (See Figure 6.4.) In all three countries, the origin of their design ideologies had roots in cultural history. At their source was a deep appreciation of the Norse legends, reinforced by the very nature of the land and the sea and the relationship of the people to the land and the sea. The forests of Sweden and Finland, the coastlines and archipelago of Denmark, and the pervasiveness of the open sea played a decisive role in the development of the cultural makeup and, therefore, of the history of design in the region.

Denmark. The built environment—design and architecture—visually exudes Danish values; Context and design are inextricably linked. Denmark's historical association with agriculture, fisheries, and exceptional crafts, especially in the nineteenth century, provided fertile ground for the continuation of a very natural, humanistic design in the period after World War II. But the seeds that spawned Scandinavian Modern were found as early as the turn of the twentieth century in the works of Kaare Klint, Georg Jensen, and Gerhard Henning. Later, and in the period between World War I and II, the Functionalist movement that was permeat-

ing many parts of Europe was not to have any overwhelming impact on Danish design. The traditions of natural materials and the adherence to superior craftsmanship were too well entrenched, although some formal attributes of Functionalism slowly began to appear. Examples included the hanging lamps of Poul Henningsen, the silverware of Kay Bojesen, and the furniture of both Kaare Klint and Mogens Koch. All contributed to the advancement of Danish—as well as Scandinavian—design.

It was the 1950s that saw the greatest triumphs in Danish design. The forms took on a less severe look than those of the 1930s and, in certain design areas such as consumer goods, the traditions of small-production crafts met head-on with the ideologies of mass production. Instead of the expected devaluation of design quality—something that had occurred in England, for example—the opposite happened in Denmark. The design qualities that had become customary in crafts-based production were transferred to mass-produced designs.

Today's Danish design community is relatively large. Among its outstanding individuals, we find Hans Wegner, Arne Jacobsen, Poul Kjaerholm, Verner Panton, Rud Thygesen, Erik Magnusen, and Johnny Sorensen. Some Danish design companies remain in the forefront, including Lego, Stelton, Bang and Olufsen, and Fritz Hansen.

Sweden. The evolution of design ideology in Sweden paralleled quite closely that of Denmark. There were some differences, however. One of these was Sweden's link with the Art Nouveau style that originated in Vienna; another was the stylistic direction advocated by Charles Rennie Mackintosh, the Scottish architect and Designer. As a result, the visual lines of Swedish design were more geometric and disciplined, as can be seen in the chairs of J. A. G. Acke, Carl Westman, and Carl Bergsten.

The years between 1920 and 1940 saw the Functionalist movement take hold in the community, although it never manifested itself with the same vigor as it did in Germany. The first design examples to exhibit this change in visual direction appeared after World War I with such everyday things as tableware, glassware, and furniture by Gunnar Asplund, and, of great importance, the chairs of Bruno Mathsson.

The 1950s and the 1960s were outstanding years for Scandinavian design. However, the presence of large-scale industry in Sweden such as Volvo and Saab, as well as a more functionalist design approach, provided a different genre of product. Crafts-based industries, especially in glassware and ceramics, were still at the heart of the Swedish manufacturing sector, but they too became larger in scale. Gustavsberg, which was initially a small ceramics company, became a world leader in many product areas. Orrefors and Kosta Boda followed similar paths, starting out as crafts-based glassmakers and becoming world-renowned companies in the design and manufacturing of glassware.

But it was the much larger companies—Volvo, Saab, Erikson, IKEA, and Electrolux—that positioned Swedish design at the forefront of enlightened use and management of design within industry. Design concepts as well as attitudes that are now considered good design practice can often be traced to Swedish design. These include enhancing passenger safety in automobiles and designing for the physically challenged, concepts that were developed well before universal design surfaced in the United States.

Few things represent modern Swedish design or express Swedish values better than IKEA, the furniture and furnishing retailer. Although a global empire with 186 stores in thirty-four countries today, IKEA had a very modest beginning. Ingvar Kamprad, its founder, began by selling pens, wallets, picture frames, and other small items door to door. But from the very beginning, he had a mission in mind: "to create a better everyday life for the majority of people." Today, IKEA's vision has not changed: good design at low prices. Customers can enter an IKEA store and totally furnish their homes—beds and linen, dining tables and dishes, sofas and cushions. What few people realize, however, is that IKEA does not manufacture anything that it sells. What it does do—and it is the world's expert at it—is design these everyday things and then find manufacturers to make and ship them worldwide.

Finland. Finland's design history shares many similarities with Denmark and Sweden but, again, there are notable differences. The domination of the Finns by the Russians from 1809 to 1917 created a state of unrest in Finland and inspired the Finns to search for their cultural roots. The untamed forests of Karelia attracted many architects and Designers who were searching for traditional motifs. This revival was primarily reflected in weavings used as rugs, bench covers, and wall hangings. In the early 1900s, Eliel Saarinen initiated the modern Finnish tradition in design, which he later continued in the United States at Cranbrook. By the 1930s, Finnish Designers were expressing themselves as equals to their Danish and Swedish counterparts. And the heart of this early Finnish design activity was to be found in one person—Alvar Aalto. His design repertoire spanned the total breadth of design, from vases to buildings. One other Finnish Designer—Tapio Wirkkala—had a similar influence. While his work did not have the range of Aalto's, Wirkkala explored in much greater depth the specialized areas of small objects meant for human use, such as flatware, glassware, and ceramics.

Like its Scandinavian neighbors, Finland was very much in step with the Scandinavian Modern movement that occurred after World War II. Although conforming to the more general look that this style possessed, Finnish design had its own qualities, as exemplified in the works of Antti Nurmesniemi, Timo Sarpaneva, and Armi Rattia. Today, the names of several Finnish companies, such as Nokia, Iittala, and Fiskar, are well known.

British Stoicism

Of the Western nations that have contributed to design in the Age of Self, none has a longer history than Great Britain. Many events after the Industrial Revolution fortified Britain's presence in the design world. Some of these were mentioned earlier and bear repeating; others have not and need to be highlighted.

As previously discussed, the onset of industrialization created a rift between the advocates of crafts-based industry, where the artisan was in control, and the factories, where the machine had taken over. This debate spawned many informal discourses; it also led to the establishment of the Society for the Encouragement of Arts, Manufacturers and Commerce in 1754. This group still exists today but under the name of the Royal Society of Arts. Other important events were the founding of the Normal School of Design (now the Royal College of Art) in 1837, the publication of the *Journal of Design* by Henry Cole in 1849, the Great Exhibition in 1851, and the opening of the Ornamental Art Collection (now the Victoria and Albert Museum) in 1852. Just prior to World War II, the Design Council, a government agency with the mandate to promote the use of design in industry, was founded.

From this rich design heritage, contemporary Britain produced some very talented Designers and many remarkable designs. In graphic design, for example, Stanley Morison adapted several classic typefaces to the rigors of print technology and produced Times New Roman for the *London Times* newspaper. Equally important was the visual identity and wayfinding system developed for the London subway system by Frank Pick. Both designs are still in use seventy years after their first appearance. The late 1950s saw the first version of the London taxicab that, even today, is one of the finest examples of good design you will find anywhere. Equally outstanding was the design of the Austin Mini by Alec Issigonis in 1959. This ingenious automobile predates most of the small urban cars that are so prevalent today, and has been revived by BMW as the new Mini Cooper. In the mid-1960s, Robin Day introduced the Polyprop plastic chair, Alex Moulton developed the Moulton bicycle, and

Terence Conran opened his first Habitat store. The list of Britain's outstanding designs is a rather long one and includes everything from flatware by David Mellor to the Jaguar and Lotus motorcars. In the 1970s, Kenneth Grange began designing kitchen appliances for Kenwood and went on to do cameras for Kodak, shavers for Wilkinson, and high-speed trains for British Rail. Today, product Designers such as James Dyson and architects such as Richard Rogers and Norman Foster have continued the long-standing tradition of excellence in British design. (See Figure 6.5.)

This impressive design history could easily lead us to believe that British industry has a sound understanding of good design practice. Unfortunately, this is not always the case. Even today, there is a chasm in Britain between design in theory and design in practice. The clients of many of Britain's leading Designers are based outside the country; in fact, many firms that regularly seek British design expertise are Japanese, German, French, and Italian. There may be a strong correlation between this particular phenomenon and the demise of the automobile and motorcycle industries in Britain. In many cases, the original designs were highly innovative, but failure on the part of certain British manufacturers to respond to market changes placed them at a disadvantage with their competitors. A traditionalist mind-set may have been appropriate for the British market, but not for Users outside its borders. In what could be interpreted as a form of colonial irony, the Indian automotive giant Tata Motors announced in early 2008 that it was about to take control of two jewels in the crown of British automotive history: Jaguar and Rover.

German Rationalism

Given that the roots of Modernism were firmly embedded in the industrial culture of pre–World War II Germany, it was inevitable that a strong sense of design would emerge in the postwar era. The war had a devastating effect on Germany's industrial base and, as in most of Europe, this period was one of reconstruction in Germany. Interestingly enough, this strange twist of fate presented a fallen nation with the opportunity to start anew. Two events were significant in establishing the position of German design in the coming decades: the establishment of the Hochschule fur Gestaltung (HFG) in Ulm and the unique design direction taken by Braun AG, a company that came to epitomize German design in the 1970s.

Perceived by some people as a kind of revival of the Bauhaus, the Hochschule fur Gestaltung opened its doors in Ulm in 1955 under the direction of Swiss Designer Max Bill. The school quickly gained a reputation for its rigorous programs and discipline in design. But, like the Bauhaus, the HFG was forced to close in the mid-1960s. However short its existence may have been, the HFG's influence on design and Designers was substantial.

The new direction in design education at the HFG did not go unnoticed by certain industrialists, particularly by those at Braun AG. Under the leadership of Erwin and Arthur Braun, the sons of company founder Max Braun, the firm decided to set and maintain the highest possible standards for design. In 1951, Dr. Fritz Eichler, one of Braun's resident gurus, vigorously revived a design direction that had been initiated at the Bauhaus. This approach involved a critical analysis of product structure into its composite geometric forms. By 1955, Braun had its first design director in the person of Hans Gugelot. With the co-operation and assistance of the HFG, Gugelot introduced what was to become 'the Braun look.' In that same year, Dieter Rams joined the company. He later became the design director, with exclusive responsibility for the design of all Braun products. Today, Braun design may no longer be at the forefront of design thinking, but its legacy lives on at Apple. Most of the recent Apple products—especially the iPod and PowerBooks—show a genealogical link to Braun's design principles, both in form and in function. The forms remain simple and the colors consistent because of a rationale approach to designing.

German design is synonymous with Modernism. (See Figure 6.6.) In many ways, it reflects everyday German culture such as a sense of order and logic. This degree of integration between design and societal values is matched only by some of the Scandinavian countries. Not only is design viewed as a gauge of the rigor and orderliness of German culture, it is also viewed as a vehicle to promote social equality. Design objects are not considered luxury items exclusively for the rich; they are meant for all Germans. A Mercedes-Benz car is not elitist in image or in price; it is the equivalent of the Buick in the United States. Products manufactured by Braun, BMW, Siemens, AEG-Telefunken, Bosch, Volkswagen, and Audi—all internationally known product brands—exemplify superiordesign quality yet are broadly available. German design today can best be described as rational, objective, and no-nonsense. It attempts to resolve the human/product interface in the most logical way possible, never allowing itself to become arbitrary.

In their attempt to create this very objective non-style—a style devoid of whimsy—German Designers have achieved just the opposite: a very identifiable style.

It is difficult to discuss modern German design without making some reference to the German automobile industry. To many Americans, there is an almost symbiotic relationship between the German car and German design culture. They seem to coexist, one feeding off the other to the point that a description of one is a description of the other. Since World War II, German cars such as the Volkswagen, Mercedes-Benz, the BMW, the Audi, and the Porsche have been exemplars of superb German design. Without exception, they are all well-engineered machines with a discreet blend of design, aristocracy, and egalitarian availability. They may be the almost perfect physical embodiment of the German ethos.

Italian Flamboyance

In many respects, modern Italian design may be perceived as leading edge today, but this was not always the case. A few meaningful examples of pre-World War II design do exist, such as Giuseppe Terragni's Follia chair of 1935, Emanuele Rambaldi's chair of 1933, and Montalcini's Chichibio service table of 1932. But even as far back as the turn of the century, Italy lagged behind her European neighbors with respect to certain mainstream currents. Art Nouveau is one such example. Whereas this innovative direction in art and design flourished elsewhere on the European continent, it was late in developing in Italy principally because of "a cultural resistance that was stronger and more widespread than in other countries."[viii] Paolo Portoghesi, the Italian architect and historian, stated this fact quite succinctly when he wrote, "the Italian pavilion [in Paris, 1900] revealed the backwardness of the country's art and the extent to which it was retarded by adherence to the outworn modes of an academic historicism, aggravated by nationalistic rhetoric."[ix]

In fact, Art Nouveau and its exuberance of expression were rejected in favor of certain austere English and Dutch styles, but not by everyone. A few Designers began exploring new avenues in design. One of these was the poet Filipo Tommaso Marinetti. In his Futurist manifesto of 1909, he proposed a new direction, one of "protest against the past, a hymn of praise to the present, and a prophecy to the future." The Futurists wished to be in step with the present. They especially looked to the machine as the expression of the future with its imagery of speed, modern life, and science. The period between the two world wars did not prove to be any more auspicious for Italian design. The glow was not to be felt until the 1960s and 1970s. Vittorio Gregotti, the noted Italian design historian, maintained, "how limiting were the optics which had Italian design deriving from German rationalism and in particular from the Bauhaus."[x] The Italian architect Leonardo Benevolo expressed much the same sentiment when he wrote that "Italian architecture and industrial design were hopelessly behind the times [in the 1920s]."[xi]

When changes finally came, the interpretive medium for modern Italian design became the industrially manufactured object. It was strongly influenced by certain avant-garde art movements, especially the sculptural expressions found in these art movements. For Italian Designers, art and industry could coexist; however, there was a downside. This close tie to the avant-garde quickly began to define many facets of Italian design as elitist and status-ridden, especially in the eyes of those people who perceived art as an unnecessary luxury. In many respects, design was not yet seen as an instrument to influence everyday life or the built environment on a large scale. In other words, design was not taking on a socially meaningful role as it had in the Scandinavian countries or in Germany. This elitism was not only artistically driven but was also closely coupled with artisan craftsmanship, an extremely strong facet of the Italian industrial sector. The traditional, old-style artisans brought a certain attitude to the overall quality of manufactured goods—love of detail, small-quantity production, and experimentation. The designs themselves "often possessed a wonderful formal logic, were sometimes spontaneous and playful, but were invariably convincing and marked by strong individualism."[xii]

It was the combination of the two elements—contemporary arts and craftsmanship—that formed the foundation of modern Italian design. Some of the early pioneers who were active in the 1950s included Osvaldo Borsani, who designed the M. P. 40 lounge chair in 1955; Gio Ponti with his structurally minimalist Superleggera side chair in 1957; and the Castiglioni family (Achille, Pier Giacomo, and Livio), whose presence would be felt throughout the next several decades with their Mezzadro stool in 1957 and graceful San Luca chair in 1962.

The search by Italian Designers for individualism of expression led to the use of plastic, a new material that offered unexplored directions in form giving. This contrasted sharply with plastic's raison d'être in North America, where it was viewed as an inexpensive substitute for materials such as wood and marble. Plastic gave Italian Designers the opportunity to explore design in sculptural as well as functional terms. Some of these first experiments by Joe Colombo, Angelo Mangiarotti, and Marco Zanuso helped to give Italian design its unique formal characteristics. In the wake of these individuals came an impressive number of other talented Designers, including Vico Magistretti, Anna Castelli, Giancarlo Piretti, Alberto Rosselli, Mario Bellini, Ettore Sottsass Jnr., and Tobia and Afra Scarpa.

The cultural leadership role played by certain Italian corporations is equally noteworthy because corporations do not typically perceive themselves as players in a nation's cultural life. This is not the case for Olivetti. The company's story begins with Adriano Olivetti who in 1936 retained Marcello Nizzoli (1887–1969) as the Designer to the company. Nizzoli's designs—first with the Lettera 22—established the reputation of design excellence. In the 1950s, the company commissioned many well-known Designers including Ettore Sottsass Jnr., Mario Bellini, and Rodolfo Bonetto. Olivetti's first foray into the field of design marked the beginnings of design rationalism, Italian-style. Penny Sparke, the British design historian, described this new direction as "a new aesthetic, which was to combine prewar Rationalism with organic form."[xiii] But it remained dormant until World War II when it was to become the foundation of Italian design ideology and eventually the so-called Italian design of today. Olivetti never had any doubt that the corporation had a responsibility to both people and place.

Even at its height, the Italian design community never fully and unquestionably embraced the fundamental tenets of Modernism. For example, Italian design of the 1960s and 1970s reveled in unusual shapes and colors totally out of character to German Modernism, perceived by many Designers as the unadulterated version of Modernism. (See Figure 6.7.) Consequently, it came as a surprise to no one when the first signs of Postmodernism in Europe surfaced in Italy. Modernism no longer seemed to provide the intellectual basis for design as if there were something missing to justify the changes that were occurring in contemporary society. Consequently, in the eyes of many observers, the strong self-expressive character of Italian design as well as its very close link to the artistic and cultural communities made Italy a fertile ground for Postmodernism in design. Designers such as Ettore Sottsass Jnr., who approached design at Olivetti with a strong dose of Modernism, explored with equal energy the new design expressions that would soon become known as Postmodernism, discussed in greater detail later in the chapter.

American Commercialism

The period after World War II gave rise to a different lifestyle in the United States than in Europe. The United States had experienced neither the physical destruction nor the demoralization felt in Europe after the war. The Allies, which included the Americans, were the victors. Just as important was the fact that the United States was on the verge of becoming the world's dominant military and industrial power. Not surprisingly, industry was going to define post-war America. But the country faced a challenge in converting industry from a state of military production to a state of peacetime needs. (See Figure 6.8.)

One of the first examples of this conversion—one that directly touched design—was the Organic Design in Home Furnishing competition organized by Bloomingdale's and the Museum of Modern Art. The eventual winners were Charles Eames and Eero Saarinen, two Designers who were to leave an indelible mark on American design. Their submission, a chair, was described as a "complete rejection of the right angle, out of the two-dimensional world of bentwood and steel chairs of the Breuer or Aalto type into a new sphere of 'sculptured' furniture based on the latest technology."[xiv]

In the years that followed, several American Designers added impetus to this newfound direction. Many of them, including George Nelson and Alexander Girard, often worked for a handful of dedicated manufacturers, including Herman Miller and Knoll. In fact, Nelson eventually became design director at Herman Miller in 1946. Eames continued his work with Herman Miller and along with his wife, Ray, developed an enviable range of furniture and other designs. Other Designers, including Saarinen and Harry Bertoia were associated with Knoll, a company that also manufactured the furniture of Mies van der Rohe and Breuer. Looking back, Nelson attributed Herman Miller's success and position in the market to the fact that the firm had always believed that design was an integral part of business and that there was a market for good design.

Other businesses and industries were quick to adopt design as a new and modern management strategy. IBM,

the computer giant, saw the immediate potential of a good design policy and went about exploiting its benefits. Under the directorship of Elliot Noyes, IBM became a design leader in corporate America. Paul Rand, the noted American graphic Designer, developed its corporate identity and with it the highly recognizable IBM logo. Certain Designers from the streamlined era remained on the scene. Henry Dreyfuss was retained by a variety of manufacturers such as Bell and John Deere. Along with his associate, Niels Diffrient, he became known as the initiator of studies in human factors and applications in design. Raymond Loewy continued to be very active after the war and retained clients such as Studebaker, Coca-Cola, and Schick.

Not to be forgotten is the automotive industry, which became famous—or as some would say, infamous—for its use and abuse of design. The purchasing spree that occurred after World War II was often fed by superficially designed cars that changed from year to year for no other reason than style. From this aberration were born the stylists—whose designs were merely icing on a cake—with their tarnished reputations and a stigma that clings to some modern design to this day.

American design and Designers were finally creating an identity separate from their counterparts in Europe. Only in the United States had the design community forged such a close relationship with business. Major manufacturing industries such as Ford, General Motors, and Chrysler all incorporated design into their operations. So did the new companies on the block such as Apple and Hewlett-Packard. Visual communication and identity programs became part of the corporate world used by airlines such as Braniff and United Airlines; retailers such as Target and Nordstrom; and food outlets such as McDonald's and Starbucks. With firms like Gensler, architecture and interior design had also acknowledged the importance of corporate America. Head offices and resorts were not merely buildings to be constructed but part of an overall business strategy that included corporate identity as a focal point. Design and business even spawned groups such as the Design Management Institute and the Corporate Design Foundation.

By the mid-1970s, American design had become clearly associated with business and management. Design as high culture played a minuscule role. To survive, let alone thrive, design had to demonstrate purpose and utility. The design scene in Europe was equally active and vibrant but for quite different reasons. There, design was seen either as a cultural manifestation or, if more closely connected to industry, something linked to production and engineering. Two similar yet quite different paths had been forged for design and designing, one for America and another for Europe. Neither one was right or wrong. They merely reflected fundamental differences in cultural values.

Canadian Pragmatism

When the word *Canada* is mentioned, design does not normally spring to mind—at least not the way it seems to do for places like Italy or Germany or Scandinavia. With Canada, one is much more likely to think of lakes and mountains, winter or UN peacekeeping missions. It is not that Canadians are not proficient at design; it is simply

that other economic, political and cultural issues have a higher profile. Design is present, but in discreet measures.

The presence and place of Canadian design can be explained to a large degree by the contextual nature of Canada. First, Canada is a relatively young country. Its European discovery began with the arrival of the early Norsemen on the shores of Newfoundland, followed much later by the Europeans: John Cabot in 1497, Jacques Cartier in 1535, and Samuel de Champlain in 1608. Second, Canada's major industries are resource-based; that is, forestry, agriculture, mining, petroleum and petrochemical. Third, Canada's population is essentially multi-ethnic and multi-cultural, a combination of native people, Europeans and, more recently, people from East Asia. Consequently, a distinct design style may such as we find in Germany or Scandinavia may not be possible given this heterogenous setting. The geographical context is significant in that Canada stretches over 4,500 miles from east to west, and slightly less from north to south. On a typical flight from the south to the north, a person would fly over forests six times the size of France, would perhaps see herds of caribou so large that they take a day to pass the same point, and would look at an area containing 30% of the Earth's fresh water. The Canadian north—the Yukon, the Northwest Territories, and Nunavut—is 25 percent larger than India, yet all of its people can be accommodated in a very large soccer stadium (about 200,000). Climate is the final contextual factor. For three to six months of the year Canada is more like one of the Nordic countries, with the temperature easily plummeting to −40°F; for the remainder of the year it is sub-tropical with temperatures sometime soaring to 95°F.

In combination, these contextual factors—history, natural resources, population, geography and climate—create an environment where design as an identifiable national style is not a significant issue, at least not when compared for a need to respect the cultural identity of individual groups or the dominance of industries in the primary sectors such as petroleum and refining. These two features of Canada have created what is commonly called the cultural mosaic, on the one hand, and a relatively small manufacturing sector, on the other. Despite their importance to most Canadians, neither of these features actively contributes to a cohesive and common design identity. In the end, however, design in Canada is like design in other countries: It generally reflects the context.

This combination of contextual factors has provided Canadian designers with a particular set of challenges. From Alexander Graham Bell and J. A. Bombardier to Moshe Safdie and, more recently, Karim Rashid and Bruce Mau, the Canadian context has played an implicit role in the design process, demonstrating the richness and context-driven quality of Canadian design.

Alexander Graham Bell is a good case in point. Bell came to Canada from Scotland in 1870. He was 23 years old. Along with his father, he worked as a speech therapist for the deaf and his invention of the telephone came about in a serendipitous way—a combination of Bell's own scientific approach, the recent invention of the telegraph and the use of a microphone. Today, Bell's contributions to telecommunications are self-evident. In Canada, his legacy to design is found with Bell Canada, a company

that continues to push the boundaries of telecommunications. The idea of connecting people in a country that is so vast yet so sparsely populated via the telephone may not have been in the forefront of Bell's mind. Nevertheless, it makes contextual sense that someone would eventually invent such a device given these particular circumstances and conditions.

The Canadian context was also a determining factor for J. A. Bombardier. His resolve to overcome the difficulties of overland transportation in the winter is a textbook case of the context/product symbiosis. The impetus came in a very personal and tragic way: His son was seriously ill and needed to be hospitalized, but the roads were impassable due to a winter storm. This combination proved to be fatal and his son died. From that moment on, Bombardier swore that he would conquer the challenge of over-land winter transportation. This he did with little realization that his ingenuity would be the foundation of a multi-national company heavily involved in all kinds of transportation design, from the one-person snow vehicles more-commonly known as the Ski-Doo to personal watercrafts, subway cars for New York City and regional jet liners.

The Canadian context also played a role in the development of the aircraft industry in Canada. The challenge for aircraft manufacturers was the design and development of airplanes that could be used in areas where there were few airports and where lakes could serve as substitute runways, both in summer and winter. Adding to this challenge was the fact that many lakes were small and most often surrounded by forests. These conditions gave birth to an aeronautical design known as STOL, or Short-Take-Off-and-Landing. This type of design is most often associated with bush planes, but also exists with commuter planes such as the DASH 7 and 8, both manufactured today by De Havilland.

Canada's involvement in World War II altered the economy, and thereby altered the manufacturing sector. The focus was on wartime production. Once the war was over, the challenge for the economy to return to peacetime design and production. However, two conditions directly impacted this return. On one hand, many industries had developed new materials and processes for the war effort; on the other hand, many of these materials and processes had no real peacetime market. C. D. Howe, a federal Cabinet minister in the government of the day, was not deterred by this economic paradox. Howe established the Committee for Reconstruction and Re-establishment and asked the Exhibition Commission to organize an exhibit of industrial discoveries from the National Research Council of Canada and its efforts during the war. Within the framework of the National Gallery, one of the first publications on design, *Design for Use in Canadian Products,* was published in 1946. In the same year, the Affiliation of Canadian Industrial Designers was formed and, by 1947, the group had incorporated itself as the Association of Canadian Industrial Designers.

Over the next 20 years, design became an integral part of several leading industries including telecommunication, transportation and furniture. Thus Expo '67—the world exposition of 1967—came at a very opportune time in Canadian design history. It became the most important post-war design event in Canada—a celebration of design not only from Canada but also from around the world. On a few islands in the St. Lawrence River, next to the city of Montreal, architects and designers from the world over came to share their accomplishments. Notably, there was Buckminster Fuller's geodesic dome, the largest geodesic structure built, and Moshe Safdie's Habitat, a mass-produced housing concept. Even the City of Montreal contributed to the design phenomenon by building a state-of-the-art subway. Everywhere you turned and looked, the built environment had become an exemplar of good design.

In the years that followed Expo '67, many Canadian designers and architects left their mark on Canadian society. Douglas Ball became internationally known for his outstanding office furniture; Ian Bruce was the driving force behind the internationally known Laser sailboat; and John Tyson designed what is possibly Canada's first modern telephone, the Contempra, and went on to lead the design team at Nortel.

Many Canadian manufacturers have also demonstrated the wise use of design in their operations. Bombardier, especially in its Skidoo and Seadoo divisions, incorporate design in all product lines. Canadair, Nortel, Mitel, Newbridge, Umbra, and Research in Motion (known for the Blackberry) have also become world leaders in part because of the astute application of design, as have furniture makers Teknion and Keilhauer.

Design also found a place with Canadian government and many of its agencies. Both the Canadian National

Railways and the Canadian Broadcasting Corporation have developed award-winning corporate identities. Not to be outdone, the Government of Canada has also applied good design practice in its overall visual identity, as well as its stamps and currency.

Canadian architects have also influenced Canadian design. Moshe Safdie has already been mentioned. The Habitat project at Expo '67 was only the first of numerous architectural projects in which Safdie questioned established norms in architecture. Douglas Cardinal has taken the contextual factor one step further. As a native Canadian, he brings a cultural perspective to his work; his designs are distinctively native in origin.

More recently, two Canadian designers have become active on the world stage. Karim Rashid has become a leading designer of the Postmodernist genre and Bruce Mau has challenged design practice with his interdisciplinary approach as embodied in the Institute Without Boundaries. From Mau's perspective, design needs to set aside its many silos, which isolate one design discipline from another, and begin to act in a concerted effort in order to address issues that go well beyond the expertise of one design discipline or another.

Japanese Globalism

Design in Japan presented a very different picture than in Europe or the United States. Until 1853, when U.S. Admiral Matthew Perry arrived in the Bay of Tokyo, Japan had been totally closed to foreign influence. Japanese culture had evolved as a kind of hermetically sealed society. Even up to and including World War II, the influence of Japan on the international design scene was insignificant. Following Japan's defeat to the Allies and its subsequent wish to emulate the Americans, the world began to be aware of this sleeping industrial giant.

The designs that were to eventually materialize in those early years of industrialization were quickly associated with plagiarism, blatant copying, and poor quality. The first post–World War II products from Japan were cheaply made and did not have the high quality with which we now so readily associate the label "Made in Japan." However, Japan recognized as early as the 1950s that there were substantial benefits to be gained by having an enlightened design policy. And unlike its European rivals, especially the Scandinavians who were still attached to the long traditions of the crafts, Japan concentrated its efforts on the new and rapidly evolving technological sectors. Watches, cameras, hi-fi equipment, and motorcycles became the first products on Japan's agenda, an approach that placed Seiko, Canon, Sony, and Honda in the world arena of design. (See Figure 6.9.)

Since the early 1960s, the world has witnessed the emergence of Japan as a major industrial and economic power, one of the few non-Western countries to attain that status. Inevitably, this has meant a much greater presence of Japanese design in the marketplace throughout the world, more specifically in Western Europe and North America. In many ways, design in Japan has not evolved in ways similar to that of its counterparts in Europe and North America and, consequently, does not lend itself to the same kind of historical overview. Five of these differences are worth noting.

First, the notion of self-expression or individualism in design is virtually nonexistent. To study a design as an extension of a Designer's particular and personal belief system would be almost futile. In most instances, Japanese design is not self-referential.

Second, most Japanese designs appeal to several of our senses. Unlike many Western designs for which visual aesthetics are the principal if not the only focus of the attention, Japanese Designers often give as much care to tactile and auditory qualities as to visual ones.

Third, Japanese designs usually have an overall 'spiritualism' about them. Edward T. Hall made reference to this fact when he stated, "In Japan . . . emotions or feelings are ranked very high . . . Logic, as we think of it, is ranked low. Our ranking of these two sets is, of course, almost the reverse of the Japanese."[xv] The dilemma of trying to use a framework of Western thought and logic to conduct a meaningful analysis of Japanese objects becomes obvious. Kenjii Ekuan, one of Japan's foremost Designers, alluded to this when he stated that "the various spirits of millions of gods are instilled in *dogo*, or tools." Ekuan elaborated further on this when he noted that, "a thing is made for the purpose of manifesting a spirit."[xvi] As an example of this difference in design motive, Ekuan concluded that the technology of the camera and the associated paraphernalia are more a desire on the part of man for spiritual realization of image-making than the desire to possess the latest gadget. The analysis of a Japanese design on strictly visual terms is therefore superficial; it fails to come to grips with the 'spiritualism' of the object in question. Most Western Users of design

would have great difficulties in dealing with spiritual evaluation of everyday things.

Quality is the fourth important characteristic of Japanese design and is deeply rooted in traditional culture. Quality was present in the history of common Artifacts and vernacular architecture, and its underlying premise has permeated more recent developments in contemporary Japanese life.

Lastly, Japanese culture has become known for its power of adaptation. To many observers—specifically, to some in the West—this ability amounts to nothing less than plagiarism. But for the Japanese, it is a form of genuine flattery. Doing what others have done is the highest compliment that can be paid to the original creator.

The Asian Tigers

In the context of design, the Asian Tigers are generally considered to be Hong Kong (now part of China), Taiwan, Singapore, and South Korea. Since the 1980s, all four countries have grown into credible centers of design and design production, especially as the Makers of everyday things such as clothing, electronic devices, small appliances, and, more recently, automobiles. In some respects, and perhaps because they so effectively applied the Japanese model, they have challenged Japan's supremacy as the center of the Asian-Pacific industrial economy.

The economic model for all four countries has been somewhat similar. Step one, take full advantage of a skilled and industrious workforce to provide the necessary labor for the making of everyday things. Step two, create a close connection between the nation's government and its manufacturing base, including, in many cases, a very visible government promotion of design. Step three, move from the mere making of everyday things to the designing of them. South Korea has probably been the most successful at implementing this model, as can be attested to by popular brands such as Samsung (cell phones), LG (small and large appliances), and Hyundai and Kia (automobiles). India and China are next, neither of which is far behind the Asian Tigers. Their design presence will grow dramatically over the next decade. India is already a significant center for the outsourcing of engineering and software design, and China will move well beyond being just a center of manufacturing only to becoming a world center of design.

From Modernism to Postmodernism

Modernism was the leading design ideology of the twentieth century and radically changed designing. It prescribed a direction that was rational and logical, resulting in everyday things that originated from the mind and not necessarily from the heart. However, it is important to remember that as logical and appropriate as this set of rules may first appear to be, Modernism embodied a northern European ethos. Consequently, it was not and could never be representative of a set of universal values. Not surprisingly, the manifestations of Modernism were not consistently applied. The underpinning principles may have been essentially the same for all Modernist Designers, but their interpretation was very much conditioned by Context. The austere rendition of Modernism by German Designers was certainly different from the humanistic expressions of Scandinavia Designers or the exuberance of Italian Designers.

Nevertheless, certain principles were common in these interpretations. Most importantly:

- Modernism was rational and logical; it was not arbitrary. Objectivity was the order of the day.

- Modernism meant honesty; it was not deceptive. Therefore, everyday things should authentically represent both form and function and not be something less such as taking on the style of an out-of-context historical period.

- Modernism was about function; it was not useless. Everyday things needed to be purposeful and not trivial.

- Modernism integrated aesthetics in a rational way. The visual attributes of everyday things were not mere decorations applied at the end of the designing process.

- Modernism meant as little design as possible. Economy—of material, of use, of almost anything—was primordial.

- Modernism was no-nonsense design.

By the 1970s, Modernism had become the reigning dogma in designing. To no one's surprise, it became vulnerable to criticism. It may still have been novel in the marketplace and in the public realm but, to Designers, it was yesterday's news. Modernism was well ensconced both in design schools and in design practice but was becoming predictable, perhaps too much so. Furthermore, negative criticisms of Modernism's failures became common. Tom Wolfe's treatise of on the subject, *From the Bauhaus to Our House*, for example, did not pull many punches in its ridicule of Modernism and how it had failed to resolve problems in urban development, architecture, and design given its high expectations.[xvii] Challenges to the dictates of Modernism were also occurring in the European design community.

Clearly, the pendulum was beginning to swing away from Modernism and toward something else. But what was that something else to be? In America, it was the architectural and design explorations of noted American architects Robert Venturi and Michael Graves as well as the architectural writings of Charles Jencks that began to question Modernism. Venturi was especially vocal, calling for the inclusion of the values and tastes of common people in architecture while at the same time admonishing those architects whose concerns were limited to trophy houses or buildings as a form of ill-placed self-aggrandizement. As he so adroitly pointed out, less was not more—less was a bore. In the book *Learning from Las Vegas*, co-authored with Denise Scott Brown and Steven Izenour, Venturi articulated and expanded on this premise at length. For many Designers like Venturi, Modernism had ceased to be a reflection of the times; it was something of the past. Much like functionalism and rationalism had been a reaction to the aesthetic exuberances of the late nineteenth and early twentieth centuries, the stage was set for a similar reaction to Modernism.

The architectural and design work of Michael Graves certainly explored this new direction. His use of a visual language imbedded with elements of historicism and eclecticism was contrary to the cold and impersonal logic and rationale that we had come to expect of Modernism. Graves's buildings and products for Target, which came later, became feasts for the eyes, a kind of smorgasbord of multi-colored forms and shapes. Even a superficial analysis of Graves's everyday things for Target would reveal an immediate and very obvious difference with, for example, the very Modernist everyday things produced by the Danish company Rosti, the Swiss company Bodum, or the American company Dansk. These three exemplified the best of Modernist ideology and generally followed the rules of understated visual expression, as defined by the Modernist mantra "Less is more." For Graves, however, celebration was much more the order of the day. Everyday things did not have to be staid; there was no reason they could not be both useful and visually exciting.

More recently, Frank Gehry, the Canadian-born architect and Designer, has established himself as the premier advocate of an architectural and design expression that has pushed the dictates of what has become known as Postmodernism even further. Moreover, this expression has been much more than mere visual provocation, which is often our first reaction to Gehry's designs. (See Figure 6.8, Gehry's Walt Disney Concert Hall.) For example, the Guggenheim Museum in Bilbao, Spain, has been declared one of the most important buildings of the twentieth century. By its form alone, it certainly qualifies for that title. However, the technology behind the building—both the computer technology to design it and the construction technology to build it—equally qualify the museum as important. And Gehry has not limited his explorations to architecture. He has also applied his imagination and creativity to furniture. In his early years, he explored the innovative use of cardboard in chair making; later, it was a similar exploration with bent strips of wood, which culminated in a line of wooden chairs for Knoll, the American furniture Maker. In 2003, Gehry ventured into yet another area of material exploration and produced the aluminum Superlight chair for Emeco.

Although first considered revolutionary and controversial, Postmodernism provided a necessary elixir for design and Designers alike. If nothing else, it demonstrated that sacred cows could be burned without serious repercussion. More importantly, it brought a new and vitally refreshing perspective—both spiritually and visually—to a school of design thought that had become somewhat stuffy and stodgy.

Similar unrest was occurring in Europe as well. There, the charge for change was led by several Italian Designers including Ettore Sottsass, Jnr, and Andrea Branzi. They too rebelled against the predictability of Modernism and its tenets. But Sottsass and Branzi were not alone. Along with Michele de Lucchi and Matteo Thun, they formed a group called Memphis. Under this banner, they and others experimented with a revolutionary product language as a way of questioning the quasi-sacred qualities of Modernism. Theirs was a kind of palace coup intended as a kick in the pants to those Designers who continued to blindly follow the predictable dictates of Modernism. Andrea Branzi made it quite clear that Sottsass and colleagues never intended the Memphis movement to be

taken as seriously as it was.[xviii] Much to the chagrin of the Memphis founders, eager young Designers as well as overzealous scholars attempted to uncover more profound meanings other than what actually existed in the works produced by the group.

Memphis was not the only group leading the charge in Italian Postmodern design. There were individuals such as Gaetano Pesce (see chapter 2), who explored the visual essence and poetic presence of everyday things, especially furniture. And there were companies such as Alessi, whose design presence has not gone unnoticed. Alessi began as a small metalware manufacturer founded in northern Italy in 1921 by Giovanni Alessi. By the mid-1930s, Carlo Alessi, Giovanni's son, introduced the idea of using Designers in the development of new products, most of which were meant for restaurants and the catering trades. Today, the company exports 65% of its production to over sixty countries. Designers such as Michael Graves, Richard Sapper, Philippe Starck, and Ron Arad, to name only a few, are regularly commissioned to create highly innovative everyday things for Alessi, in step with both the tenets of Postmodernism and the company's vision of "offering the consuming masses veritable artistic items at low prices."

More recently, Canadian Designer Bruce Mau has redefined design in this Postmodernist era by questioning the disciplinary boundaries and paradigms of the past. For Mau, these disciplinary boundaries are artificial and the paradigms are no longer meaningful. He regularly collaborates with some of the world's leading architects, artists, writers, curators, academics, entrepreneurs, businesses, and institutions. Mau's reputation has become international and his impact has been felt over a wide range of business and cultural disciplines alike.

As can be expected of any movement that purports to be reactionary, Postmodernism's chief characteristics were quite the opposite of its predecessor. Therefore,

- If Modernism was rational and logical, Postmodernism was not, or it at least approached design with a different sense of logic. For Postmodernist Designers, design did not have to always make rational and logical sense.

- If Modernism was honest and not deceptive, Postmodernism allowed itself to be frivolous and often even humorous and witty. Design did not always have to be so serious.

- If Modernism was about function, Postmodernism redefined the meaning of function and adventured well beyond mere utility.

- If Modernism integrated aesthetics in a rational way, Postmodernism proposed an approach to aesthetics that did not necessarily follow past logic. The use of color, for example, did not always have to be rational.

- If Modernism meant as little design as possible, Postmodernism was about exuberance and celebration.

- If Modernism was no nonsense, Postmodernism often presented an almost irreverent message about design.

In retrospect, Postmodernism in design was nothing less than a reaction to Modernism. And reactions in the world of art and design—that is, established movements being displaced by newer, reactive ones—are nothing new. They are inevitable, as history has shown over and over again. Modernism itself was a reaction to the excessive decoration in design and architecture of the late nineteenth century, much like Art Nouveau was a reaction to the mechanistic tendencies of the Industrial Revolution.

With Postmodernism, the past had become the present, or at least a kind of reinterpretation of the past with a dash of the future. Designing was not cyclical; if anything, its evolution was more like a spiral. It moved forward in circles, retrieving from the past but never staying there, like a long spiral. The pattern had occurred before and will occur again.

Tools
The Age of Self saw the final split in the Designing Triad—that is, a point where the Designer, the Maker, and the User became independent agents even as they existed and functioned in an interdependent relationship. Makers continued to have prominence, but slowly Designers began to play an interdependent role with the Makers. Such was the case with Ferdinand Porsche, Coco Chanel, and Charles Eames—three Designers of great significance who interjected a great deal of self into the designing process.

Ferdinand Porsche

Most people know Porsche as one of the premiere sports-car manufacturers; few people, however, know much about its founder, Ferdinand Porsche (1875–1951). This Austrian engineer spent the majority of his life in Germany. Very little in Porsche's early automotive design career in the early 1930s foretold of the world-class reputation his automobiles would eventually gain. The sports automobile that we have come to revere today had a very humble beginning as the *Volkswagen* or "people's car," commissioned by Adolf Hitler in the mid-1930s. The German government of the day had a very strong socialist agenda, and the idea of a car for everyone sat well with the government leaders. More than that, German officials calculated that individual car ownership among the German populace would foster a public demand for roads that would allow the government to move forward with its massive project of building national highways, or autobahns. Such a network of highways would also allow the military to travel quickly to almost any point in the country and beyond.

The engineering curiosity of Ferdinand Porsche led him to see that the basic concepts behind the Volkswagen—rear engine, rear-wheel drive, air cooled, and aerodynamic styling—were ideally suited to a performance sports car. After World War II, Porsche began to develop such a car, basing his concept on what he thought a car should be rather than on the opinions of others. Having returned to his native Austria, Porsche launched his first sports car, the two-person 356 roadster, on June 8, 1948. The 356 embodied Porsche's own philosophy about design: every aspect and every detail was rationalized and justified to the utmost degree. Nothing—absolutely nothing—was left to chance. And if, in the end, the 356 seemed to be similar in concept to the Volkswagen, it was because all four of the aforementioned attributes were rational and logical. In the 356, of course, they were more refined and advanced. After all, the 356 was designed as a two-person performance car for the twisting mountain roads of Austria, not a four-person sedan for the autobahns of Germany.

The debut of the 356 in Austria was the beginning of what would become a legend in automotive design and construction. The performance specifications originally required for the driving conditions of Austria were just the first step for world-class performance. Over the next decades, various Porsche models conquered and at times dominated the major road-racing circuits of Europe and the world, including Nurburgring in Germany, Le Mans in France, and the Targa Florio in Italy. The same story was to repeat itself in road rallies as well as all major GT racing events for the next decades.

For Porsche, racing was not for the sake of winning or for the thrill of competition. Racing was a living laboratory for its production cars. The time and money invested in racing was reflected in the automobile that someone could purchase at a local dealership. Consequently, the Porsche 911, first launched in 1964 and still produced today, is a direct descendent of the 356. (See Figure 6.10.) Ongoing modifications to the car as the direct result of racing and research and development occurred in the intervening years. The philosophy of the past—compelling Porsche to question and justify every aspect of the car's design—remains just as pertinent today. The man is still embodied in every car.

As a meaningful footnote in this age of green design and sustainability, around 60% of all Porsches ever built are still running.

Coco Chanel

Very little in Coco Chanel's childhood predicted the phenomenal success that she would achieve and the fashion empire that she would build in her lifetime. After all, Chanel, the company, is a leading—if not the leading—brand in haute couture, perfumes, and accessories. Its logo of two intertwined Cs is recognized the world over as a sign of refined taste and elegance. Yet, Coco Chanel (1883–1971) was not born into a world of refined taste and elegance. On the contrary, Gabrielle Bonheur "Coco" Chanel's early years were quite modest. She was born in Saumur, France, and lost her mother at the age of six. Shortly thereafter, her father abandoned her and her siblings to the care of relatives.

She had a brief career as a singer, where she first used the name Coco. Her career in fashion, however, only began as the result of romantic liaisons with two well-connected gentlemen. These relationships made it possible for Chanel to open a millinery shop in Paris, where her simple hats found favor with the public. Simplicity became her trademark and remained her forte as she expanded her activities into clothing such as skirts, jackets, chemises, and dresses. In 1922, she launched Chanel No. 5, the perfume that would become the bedrock of her growing empire. No other fragrance has had the impact that Chanel No. 5 has had on the marketplace and on fashion. A few years later, she introduced her signature cardigan jacket and 'little black skirt' to the market, both of which became closely linked to her reputation as a Designer of simple and elegant garments.

Perhaps more significant than visual simplicity was the liberation—both physical and symbolic—that she introduced to women's clothes. Chanel deliberately avoided the constrained look that the popular corset created; rather, she opted for clothing that was more comfortable and that provided a more relaxed appearance. Symbolically, she was liberating women.

Chanel's career and reputation suffered somewhat during and after the Second World War because of a romantic relationship that she had with a German military officer. She felt the need to leave France, went to live in Switzerland, but returned to Paris in 1954. Fortunately, the popularity of Chanel's designs—clothing that was simple, elegant, and comfortable—had not waned in her absence. The public's desire for such fashion remained strong, and her company continued to grow into the multinational that it is today. As for Chanel, she continued to design until her death in 1971.

Charles and Ray Eames

Few names resonate in American design and with American designers as do Charles (1907–1978) and Ray Eames (1912–1988). As a couple, they became the quintessential designers of the twentieth century century via their contributions to design, furniture, architecture, visual communication, and film—all of which were distinctive by their innovation, attention to detail, and quality. As prolific as they were, Charles and Ray came to design via very different routes.

For Charles, there was never any clear indication in his youth that he would become such a prodigious designer. As an adolescent, he worked as a laborer, was fascinated with engineering and architecture, and eventually became a student in architecture at Washington University. However, he never completed his studies. To his misfortune, it now appears that Charles had selected the wrong role model in Frank Lloyd Wright. In the eyes of faculty members in many American schools of architecture in those days—including those at Washington University—Wright was not a favorite; he was considered too revolutionary and not someone to be emulated.

In retrospect, Charles' career seems to have benefited from a fateful series of incidences that occurred at the most appropriate time. His departure from architectural studies was certainly one of these incidences; so was his relationship with Eliel Saarinen, the Finnish master architect. Saarinen invited Charles to move to the Cranbrook Academy of Art in Michigan, where he could continue his studies in architecture. This he did and eventually became the head of industrial design. Not only was this move to Cranbrook a fortunate turn of events for Charles but it also brought him into contact with Eliel's son, Aero. Together, Charles and the younger Saarinen would design the prize-wining entry for the Museum of Modern Art's 'Organic Design in Home Furnishings' competition and steer American design into new directions.

For Ray, the journey was somewhat different. She began her design career as a painter, established herself in New York, and, in 1936, became a founding member of the American Abstract Artists. In 1940, she enrolled at Cranbrook Academy of Art, where she met Charles. This was in the same year that Charles and Aero Saarinen were working on the aforementioned 'Organic Design in Home Furnishings' competition. Charles and Ray married the year after and began their life-long design journey together.

For the Eameses, explorations in new design directions became their trademark and became evident in three areas. There were films, especially *The Power of Ten* made in 1977, but others such as *A Communications Primer* in 1953 and *Toccata for Toy Trains* in 1957; there were the exhibitions such as *Glimpses of the USA* in Moscow (1959), *Mathematica* for IBM (1961), and the IBM Pavilion at the 1964 New York World's Fair; and, of course, there was the furniture, which remains their legacy. (See Figure 6.11) Not only did the furniture explore new forms in the spirit of Modernism, but it also embraced the latest developments in technology, from molded plywood and cast aluminum to glass-reinforced plastic. Many of the pieces were developed in collaboration with Herman Miller and remain in production to this today.

Structures

Structures or buildings of one kind or another have generally followed a pattern in which an architect, or Designer, creates a concept to be constructed by a builder, or Maker. There is a client, of course, but the client is not always the User. A client for a new museum, for example, may be its board of directors. As important as these people are to the design project, they are not the museum's everyday Users; the everyday Users are the people who frequent the museum.

What characterizes the Age of Self is the aforementioned split in the Designing Triad—distinct roles played by the Designer, Maker, and User in an interdependent relationship. For the architect, this distinctive role was self-referential—that is, there was a clear expression of self in the visual expression or aesthetic of the building.

This shift did not occur fully until the early twentieth century in architecture with pioneers such as Adolf Loos, Peter Behrens, and Joseph Maria Olbricht. In the eighteenth and nineteenth centuries, mainstream architecture in both in Europe and America was essentially revivalist and greatly influenced by the symbolism of the past. Self-reference was not obvious. This was certainly the case with the U.S. Capitol Building, designed by Thornton-Latrobe-Bulfinch between 1793 and 1830. With its dominant dome and countless columns, it is a flashback to the past classical style of architecture and very reminiscent of St. Peter's in Rome, which was designed centuries before. In principle, Westminster Palace, which houses the British Parliament in London, is no different. Designed by Sir Charles Barry between 1836 and 1868, it has all the visual trappings of neo-Gothic design, much like the Paris Opera designed by Charles Garnier and opened in 1875 has all the visual trappings of what is called the Beaux-Arts style in architecture. (See Figure 6.12.) Self-expression and individualistic design creativity—the hallmark of twentieth-century architecture—were not yet in evidence.

In all three cases— the U.S. Capitol Building, Westminster Palace, and the Paris Opera—as well as countless others, public architecture was undertaken much as it had been for centuries. The independent contributions of the Designer, Maker, and User were not yet clearly differentiated. The Designer, or architect, was not using the Artifact, or building, as a form of self-expression. If anything, many of these buildings reflected a past era conditioned by symbols from religion or mythology and very little of the present. Neither was the Maker having any impact by way of the latest technology. After all, Britain and most of the developed world were engulfed in the age of industrialization and the massive societal changes that resulted from steam locomotion, factories, and machinery; yet the U.S. Capitol, Westminster Palace, and the Paris Opera reflected very little if any of this reality. And the User's role was also less important and subservient to the obvious symbolism implicit in buildings as monoliths. One exception to this rule, as noted in the previous chapter, was the Crystal Palace.

The Dymaxion House

Industrialization and technology had become much more ingrained in mainstream society by the early twentieth century. Their application was becoming more evident, especially in manufacturing, transportation, and communication. Not so, however, in architecture and the construction trades. Compared to other industrial sectors, buildings were the result of a complex craft-oriented process executed in an antiquated way. It has been said that if the automobile industry had evolved like the building sector, we would still be driving buckboards. As often is the case, there were exceptions. The Dymaxion House designed by Buckminster Fuller was one of these.

Maybe because he was not an architect trained in the traditional sense but more of a highly creative engineer closer to what we consider a Renaissance Man,

Buckminster Fuller never approached a challenge in a conventional way: his solutions were always imaginative if not revolutionary. This was certainly the case with his concept for the geodesic dome and also for the Dymaxion House. The Dymaxion concept saw the light of day around 1927 and was based on two principles. The first was the advantages of mass production, which had already become self-evident in the automobile industry; the second was the dome and the many inherent properties possessed by a dome—structural integrity, minimal volume, and superior venting. In combination, the industrial-scale production of dome-like houses became a logical and rational step for Fuller.

Fuller's idea for such a house became more realistic after World War II because of two intersecting factors: America had a great deal of manufacturing capacity that had to go from wartime to peacetime production; and soldiers returning from the war would begin to raise families and need houses. The house that Fuller had in mind was designed to take advantage of the former for the benefit of the latter. (See Figure 6.13.) It was circular in shape and provided a little over 1,200 square feet of living space meant for a family of four. More significantly, it had a central core that served to heat, cool, and vent the house, and was made of aluminum. The latter material was used because of the many factories that had acquired the technology as the result of aircraft manufacturing during the war.

As thoughtful and innovative as the Dymaxion House was in concept, it was a commercial failure. Only two prototypes were ever built, and one remains in the Ford Museum as evidence that logical, rational thinking does not always culminate in business success. This is often the risk with innovation. Perhaps Fuller's most significant omission when designing the Dymaxion House was not realizing that most Users want a home and not necessarily a house. From that perspective, the Dymaxion House failed. It was a mechanistic marvel, both in concept and production. However, it was devoid of any humanistic qualities. No matter how great one's intellectual capacity may be to accept Fuller's revolutionary idea of a house, a round, aluminum dome is not what a normal User intuitively envisions as a home. A home has square rooms in which you place furniture and a roof with a peak and windows with curtains. The Dymaxion House provided none of these. Worse, it was contrary to the architectural conventions of the times, which advocated for visual integration with existing architectural styles and consideration for the site.

Levittown

The inability to perceive a house as a home and all of the socio-cultural implications attached to such a misperception proved to be the demise of the Dymaxion House. This same misperception would also prove to be the principal reason why architects failed to have a major impact on the housing industry after World War II. It is estimated that over 90% of buildings built in America today are not designed by architects. Architects, or Designers, did not appear to comprehend that the majority of people, or Users, wanted homes, not houses. The inability of Designers to provide what Users wanted opened the door for builders and developers, or Makers, to fill the void. Levittown—both the original suburb outside New York City and the sequel in Pennsylvania—was probably the first of what would become a pattern of suburban developments built by myriad developers. In almost every case, the houses, or Artifacts, were designed to be homes with a much greater regard for the desires of the Users rather than the aesthetics of the Designers.

The first Levittown is on Long Island in New York State and was launched in 1947 as a post-war project because of a need for inexpensive homes for veterans. The community derived its name from the builder, the firm of Levitt & Sons. The second Levittown, in Bucks County near Philadelphia, was started in 1952. It too offered entry-level homes for new home buyers in the bustling era immediately after the war. At its completion, Levittown (NY) was a community of well over 17,000 homes, and William J. Levitt, the founder of Levitt & Sons, appeared on the cover of *Time* magazine.

Both Levittowns reflected the spirit of the times. Not only were they part of the general growth in a post-war economy, but like the automotive industry they also incorporated some of the principles of mass production. For example, house models were standardized, and lumber was pre-cut in a California factory owned by Levitt and shipped to the building site. At its height, the construction crews were making thirty houses a day. Not only had developers, such as Levitt, come to understand the difference between a house and a home, they also perceived that with the application of mass-production techniques, the house would be a commodity.

Predictably, the suburbs became possible because of the returning veterans and a booming post-war economy. However, that was not the complete story. People cannot move to the suburbs and travel to and from work without some form of transportation. It was the modern automobile—now truly an everyday thing—that made the transportation connection between home and work feasible. Without the automobile, the growth of suburbs would not have occurred, at least not to the degree that it did. In this instance, tools and buildings were intricately interconnected. One could neither evolve nor grow without the other.

Habitat '67

In the years following World War II, mainstream architecture continued in its prescriptive mission. Its prominence was increasingly visible in public buildings of one kind or another—airports, museums, hospitals, libraries, and universities. Involvement in private homes was more often than not limited to one-of-a kind houses for individual clients. Except for examples of public housing here and there, most of these commissions were the so-called trophy houses.

A young architect by the name of Moshe Safdie had a different idea for a housing project, one that would integrate mass-production technology all the while creating individualized living spaces for its occupants. Safdie was completing his architectural studies at McGill University in Montreal with a thesis focused on a multiple-story, apartment-like project that would use techniques practiced in the concrete industry. Imagine a larger-than-life Lego set whose bricks are made not of injection-molded plastic but rather of cast-concrete produced in a factory and put together as modules. Once complete with plumbing and wiring, these apartment modules would be shipped to the building site and stacked one on top of the other. Such was the idea behind Habitat '67. (See Figure 6.14.)

Although Safdie's project was a student thesis, it was his good fortune that it occurred at the same time as Expo 67, the 1967 World's Fair in Montreal. Under the theme of Man and His World, Expo 67 was ideally suited for the building of a prototype of Safdie's habitat concept. In the months leading to the official opening of the fair, Safdie supervised the construction of Habitat '67, as the building concept came to be called, and saw it to completion. Forty years later, Habitat '67 is a thriving community in Montreal with a waiting list for people who wish to live there. In its original version, Safdie's idea was predicated on the use of industrial methods and factory production as a strategy to reduce the cost and to make housing affordable. Unfortunately, the popularity as well as the design cachet of Habitat '67 has made it an address of choice with a subsequent rise in the cost to live there.

Signs

Signs as elements within an alphabet have not gone through any revolutionary changes since their inception nearly two thousand years ago. Moving from pictographs to letterform was revolutionary because it created the basis for a visible language. But variations on a known theme—as we see with the redesign of one font or another based on the same alphabet—is evolutionary. This is especially true of the Western alphabet, which has not gone through any momentous change during the same period of time. In other words, the use of a specific sign as the basis for a visible language is not that different today than it was in ancient Rome. What has evolved are varia-

tions on a theme—that is, the seemingly infinite number of visual interpretations by Designers of letterforms in different font designs. Two excellent examples make the point.

The first example is the vastly popular typeface Times New Roman, designed by Stanley Morison in 1931 as the result of criticism Morison had made about *The Times* newspaper in London and its continued use of an antiquated font. Morison's design, based on another typeface, Plantin, eventually replaced Times Old Roman. If further validation of Times New Roman was needed after its adoption by *The Times*, it occurred when Microsoft, some sixty years later, installed it as its default font on Windows.

The second example is the typographical designs of Adrian Frutiger, born in Switzerland in 1928. In an age of computers and electronic media, Frutiger has aptly demonstrated that the design of typefaces continues to be an ongoing necessity. Among typeface Designers, he is one of the most prolific. Frutiger is best known for two typefaces: Univers and Frutiger. Univers was designed in 1956 and is a sans-serif typeface that reflects Modernist ideals: it is as minimalist as anyone could expect and is based on a logical system. It is similar to two other typefaces, Folio and Helvetica. All three are based on Akzidenz-Grotesk, a much older typeface dating back to 1896. Like Univers, Frutiger, the font that bears the name of its Designer, is a sans-serif typeface. It was deliberately created as part of the wayfinding system at the Charles de Gaulle International Airport in Paris and installed there in 1975. Because Frutiger wanted a typeface that had a modern appearance as well as being legible in various sizes and at different angles, he opted to design a new typeface rather than use an existing one such as Univers.

Both Morison and Frutiger have shown the importance of design at the level of micro details to address readability and legibility. However, the twenty-six signs of the alphabet remain and the changes have been evolutionary. That said, a revolution in signs has begun that is as significant as the one that shifted communication from a symbol-based system with petroglyphs and pictograms to a sign-based visible language. The digital age, with its strings of ones and zeros, has already created major shifts in how signs affect human communication—not only its visual quality but also its communicative effectiveness and impact. What is changing is the concept that underpins the sign itself through the shift from an analog model to a digital one, a shift that is revolutionary in every sense of the word for two important reasons.

First, digitization places into question the concept of originality. In the analog world, a duplicate is a facsimile of an original. It is almost as good as the original but never quite. Look closely at a duplicate 35mm slide and you will see that it is not exactly the same as the original. The colors may not be as faithfully reproduced or the image may not be as sharp. But a digital copy is as accurate as the original. So what does *original* mean in a digital age? There is no clear answer. Perhaps the non-existence of an original creation is what allowed so many people to download music off the Internet with little guilt that they were copying. And why should there have been? The copy was as good as the original, which therefore did not make it a copy in the first place. The argument may

be a convoluted form of logic perhaps, but major record labels are suing people for this illegal act of copying nonetheless.

Second, digitization increases accessibility. In the analog world, for example, documents are only accessible as hard copies—letters, photographs, books, magazines, and newspapers. Without a hard copy, you cannot access the information. Not so in the digital world. Documents of all kinds can be shared, transmitted, or posted with great ease. Because of this increased accessibility, communication is not only enhanced but is also accelerated. Think of the Internet, the World Wide Web, blogs, podcasts, and even e-tickets in the airline industry. Not one of these methods of communication could have existed in the analog age.

The simplicity behind the ones-and-zeros-based code that underpins the operating systems of computers is perhaps invisible. However, that too is changing. Bar codes—those thin and thick lines found on the tags of most products today—are undecipherable visual signs to the naked eye but are a source of detailed information to a bar-code reader. Airlines now use this visible code to sort luggage, and transport companies—both rail and road—use versions of bar codes to expedite their cargo. Today, bar-code readers of one kind or another are available for most smartphones. They allow people to access information as never before, both quickly and conveniently.

It is the ease with which a digital message can be replicated, distributed, and read that makes it so potent. After all, the effectiveness of communication only increases as its operational parts—signal, output, and input—are seamlessly knitted together. Certain politicians have learned that lesson only too well. Their attempt to conceal or embellish a story can come to a crashing end because of the availability of digital information, which can be found and distributed quickly via communication outlets such as YouTube—a distribution channel totally driven by the concept of self. Analog information could never have this immediate impact.

Is the analog world about to go away? Not likely. The digital age will not simply displace the analog world—it will complement it. Letters, photographs, books, magazines, newspapers, and other communication devices will be around for some time yet.

Summary

The Designer/Maker as one entity dominated design and designing for thousands of years. This was the Age of Surplus in which the notion of self-expression was not a basis or motivation for designing. If everyday things embodied self, it was in the making process as manifested in crafting. Crafting was not only found in most everyday things but also in the arts, such as painting and sculpture. And crafting could occur only because of a person—a skilled artisan or a gifted artist. Consequently, names of Designers began to be linked directly to everyday things. However, the skilled artisan or gifted artist was still the Designer/Maker. Perhaps the only exception was the architect of the time, who was rarely ever the Maker but certainly retained control over the making of the building.

The fissure between the Designer/Maker began to become apparent when the making process became industrialized. Suddenly, the place of the Designers was in question. It was not clear whether Designers had any role to play in the making process because a great deal of their contribution had become nothing more than decorative or applied. Machines could now produce this kind of decoration without Designers, albeit by copying what the same Designers had originated. Fortunately, there were a few industrialists who were more insightful, including Wedgwood and Thonet. So were the founders of the Deutscher Werkbund and what they referred to as the divide between the inventing and accomplishing spirits. From their perspective, it would be the cooperation and collaboration between Designers and Makers that would move designing forward.

Progressively and in the century that followed, Designers did separate from the Makers and, over time, names of individual creators and innovators surfaced with regularity and consistency. These Designers came from all areas—architecture, engineering, fine arts, and design. And with each, a trail was blazed for the many that would follow. What was a novelty only one hundred years ago had now become a common occurrence. Today, no one bats an eyelash when yet another Designer makes an entrance onto the world stage.

Further Reading

Ambaz, Emilio. *Italy: The New Domestic Landscape.*
Bayley, Stephen, ed. *The Conran Directory of Design.*
Blake, Peter. *Form Follows Fiasco: Why Modern Architecture Hasn't Worked.*
Branzi, Andrea. *The Hot House: Italian New Wave Design.*

Dormer, Peter. *Design Since 1945*.

Eidelberg, Martin, ed. *Design 1935–1965: What Modern Was*.

Ekuan, Kenjii. *Japanese Design and Modern Technology*.

Friedman, Thomas. *The World Is Flat*.

Giard, Jacques. *Design FAQs*.

Hiesenger, Kathryn B. *Design Since 1945*.

Hollis, Richard. *Graphic Design*. London.

Horn, Richard. *Memphis: Objects, Furniture, and Patterns*.

Huygen, Frederique. *British Design: Image & Identity*.

Ikko, Tannaka, and Koike Kazuko, ed. *Japan Design*.

Julier, Guy. *Dictionary of 20th Century Design and Designers*.

Mang, Karl. *History of Modern Furniture*.

MacCarthy, Fiona. *British Design Since 1880*.

Massey, Anne. *Interior Design of the 20th Century*.

McFadden, David Revere, ed. *Scandinavian Modern Design: 1880–1980*.

Meggs, Philip. *A History of Graphic Design*.

Pile, John. *A History of Interior Design*.

Raizman, David. *History of Modern Design*.

Sparke, Penny. *Ettore Sottsass Jnr*.

_____. *An Introduction to Design & Culture in the Twentieth Century*.

Wingler, Hans M. *The Bauhaus*.

Wolfe, Tom. *From Bauhaus to Our House*.

Woodham, Jonathan M. *Twentieth-Century Design*.

Yoshida, Mitsukuni, et al. *Japanese Style*.

Endnotes

[i] Even today, developers (Makers) do not always hire architects (Designers) to design houses but rely on draftsmen or other sources for ideas.

[ii] Coulton, J. J. *Ancient Greek Architects at Work: Problems of Structure and Design*.

[iii] Julier, Guy. *Dictionary of 20th Century Design and Designers*.

[iv] The quotation appeared in an exhibition of The Werkbund at Carleton University (Canada) in the 1980s.

[v] Gideon, Siegfried. *Mechanization Takes Command*.

[vi] In the end, it was the political pressure of the government in power—the National Socialist Party led by Adolf Hitler—that brought the Bauhaus to its knees.

[vii] Wingler, Hans M. *The Bauhaus*.

[viii] Ambaz, Emelio. *Italy: The New Domestic Landscape*.

[ix] Ibid

[x] Design Center Stuttgart. *Mobel aus Italien*.

[xi] Ambaz, Emelio. *Italy: The New Domestic Landscape*.

[xii] Mang, Karl. *History of Modern Furniture*.

[xiii] Sparke, Penny. *Ettore Sottsass Jnr*.

[xiv] Mang, Karl. *History of Modern Furniture*.

[xv] Hall, Edward T. *Beyond Culture*.

[xvi] Ekuan, Kenji. *Japanese Design and Modern Technology*.

[xvii] Peter Blake's equally scathing book, *Form Follows Fiasco,* stated much the same as concerns the failure of Modernism to solve significant societal challenges as intended by some of its founders.

[xviii] Personal conversation between the author and Andrea Branzi.

Figure 1.1: Natural and Artificial Worlds

Lakes are natural, such as this one in the Canadian Rockies; swimming pools are artificial, such as in this resort hotel in Arizona.

Figure 1.2: Natural and Artificial Worlds

Forests are natural, such as this aspen forest in northern Arizona; wooden sailboats are artificial, such as these two sailboats in Copenhagen.

Figure 1.3: Natural and Artificial Worlds
Sandy beaches are natural, such as this one on the Pacific coast of Mexico; glass—made from sand—is artificial, such as these glass birds made by the Finnish company Iittala.

Figure 1.4: Natural and Artificial Worlds
Sea food is natural, such as these clams, mussels, and oysters in a Korean village market; sushi—a combination of seafood, rice, and wasabi—is an artificial creation.

Figure 1.5: Water and Transportation
Venice is like no other city. It is planned around the use of canals as the day-to-day mode of transportation—from vaporetti (top) to gondolas (bottom, left and center) and water taxis (bottom, right).

Figure 1.6: Hieroglyphs and Pictograms

Egyptians used a form of written language based on pictographic images called hieroglyphs such as these on tablets in the British Museum (top, left) and the Louvre Museum (top, right); today, we use similar principles of visual communication when pictograms are created for events such as the 1976 Olympic Games in Montreal (bottom row).

Figure 1.7: Mechanistic Design

The Eiffel Tower, designed by Gustav Eiffel and built in Paris for a world exhibition in 1889, was an exemplar of mechanistic design. Many Parisians objected to this engineering marvel and perceived it as visually ugly. Today, it has become an icon of Paris and draws tourists from all over the world.

Figure 1.8: An Antidote to Mechanistic Designs

To Art Nouveau architects and designers, the lack of visual aesthetic quality in designs such as the Eiffel Tower needed to be addressed. Many did so by introducing a more humanistic expression, such as can be found in Hector Guimard's light standards for the Paris Metro, which appear like large plants (top). Detail of a light standard (bottom).

Figure 1.9: The Inventive Mind of Leonardo da Vinci

Leonardo da Vinci, the Italian Renaissance man, was perhaps one of the earliest Designers to perceive nature as a source of ideas. This was certainly the case with da Vinci's flying devices such as the glider exhibited in the Victoria & Albert Museum in London. The design of the wings is derived from the wings of birds, which he studied at length.

Figure 1.11: Macro- and Micro-contextual Features

Chairs reflect cultural values, such as the desire to sit and the status that derives from sitting. These values are often implicit and are macro-contextual. Color, material, and form are different. They are explicit and micro-contextual. Cafeteria chair (top, left); first-class rail passenger seat (top, right); vernacular Mexican chair (bottom, left); plastic side chair (bottom, right).

Figure 2.1: Everyday Things as Signs and Symbols

The design features of everyday things—form, shape, color, proportion, scale, etc.—are a combination of signs and symbols. Consequently few people mistake a church for a pick-up truck (the mission at Oquitoa and pick-up trucks in Alamos, both in the State of Sonora, Mexico).

Figure 2.3: Communication Not at First Evident

Gaetano Pesce's sofa is based on a metaphor: a sunset on the urbanscape of a city. It avoids the generic visual language that we normally associate with a sofa.

Figure 2.4: Same Message; Different Signs

The exit signs in public buildings exist to aid people in case of an emergency. Yet, the use of red or green could be confusing. Not only are the colors different but they also send a very different signal: generally, green means go whereas red means stop.

Figure 2.5: H/C and L/C Communication
The Vietnam War Memorial (left) is High-context Communication. A great deal of the message resides with the viewer. The Vietnam War Memorial (right) is Low-context Communication; its message is very explicit and leaves little to the imagination.

Figure 2.6: Villa Savoye

Le Corbusier designed Villa Savoye applying the tenets of Modernism. The house is an excellent study in rational and logical thinking in design, a direction that was typical of architecture and design in northern Europe in the 1920s.

Figure 2.7: Same Function; Different Forms

The two trucks pictured above—the Hummer H3 and the Chevrolet Colorado pick-up—share the same technology or platform. Yet they appear to be two completely different vehicles and are designed to appeal to two very different types of Users.

Figure 2.8: Same Sign; Different Meaning

Many people in the West have only one image of the swastika: Adolf Hitler and the horrors of World War II. In the East, the swastika has a very different connotation. It has been used in the Buddhist religion to symbolize the feet or footprints of the Buddha. The symbol, which was also used widely in the ancient world including Mesopotamia, the Americas, India, and Scandinavia, became common in China and Japan with the spread of Buddhism. The photographs above show the swastika in a brick pattern (top), in a museum banner (left), at a temple (middle, right), and in a metal fence (bottom, right). All photographs are from the Republic of Korea.

Figure 2.9: One Sign; Many Meanings

The cross is a very common sign. It is used as national symbols in the flags of countries such as Denmark (top); Christian churches such as this chapel in Sedona, Arizona (bottom, right); by life-saving agencies and services such as this US Navy hospital ship (second from the top, left); as corporate symbols such as the Swiss airlines (second from the bottom, left); and as branding such as these Swiss Army products (bottom, left).

Figure 2.11: Location of Controls and Gestalt

Modern automobiles provide controls for a variety of functions. To avoid confusion among these, Designers group them logically and use different shapes and forms to distinguish one from the other. The Audi console pictured above separates the radio functions from the ones for climatic control, and then goes on to use various rectangular and circular shapes to identify particular controls.

Figure 2.12: Consistency of Visual Identity

Pepsi's and Coke's visual identities show consistency around the globe. Although the language in the two signs in Bangkok shown above is not English, a person who knows the visual identity of either brand would recognize them almost immediately. By being visually consistent wherever they are sold, Pepsi and Coke increase the certainty of brand recognition.

Figure 3.2: Some Everyday Things Extend Our Muscles

There was a time when people built roads by using their muscles, such as this worker in Mumbai, India (top, left). Today, human muscle has been replaced with mechanical ones, such as this road-working equipment (top, right).

Figure 3.3: Some Everyday Things Extend Our Senses

Mechanical and electronic devices enhance human senses. The hiker uses binoculars to increase his range of vision (bottom, left); the US Navy plane uses radar (the large dome on top of the fuselage) to see in the dark, through clouds, and in fog (bottom, right).

Figure 3.4: Chateau de Chenonceau in the Loire Valley

Beginning in the tenth century, French kings as well as members of the French nobility built castles and chateaux in the Loire Valley southwest of Paris. The Chateau de Chenonceau was one of these and is a blend of Gothic and Renaissance architecture. It was built in the early fifteenth century but underwent regular changes and renovations.

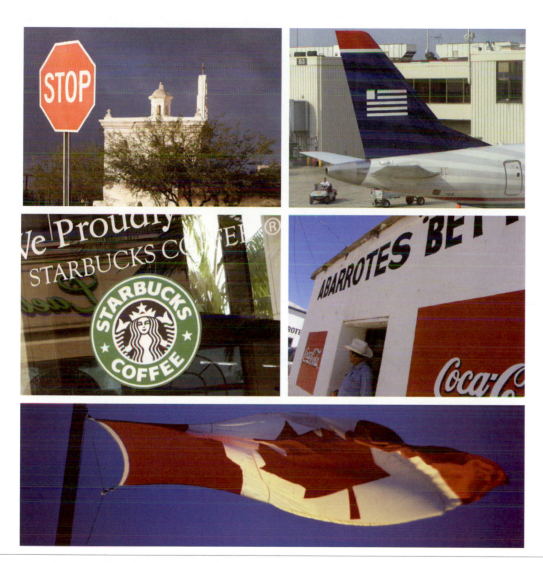

Figure 3.5: Signs and Symbols Are Everywhere

The octagonal red stop sign signals drivers to come to a complete stop. As a symbol, it connotes a society that has a sense of order. Commercial signs, such as the US Airways and Starbucks logos, identify the company as well as symbolize an expected level of service. In rural Mexico, the Coca-Cola sign is recognized by the villagers as a place not only to buy the product, but also to belong to a group. By way of another example, national flags serve as both signs and symbols.

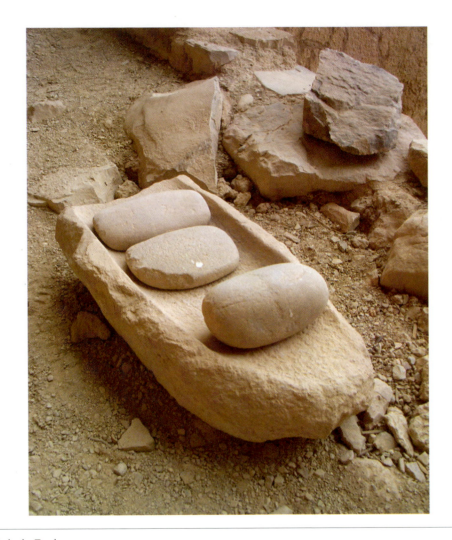

Figure 4.1: Salado Tools

The Salado people populated parts of Arizona at various times and as recently as five to six hundred years ago. Like other tribes who relied on the land for food, tools, and shelter, the Salado made use of stone for grinding corn and other seeds.

Figure 4.2: Birch-bark Canoe

The native people of northeast North America used the birch-bark canoe extensively in order to travel, hunt, and fish. The canoe's design was an ingenious combination of functional form and local material—birch bark, cedar, roots, and spruce gum.

Figure 4.3: Cliff Dwellings in the American Southwest

Throughout many areas of the American southwest, especially Arizona and Colorado, native people often built dwellings into the cliffs. The four pictured are all from Arizona: the White House in Canyon de Chelly (top), Walnut Canyon (bottom, left), Mummy Cave at Canyon de Chelly (bottom, center), and the Upper Tonto ruins (bottom, right).

Figure 4.4: Arcosanti

Arcosanti is the physical manifestation of arcology—a concept developed by the architect Paolo Soleri. Arcology fuses architecture and ecology in such a way that people can inhabit the land in a sustainable way. This approach includes the designing and making of many everyday things. The picture in the lower left is the area designated for the making of the Soleri bells, which are cast in an artisanal fashion.

Figure 4.5: Petroglyphs

Petroglyphs are etchings on stone done by early societies. The ones pictured above are from the Anasazi people of the American southwest: V Bar V Ranch, Sedona, Arizona (top); Palatki Ruins, Sedona, Arizona (bottom, left); and Baird Ranch, Winslow, Arizona (bottom, right).

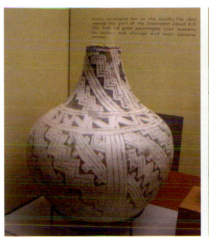

Figure 5.1: Navajo Pot and Bowl

The Age of Surplus created the need to store what was cultivated and harvested. Pots, bowls, and baskets became common everyday things.

Figure 5.2: Pei Pyramid at the Louvre

The pyramid is a classic building form. It is found in ancient cultures such as Egypt and Mexico, and is a source for inspiration even today. Such is the case with the addition to the Louvre Musem in Paris in 1989 by the American architect I. M. Pei.

Figure 5.3: Columns in Athens, Montreal and Milan

Columns have been a mainstay in architecture, such as with the Parthenon in Athens (top, left), and are often used to express prestige and status, such as with the Museum of Fine Arts in Montreal (top, center), which is a relatively recent building. In the case of a railway station in Milan (top, right), architect Gae Aulenti used the columns in a more playful way.

Figure 5.4: Arc de Triomphe and Arc de la Défense, both in Paris

Like columns, arches have also been part of western architecture for centuries. Napoleon Bonaparte recognized the importance that an arch would have in his quest to honor his victories and, in 1806, he commissioned the Arc de Triomphe, which is now a Paris landmark (left). More recently, l'Arc de la Défense was erected in the newly developed business district of Paris.

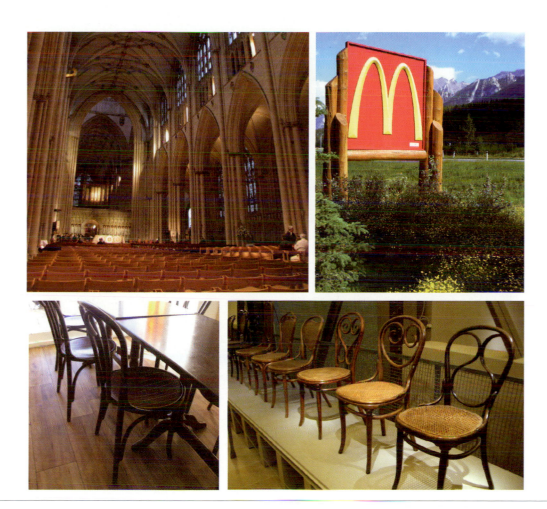

Figure 5.5: Gothic and Golden Arches

In architecture, Gothic arches are almost always used as a formal device to bestow prestige and an air of reverence to a building, such as we see at York Minster in England (top, left). Arches often occur elsewhere such as the golden arches of this McDonald's located in Canmore, Alberta (top, right).

Figure 5.6: Thonet and Bentwood Furniture

Thonet developed a bentwood process meant for the furniture industry and introduced the bentwood chair to the world. Bentwood chairs at the public cafeteria at Blenheim Palace in England (bottom, left); other models on display at the Musée d'Orsay in Paris (bottom, right).

Figure 5.7: Saltaire, Yorkshire, England

Sir Titus Salt believed that there were economic benefits to be gained by supporting his workers. As a result, he built a community (top, left) for his employees next to his mills (top, right).

Figure 5.8: Shaker Community, Hancock Village, Massachusetts

Members of the Shaker sect built self-sufficient communities such as this one in Hancock Village. Brethrens' workshop (bottom, left); and round barn (bottom, right).

Figure 6.1: Roskilde Church in Denmark

The Roskilde church is a brick construction (top, left), unlike stone masonry found in many Gothic churches.

Figure 6.2: Gaudi Buildings in Barcelona

Art Nouveau influences abound in the architectural work of Antonio Gaudi. These buildings in Barcelona are indicative of this architectural style. Sagrada Familia (top, right); Casa Batllo (bottom left and right).

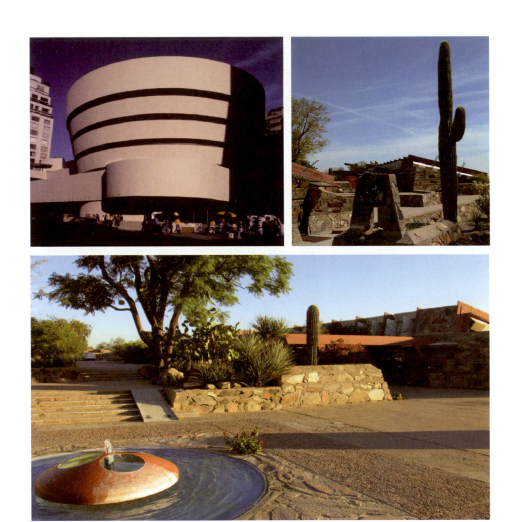

Figure 6.3: Frank Lloyd Wright

Frank Lloyd Wright was very sensitive to the importance of place when designing a building. The Guggenheim Museum (top, left) fits extremely well in the urbanscape in New York City much like Taliesin West is designed to fit into the landscape of the Sonoran desert in Arizona (top, right and bottom).

Figure 6.4: Scandinavian Designs

Denmark: Henningsen lamp; phone booths in Copenhagen (top row).
Sweden: Volvo station wagon; IKEA store (middle row).
Finland: Aalto bentwood chair; Temppeliaukio (Rock) Church in Helsinki (bottom row).

Figure 6.5: British Designs

London Underground map (top, left); British Museum addition by Norman Foster (top, right).
Double-decker bus (middle, left); London cab (middle, right).
High-speed train (bottom).

Figure 6.6: German Designs

Wayfinding at Frankfurt airport (top, left); Munich Olympic Stadium (top, right);
Braun food processor (middle, left); Wassily chairs (middle, right);
Bosch coffee grinder (bottom, left); Volkswagen New Beetle (bottom, right).

Figure 6.7: Italian Designs

Vennini glass (top, left); Lamborghini Gallardo (top, right);
Brionvega radio (middle, left); Magistretti lamp (middle, right);
Zanuso chair and Munari lamp (bottom, left); Olivetti Valentine typewriter (bottom, right)

Figure 6.8: American Designs

Chevrolet SSR (top, left); Bertoia Bird Lounge Chair (top, right)
Walt Disney Concert Hall (middle, left); Aeron chair (middle, right)
Boeing 737 (bottom, left); Ford Mustang (bottom, right)

Figure 6.9: Japanese Designs

Panasonic CD player (top, left); Lexus RX 330 (top, right)
Shinkansen bullet train (middle)
Honda Element (bottom, left); Kuramata dresser (bottom, right)

Figure 6.10: Porsche Models

Porsche Speedster (top, left); Porsche Spyder (top, right)
Porsche Boxster (middle)
Porsche 911 (bottom, left); Porsche detail (bottom, right)

Figure 6.11: Chairs by Charles and Ray Eames
Airport seating (top)
Eames lounge chair (bottom, left); wire chair (bottom, right)

Figure 6.12: Garnier Opera, Paris

Garnier's Paris Opera House left nothing undecorated and used as many classical architectural elements as possible. (Top and middle rows.)

Figure 6.13: Dymaxion House

With the Dymaxion House, Buckminster Fuller wanted to use contemporary manufacturing technology and the latest materials in the design and construction of everyday houses.

Figure 6.14: Habitat '67, Montreal

Moshe Safdie designed Habitat '67 as a building-block concept that incorporated a modular approach. Housing units were made of cast concrete and then placed one on top of the other—much like a giant Lego set.

Figure 7.2: Clocks in Zurich

Public steeple clocks are common in Swiss cities such as these in Zurich (bottom, left); detail of one of the steeple clocks (bottom, right)

Figure 7.4: Public benches

Public benches vary greatly in design. Antonio Gaudi designed a long, meandering bench in Barcelona as part of the landscape (top). Most public benches, however, are stand-alone designs such as the steel bench in Venice (middle, left), a vernacular bench in Cape May, NJ (middle, right), a concrete and steel bench in Hong Kong (bottom, left) and a log bench in Banff, Alberta (bottom, right).

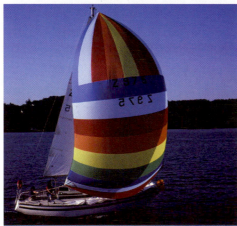

Figure 7.7: Pastimes Are Past Times

Activities of the past are often pastimes or leisure activities of today. Ballooning, for example, developed in the late eighteenth century as experiments in flight. Today, hot-air ballooning is a hobby for many people (top). Much the same pattern occurred with sailing, which used to be the only mode of trans-oceanic transportation but is now a pastime for many people (bottom, left). And kayaking is no different. For the Inuit, it was an everyday activity; for today's adventurers, it is a recreational activity (bottom, right).

Part III

Looking Back and Ahead

CHAPTER 7

Lessons Learned
Along the Way

The third section of *Designing: A Journey Through Time* brings us to the end of our metaphorical journey and to a time for reflection. What do we know now about designing that we did not know before our journey? What lessons have we learned? How will these lessons impact designing in the future? Reflections and suppositions on these and other questions provide the content for chapters 7 and 8.

Astute observations of designing activities over the last few centuries are revealing indeed. They give us an insight not only into the past but also provide a platform for launching into the future. Needless to say, society today knows a great deal more about designing—why we do it and how we do it—than it did a century ago, let alone 3.4 million years ago when someone first chipped a stone in order to design the first artificial tool. This chapter will touch on several of the important operational principles that underpin designing, especially those that provide a deeper understanding of User needs and behavior, two factors that are very important to Designers and Makers. Without Users, there is no need for designing.

Understanding The Designing Triad helps us see that designing is always contextual. That is why the next stage of our exploration begins by looking at the bigger picture of designing—Place, People, and Process, or the 3Ps of designing. People design their Artificial World in order to change an existing situation into a preferred one. Beginning from that perspective, the chapter diverges into several sub-topics or lessons—all falling within the broad area of the 3Ps but each with a particular point of view. In the end, the goal is to unpack our contextual baggage in order to understand better what motivates people to do what they do when it comes to designing. As a side note, each lesson will begin with an anecdote that illustrates the realities of Context and designing. These are not imaginary lessons but practical realities.

Lesson 1: Place, People, and Process—or the 3Ps of Designing

As a graduate student in England, I was involved in a design project with a college of architecture and a local firm of architects. The project centered on a problem faced by the management group for a retirement home. The home was a recent construction with state-of-the-art architecture and building systems including central heating. The problem that was puzzling the management group was the complaints from the residents: people were cold. The news came as a surprise because the management group regularly measured the temperature in the apartments and found it to be normal. Yet people continued to complain that they were cold. In one of those moments of insight, someone on our design team put his finger on the problem. Before moving to the retirement home, most of the residents had lived in traditional English houses. Most traditional English houses do not have central heating. Instead, each room has a fireplace, which is a visible source of heat. The problem was resolved quite simply: an artificial fireplace was installed in each room. Almost overnight, the complaints stopped.

The information from the previous six chapters may seem somewhat overwhelming. First, we were made to realize that designing is not a recent phenomenon—it is certainly not just the latest flavor of the month. It has been part of human existence for at least three million years, making designing virtually timeless. Second—and keeping this historical perspective in mind—it became evident that designing is not limited to the domain of people who are formally recognized as Designers. As we soon understood, everyone designs. The third revelation was equally profound: design and designing occur wherever people live. They are not the phenomena of the developed countries only. High-technology and high-style design may be found principally in Europe, America, and certain south-east Asian countries but, broadly defined, designing occur in all human societies. Everything else about design—color, form, shape, scale, quantity, quality and most other features—are localized details. So, what is universally important in all design and designing? Three things: Place, People, and Process, or the 3Ps of designing. Place, or Context, is where designing occurs; people in place are the ones who engage in designing; and they do so based on a contextually relevant designing process. (See Figure 7.1.)

Place
As we know, designing does not occur in a vacuum but occurs in Context, or in a place. This contextual influence occurs in ways that are both physical and metaphysical. Place may be embodied in the physical makeup of everyday things through materials such as wood from the forests of Thailand, marble from the quarries of Italy, or even plastics from the factories of developed countries. The method of production used to create everyday things—such as the handmade Artifacts of Mexico or the sophisticated technology in medical devices of the United States—may also reflect Place.

The same can also be said for the metaphysical aspects of Context. Metaphysical qualities, such as cultural values and other belief systems, may not be as tangible as physical materials but they are equally important in determining the essence of the everyday thing. Together with the physical aspects just described, they reflect the spirit of the everyday thing. Material qualities may speak to the everyday thing's visible and concrete properties, but metaphysical qualities go deeper and well beyond the obvious tangible properties. They contain and

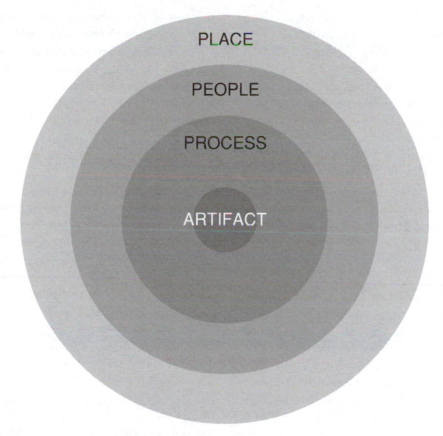

Figure 7.1: The 3Ps of Designing: Place, People, and Process

manifest the very fundamental raison d'etre of the everyday thing itself and are nothing less than its soul. We take the embedded values in most of everyday things for granted because—in a kind of invisible way—they tend to match our belief systems. We consider them to be right, logical, and rational. This is why and how we easily integrate these everyday things into our lives. They are known to us and are culturally soothing and comforting.

Insert an unknown belief system into our midst, such as Feng Shui, and we dismiss it out of hand. For many of us in the West, Feng Shui simply doesn't make sense. How can anyone base the layout of a room or, for that matter, the design of a whole building on a superstitious Chinese belief founded on some immeasurable balance of energy? Yet, the Chinese do it every day. Feng Shui is a strong metaphysical belief that plays the same role our so-called system of logic plays in Western culture. (Our system is not always consistent: we still design buildings without thirteenth floors, and many people remain superstitious about Friday the thirteenth!)

Clearly, place is implicit in the everyday thing. It has always been and will continue to be. What we as Designers can do is better understand its qualities and its presence in the everyday thing.

People

In some cases, the connection between individual people and an everyday thing can be very direct, such as a pair of prescription glasses or a made-to-measure suit. Both of these are meant for one specific person. Such everyday things are used by individuals in a very personal and unique way. In other cases, the connection is indirect. Cell-phone transmission towers or radar facilities at airports are designed things that benefit the public, not by individuals. Then there are those countless everyday things between these two extremes. In every case, however, there is a connection between everyday things and people. In all cases, the Designer's mission is clear: designing must never occur without Users in mind. They are, after all, the ultimate beneficiaries of designing.

The degree to which Designers include—or do not include—Users in the design process is never a certainty.

Engineers often leave the User out of the equation but do not do so deliberately. An engineer working on the design of a circuit board for a computer-based product or on a new plastic composite, for example, does not need to be overly concerned about the direct interaction of the User. In the case of the circuit board, the User will most likely never see it; as for the plastic, it will most likely become an inconspicuous part in one product or another. In both cases, there will be a multitude of different Users, but the contribution from the engineer will have very little direct impact on how they will use the every-day thing. The knowledge of electronics or molecular chemistry may be necessary for the engineer, but this is most likely not the case for the User. No one needs to know the intricacies of micro-circuitry to tell the time with a digital watch! In these and all other cases, however, scientists and engineers, while perhaps not focused on the individual User, are generally concerned about Users.

The disregard of Users can occur even in cases in which designing is not scientific. This happens in haute couture when Designers create new styles for fashion models who are not remotely representative of the general population. Nevertheless, most fashion Designers persist in basing their latest creations on this atypical body type. This misrepresentation is not some kind of perverse act on the part of fashion Designers but occurs principally because haute couture is closer to the fine arts than it is to design. It is a form of self-expression and has more to do with the Designer's values than the User's needs or wants. Fashion Designers and artists, for example, do not seek insight from marketing studies. Nor do they consider focus groups and ethnographic studies as important sources of user information. For such Designers, ignoring Users when designing is tempting; it certainly makes the task less complicated and frees the Designer. At best, it's illusionary; at worst, it's irresponsible.

Process

Designing is not black magic, nor does it need to be mysterious. It's a process but not a formula—and there is a difference between the two. A process is a set of deliberate actions directed toward a particular goal or objective. A formula is a prescription with well-determined variables, such as you find in the formula $E = mc^2$. With all of its possible permutations, designing is too complex a task to be easily resolved by one process and one process only. It's at this point that the intelligence, wisdom, and intuition of the Designer come into play. There are, for example, different design processes particular to graphic design, industrial design, interior design, and architecture. This is because the scope of typical design tasks can be very different. After all, the design of a book is very different from the design of a building.

The scope of the design challenge may be the most obvious difference, but it is not the only one. Various design attributes implicit in everyday things also impose certain conditions on the designing process. Physical scale is one of these. An MP3 player, for example, is relatively small; you can hold it in your hand and put it in your pocket. Not so a sailboat; it can be forty feet or more in length. While both are examples of industrial design, the designing process undertaken for the MP3 player is quite different from the one for the sailboat.

Production volume is another design attribute that can markedly differentiate the designing process. Automobiles are mass-produced, whereas upscale homes are not. Consequently, the design process used by an architect to design a unique building is not suitable for the design of a mass-produced car.

There was a time, perhaps in the very early twentieth century, when one process could be applied to designing many everyday things. Those days are behind us. Designing and making were less complicated one hundred years ago. The world was not as complex, manufacturing was simpler, and global economies were unheard of. Given these circumstances, it was indeed possible for one person, such as Peter Behrens, to design everything from graphics to buildings to products as he did for AEG. That is not so today. Although the phenomenon of superstar Designers still exists, their contribution to the total design production—certainly in total number—is minuscule. Relatively unknown or anonymous Designers do by far the largest portion of designing.

The anecdote about the 'cold' tenants recounted at the beginning of this lesson illustrated that place, people, and process are common to all designing activities. Effective design cannot occur without the inclusion of all three. However, their inclusion will not automatically guarantee design success. Design and designing are not that facile. But the chances of design success increase significantly when Designers wisely and astutely consider people, place, and process in designing.

Lesson 2: Context and Culture

Sometime ago, a young man of the Sikh faith was accepted into the Royal Canadian Mounted Police, the Canadian equivalent of the FBI. When asked to wear the "Smokey-Bear hat," or Stetson, which is part of the traditional dress uniform of the RCMP, he refused because his religion obliged him to wear a turban. As we all know, religion is very much a part of everyday culture, but not all religions manifest their beliefs in the same way. Some religions are more overt and impose dress codes. The Sikhs, for example, require that men wear turbans. The RCMP case went to Canada's Supreme Court. Because the Stetson hat was ceremonial and did not serve a specific function such as protection from danger, the judges sided with the young Sikh officer, citing the right of religious freedom. Not surprisingly, many Canadians were upset with the court's decision because they considered the Stetson hat sacrosanct. What they probably did not realize was that the Stetson hat was not unique to the RCMP. It had been originally borrowed from the USA when it was found that the traditional British pillbox hat was unsuitable in the sunny climate of the Canadian prairies.

The Designing Triad includes Context as an essential component because, as previously stated, designing always occurs in Context, and culture is clearly a part of the Context. Culture permeates every aspect of our lives and consequently affects designing. We are keenly aware of its influence, such as when we go to a Chinese restaurant. The food is different, as are the serving dishes and eating utensils.

At times, however, culture catches us off guard, as we see in the anecdote of the Sikh officer in the RCMP. Who would ever think that a hat could create such a kerfuffle? After all, it was just a hat. Nevertheless, it did raise the attention and ire of certain people, many of whom reacted passionately when told of the refusal by the Sikh officer to wear the Stetson hat.

The example of the Stetson hat demonstrates that the clothes we wear have a connection to our culture. So do the foods we eat, the habits we learn, and the values we are taught.

In simple terms, different aspects of culture are generally categorized in one of two ways. One of these is the one that we associate with high culture. This classification includes the fine and performing arts and those other cultural manifestations normally found in museums and concert halls. The other classification—the one that is more appropriate to designing—is so-called low culture. This is the anthropological definition of culture and most definitely includes designing. Anthropologists who study cultures—especially contemporary cultures—do so, in part, by observing what people do and how and why they do it. Even investigatory principles in anthropology such as ethnography apply to contemporary design. Whether we are talking of primitive tools from tribes in Papua New Guinea or sophisticated modern high-technology devices in Silicone Valley, all are reflections of cultural values. Everyday things can provide invaluable insight about people because they are mirrors—that is, they reflect people's essential values and behavioral systems.

Much the same can also be said of archeology. When archeologists study civilizations of the past, they often do so by way of found objects and buildings. The people from these civilizations have unintentionally left a wealth of information about their culture, a great deal of which is decipherable through Artifacts and other everyday things. We know, for example, about the hierarchy of early cultures or what religious belief prevailed or what rituals were at the heart of their civilization. Similarly, we understand the important signs and symbols of those times and how these went on to create a visual language, either through the developments of alphabets or actual visual styles that we directly associate with one civilization or another.

This knowledge derived from studies in culture and archaeology has served design and Designers, particularly as a source of visual language. Examples can be found throughout design history. Charles Rennie Mackintosh, the Scottish Designer and architect, was inspired by Japanese art and Artifacts, something that was made possible when Admiral Matthew Perry opened Japan to the rest of the world in 1853. Similarly, many Art Nouveau Designers found sources of visual inspiration from the objects discovered in the tomb of Tutankhamen when it was unearthed in 1922.

The imbedded value in everyday things occurs in two forms: explicit and implicit. The Designing Triad explains these as micro-context and macro-context, respectively. That is, some of the perceived physical attributes of everyday things and their meanings are often clearly evident. This is the case when a design explicitly tells us that something is meant for children or for seniors.

For example, Designers can achieve this effect by way of color (such as bright colors for children's toys) or by form and shape (such as more traditional styles in furniture for certain groups of people).

However, there are many other attributes that are not as overtly manifested but that are more implicit. Implicit or macro-contextual factors communicate values—personal, social, or cultural—that are imbedded in the type of everyday thing itself and that provide a rationale for its presence. Clothes are a good example. Annually, fashion Designers create lines of clothing for the major shows in Paris, Milan, New York, and other fashion centers. What most of us see are the styles, colors, fabrics, textures, and other micro-contextual features that determine the visual appearance of the garment. Rarely do we ever ask why we wear clothes in the first place. Why women wear skirts but men generally don't? Why some styles of clothes are appropriate at some occasions but not at others? The answers to these and other similar questions all have to do with macro-cultural factors.

There are two factors that are particularly salient in the understanding of implicit cultural or contextual factors: time and space. Both impact design immeasurably but do so quite inconspicuously. They are present in design and everyday things but in ways that are at times neither clear nor obvious. Both time and space are part of the Context referred to in The Designing Triad.

Time
We cannot escape time. It is a kind of fourth dimension and affects us—and designing—in myriad ways. To

appreciate time's influence better, however, certain particularities need to be understood.

First, time is either natural or artificial. Both facets are important but very different. Natural time is part of the Laws of Nature and, as a result, occurs regardless of cultural or personal intervention. Furthermore, it has three different but interrelated sub-units—the annual calendar, the lunar calendar, and the daily calendar, which are simple in concept yet universal in impact. In the end, no one goes untouched by these three time calendars. Agriculture is conditioned by the seasons much like fishing is conditioned by the tides. Most people rise with the sun and sleep at night. These activities, like so many others, are inextricably linked to time's natural cycle.

Artificial time is quite a different matter and includes various divisions of natural time. The twenty-four-hour day or the sixty-minute hour, for example, or even such infinitesimally small divisions of time like milliseconds, are all artificial divisions of time. In every case society has created these divisions to serve its purposes. Early sundials were just that—a way of taking the natural day and sub-dividing it into smaller segments. But the division of time also amplified society's sense of order, and it is therefore not a coincidence at all that societies with a well-tuned and imbedded sense of time also have an equally well-tuned and imbedded sense of order. In general, northern European cultures are societies in which timeliness and orderliness are inseparable. They both complement and reinforce each other. The timeliness of Swiss culture goes hand in hand with its strong sense of civic and cultural order. Not surprisingly, a great deal of modern graphic design theory originated in Switzerland and reflects this sense of control and need for order.

Natural and artificial facets of time are important, but there are others that are not as easy to quantify. One of these is the cultural perception of time. Edward T. Hall identified many of these facets of time, including:

- Personal time, in which a more subjective or personal focus affects our perception of time, validated with comments such as "Time flies" or "The time is crawling";

- Micro time, in which the system of time is a product of primary culture and manifests itself in different time tolerances for things such as waiting for someone; and

- Sacred time, where one is perceived as being in the time.[i]

Hall went on to describe other systems of time but, for our purpose, it is only important to realize two things. First, Western concepts of time are a cornerstone of Western thought and have their roots in Greek philosophy of the fifth century BCE. Second, the Newtonian belief in one and only one universal concept of time is not cross-culturally valid. Some cultures, in fact, do not even have a word for time in their vocabularies. As Hall explained, variations in artificial time have been discovered in numerous cultural groups and provide us with a fascinating perspective on how other people function given the constant of natural time.

There is little doubt that our cultural attitudes about time have affected or influenced design and everyday things. Returning to the example of Switzerland, a keen observer on a leisurely walk in Zurich would no doubt notice a varied collection of church steeples. This would not be highly unusual in an old European city. A closer observation, however, would reveal that these same steeples all have clocks prominently displayed on all four sides. As if that were not enough, all clocks show precisely the same time. For the Swiss, time and timekeeping have become a very important aspect of everyday life. Furthermore, Swiss companies involved in the timekeeping industry have flourished. Watch making is still a large part of the Swiss economy, as the manufacturing sector is closely linked to timekeeping and other scientific measuring devices. The Swiss have become known as the timekeepers of the world, and Swiss watches like Rolex are still considered the ultimate timekeeping devices. (See Figure 7.2.)

The near-obsession with time for the Swiss, however, does not stop with clocks and watches. Ride a train in Switzerland and you are guaranteed punctual service. One facet of this relationship between the Swiss and time does raise an important question: which came first, the time-keeping devices or the character trait of punctuality in the Swiss? Obviously, the question can never be answered in simple terms. Both aspects are interrelated and evolved symbiotically. However, there is little doubt that artificial and cultural times are a very strong component of the Swiss culture.

The quantifiable aspect of time can go on to take strange twists in certain cultures. For example, the American culture has a strongly developed sense of time, but in this case time equates to money. This particular mindset has gone on to define a great deal of everyday American life, becoming, along the way, an inseparable part of the belief system of many Americans. Choices are often made on a monetary basis only, with little consideration given to other factors. The result is a somewhat specious logic when discussing questions such as who is more valuable to society, the president of a leading research university or the coach of the same university's football team, who often earns three to four times the salary of the president.

Other cultures, such as those of Italy and Mexico, have not fully embraced the idea of artificial time to the same level of precision as the Swiss. For these cultures, Swiss time-keeping is tantamount to punctual paranoia. Arrive at an Italian social event at the time printed on your invitation card and you may be the only guest for the first hour or so. In cultures such as these, time is not so much a measurable quantity as it is a micro-time, to use Hall's previous classification. It takes on a value that can only be described in terms more closely allied to quality, in which we find a marriage of both artificial and natural time. This attitude of time is a very real part of everyday culture and, by extension, also influences designing. When Sottsass and Associates, a Milan-based firm of Designers and architects, was commissioned to redesign the branch offices of one of Italy's large banks, it was asked to incorporate comfortable waiting areas for the customers. From the bank's perspective, there was no point in trying to change banking procedures in order to reduce the waiting time. That would have been nigh impossible; better to provide a designated waiting area in which the customers could bide their time.

These few examples illustrate how pervasive the notion of time is and how it affects the rhythm of life. Hall studied this phenomenon extensively and elaborated on the various qualities of time. His observations led him to define two distinct time categories within which most cultures can be situated. These categories are monochromic, or M-time, and polychromic, or P-time. Monochronic time defines an attitude to time that emphasizes measurable properties of time such as schedules, segmentation, and promptness. Things happen one at a time. Polychronic is just the opposite. Everything seems to be happening at once. It is curious to note that when the concepts of M-time and P-time are layered over the concept of Christopher Alexander's self-conscious and unselfconscious cultures (explained in more detail later in this chapter) it is the self-conscious cultures that have developed the M-time system, whereas it is the unselfconscious cultures that function in a P-time system. This categorization would lead us to surmise that cultures based on the persona of the individual also created ever-smaller units of time, whereas cultures that are group-centered continue to deal with time in a more holistic way.[ii]

A particularly telling example that illustrates M- and P-time is the cultural peculiarity found in certain eating habits, especially the sequential order—or lack thereof—in which food is served. In the West, the normal procedure for most meals is to eat one serving or course after another. Typically, we speak of four-, five-, or six-course meals at which we are served appetizers or soup (or both), a main course, a salad (which can come either before or after the main course, depending on the culture), a dessert, and more. In Japan, meals need not be served in the same sequential order. There, the different dishes for a normal meal are often served all at once: the pickles, the soup, the sashimi, and the rice. Reflecting for a moment on some of Hall's findings, we can detect in these two eating patterns a similarity to monochronic and polychronic behavior: the former requiring sequential ordering and the latter allowing everything to happen simultaneously.

For Hall, time was very much at the center of fundamental patterns in our belief systems and, consequently, in design as well. Hall believed that people in Western societies were creating chaos in their daily lives by denying that part in people that encourages integration while embracing those features that fragment our life experience. Furthermore, and by associating the Western time process based on fragmentation with a linear thinking process based on a unidirectional, step-by-step approach, Hall was convinced that we in the West valued one system of thinking over all others—that of logic, a linear system that has been with us since Socrates. Over time, this pervasive mental attitude implied by this linear model has not limited itself exclusively to logical thought such as mathematics but has gone far beyond these fields and has embraced the fundamentals of truth.

This model of logic may have been valid when Western thought was limited to Europe, but the situation has significantly changed over the last century or two. Today, the global arena has become multicultural. Consequently, any one Context will reflect the values of its culture all the while selectively borrowing from others. Everything makes sense as long as it remains in Context; out of Context, however, most cultural value systems appear as meaningless collections of illogical foibles.

Space

The second important facet of culture that can dramatically affect designing is space. Like time, the concept of space is an all-encompassing variable and manifests itself differently in different cultures. To better understand the role of space and its impact on design, we need to focus on territoriality, or the spatial relationship that exists between people.

Much like the study of time, the study of space clearly illustrates that we do not all live in the same sensory world. This is not only the case for individuals within the same culture but it applies even more so across cultures. We should never forget that the sensors that contribute to our perception of space are conditioned by the cultural Context. People of different cultures see, feel, and touch in ways that are at times quite different.

In his extensive studies of space, Hall referred to *proxemics,* a term he coined for the study of the interrelationship of people and space. For Hall, proxemics was, "the study of people's use of their sensory apparatus in different emotional states during different activities, in different relationships, and in different settings and contexts."[iii] Hall's research showed that the differences in our sensory world were in those things that our senses did or did not absorb. Hall discovered that even as children we subconsciously learned to screen out certain bits of information while concentrating on others.

This screening can occur differently in different places. For example, the Japanese create privacy in a way that is quite different than the way Europeans do. A typical Japanese domestic scene would normally find many family members sharing the same small quarters with only paper walls and doors to separate them. Nevertheless, they easily create their own acoustic space, screening out distracting stimuli. Most Europeans and North Americans cannot create this kind of acoustic space; they require the visual space created by thick walls and double doors to perceive privacy. Ambient noises and sound become a distraction.

The cultural notion of visual space provides other fundamental perceptual differences. For example, we in the West tend to see space as a void that is meant to be filled. Many living rooms in North American or European homes illustrate this tendency very well. All available space—whether it is on the floor or on the wall—needs to be filled with something. Like the vacuum in nature, emptiness is abhorred. For their part, the Japanese deal with visual space in quite a different manner. Objects placed in a given space do not only create a positive volume by their physical presence but also create an equally important negative space between each object. A traditional Japanese room may appear empty to a Western eye but not so for the Japanese. For them, both negative and positive aspects of visual space need to be considered if the final arrangement is to be aesthetically pleasing.

These examples could easily lead us to believe that we in the West have neither a well developed nor a highly refined sensitivity for space, especially acoustic space. However, this is not necessarily the case and certainly not so for musicians. They would immediately recognize the analogy that exists between positive and negative space in a musical score, where the silence between notes is as important as the notes themselves.

A second relevant spatial element discovered by Hall was the role of the human olfactory apparatus. According to Hall, most Americans are especially underdeveloped when it comes to dealing with the wide array of natural smells and odors that surround them. They bathe in perfumed oils and, once cleansed, proceed to cover themselves with deodorant so as to mask the body's natural aroma. Even a person's breath is appropriately cleansed so as not to offend others. In fact, breathing on someone else is considered intimidating and is socially frowned upon. This aversion to body odor is, of course, not universal. In some countries, it is not unusual to find people conversing in extremely close proximity to one another because, as some Arabs would ask, "If you cannot actually smell the person with whom you are talking, then how can you have a meaningful conversation?"

This phenomenon of our underdeveloped olfactory sense has spread beyond the mere scope of bodily aroma and has created blandness in many other aspects of our lives. Many staples of the American diet are uniform and indistinguishable in taste. Few spices are used and nothing close to the pungent nature of a Danish blue cheese or the heartiness of a good Bordeaux wine could survive on the menu of the average American dinner table. Bread must be white and without taste, along with the cheese and wine. The rule becomes clear: all food should possess as little individual character as possible. McDonald's, the fast-food chain, understands and applies this principle extremely well. Its hamburgers are not the best by any stretch of the imagination but they are the same wherever you eat them, whether in Tulsa or Tokyo. Blandness and predictability do indeed sell.

The results of Hall's research in proxemics provided design with some important insight, especially in the area of space and how to effectively use it in design. Following in the footsteps of Heini Hediger, the Swiss zoologist, and Maurice Grosser, the American artist, Hall proposed that all personal human space did not biologically stop with the surface of a person's skin but psychologically extended beyond, in four measurable spheres, or bubbles. He identified them as intimate, personal, social, and public distances. (See Figure 7.3.) Furthermore, these four spheres were common in all cultures, although the respective distance of each sphere varied with each. Hediger had previously found that a similar series of uniform distances or spheres existed in birds and animals, and Hall and Hediger both felt that it was in the nature of all animals, including people, to create these spatial bubbles as a form of territoriality.[iv]

Intimate Distance. Intimate distance involves the space immediately surrounding an individual person and is the first level of territoriality. Hall found that this sphere itself has two divisions or phases. The first phase,

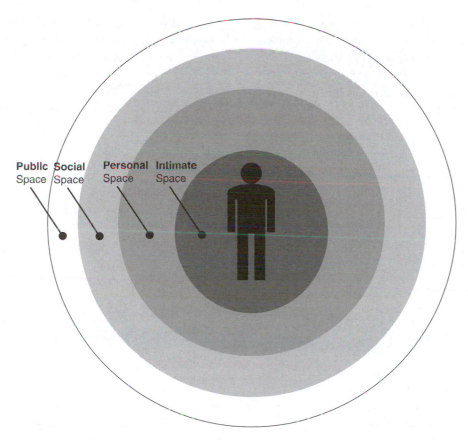

Public **Social** **Personal** **Intimate**
Space Space Space Space

Figure 7.3: Hall's Proxemic Spheres of Space

referred to as intimate distance/close phase (less than six inches), includes activities normally associated with close body contact such as love making, wrestling, comforting, and protecting. The effectiveness of distance receptors such as vision is greatly reduced at this range but the olfactory senses play a more

important role. So does tactility, for this is a sphere where skin contact occurs. Voices are subdued and whispering becomes the norm.

The second phase is the intimate distance/far phase (six to eighteen inches). Heads, thighs, and pelvis do not necessarily touch and vision becomes a bit more useful even though the other person's head is just within focus and seems distorted. Voicing is still carried out in whispers or low volume. Depending on the cultural Context, activities normally carried out in this sphere may or may not occur in public.

Many Americans would feel uncomfortable speaking to a person in public using the intimate distance/far phase. Greeks, for their part, find this close range a very comfortable distance for public discussions. Western visitors to Morocco are often taken aback when they see two men walking hand in hand in public. From their perspective, touching of such intimate nature between two people of the same gender should never occur in public.

Personal Distance. Personal distance also has two phases. Personal distance/close phase (eighteen to thirty inches) is that distance where visual distortion of the other person is no longer apparent yet the person can still be touched. Still physically close, objects can take on an unusual roundness such as is sometimes seen in a photograph taken with a wide-angle lens. Close friends can normally stay inside this sphere without creating any discomfort; others usually cannot.

Personal distance/far phase (thirty inches to four feet) is the 'arm's length' that we often talk about, especially in business relationships. At its shortest, it is the distance created by the extended arm and fingers until they touch the other person; at its longest, it is the distance between two speakers when the fingertips of their extended arms touch. Outside of this range, you cannot get your hand on someone. The olfactory and tactile senses play a minor role in this sphere.

The French, for example, are comfortable with a greater degree of daily physical contact than most Americans are. Given this fact, we can better understand the cultural habit of French students and workers who shake hands with their colleagues every morning when they meet at school or at work. There are many cultural groups who would have great difficulties in dealing with this type of recurring and seemingly unnecessary physical contact.

Social Distance. The external limits of personal distance begin to delineate social distance, again with both a close and far phase. Social distance/close phase (four to seven feet) marks the sphere of domination. Nobody touches or expects to touch a person unless there is a voluntary wish to do so. This is the distance for impersonal business, such as office work and casual social gatherings.

In social distance/far phase (seven to twelve feet), greater formality is achieved, such as the distances between senior executives seated at a boardroom table. This also partially explains the expansive offices of these same executives; it is their way of keeping their distance. This greater distance also allows one person to get on with their work even if there is someone else in the same room. For example, this spatial relationship can occur in a reception room where the secretary can continue to work even though there may be someone waiting. As long as there is an adequate distance between the two persons, neither feels that their own space is being invaded.

Public Distance. The last sphere is public distance. In public distance/close phase (twelve to twenty-five feet), a person can take evasive or defensive action if threatened. Peripheral vision now plays a role, and voicing changes. The volume goes up and words are chosen carefully to achieve full impact. At an even greater distance—public distance/far phase (twenty-five feet or more)—great formality is achieved, such as when heads of states or other famous people meet in a public arena. Because of the distance, voices and movements are exaggerated or amplified. Personal and human contacts are at the threshold of perception and interaction.

Proxemics in Practice. It does not take a great deal of research to see how the personal spheres described by Hall affect design. Public benches are excellent examples. They occur in a broad variety of models, but they can be grouped according to key design features. One is the visual demarcation of individual seats. Some public benches have them while others do not. As innocent as this design feature may first appear to be, it can be problematic when it is missing. Distinctive and recognizable visual demarcation for individual seating space makes two things quite obvious: how many people can sit on the bench and where they can sit. Remove this visible delineation and one person can easily monopolize a three-person bench because the person's position on the bench—with the accompanying spatial bubble—can delineate the actual territory in use. Other Users who come along could have difficulties determining where their territory is. At the other extreme, a bench of identical length but with obvious separations for each seat will more likely be used by several people at one time. The seating territory of each person has been explicitly delineated. (See Figure 7.4.)

The same principles apply to restaurant tables in fast-food franchises. A table capable of accommodating four people but with a groove judiciously placed down the middle will equally serve two parties of two. Without this groove, one person could easily dominate the total space. The division visually implied by the groove allows others to claim their territory and use the vacant seats.

The planning of offices is another living laboratory of territoriality. It clearly shows how people are conditioned by space and the implied meanings attached to space. For example, office layouts have long been designed and built with an implicit adherence to an elaborate system of rank and status of the User. This was especially true in the offices of government bureaucracies. Windows, fixed walls, and fixtures and fittings were all part of well-planned scheme of territory. With any given rank came a well-established and very specific amount of space. The degree of privacy related increasingly to rank. In the early 1970s, conditions changed. Curtain-wall construction became the norm in buildings, and management sciences advocated flexibility in business environments. The result was the concept of open-office planning.[v] As innovative and architecturally correct as the concept was, it met with great resistance. Many middle- and senior-level managers became very upset by the perceived loss of territory. In reality, their concern was much more with the loss of visible status implied by territory than of the territory itself.

At the other extreme, F & P Manufacturing, a Japanese subsidiary of Honda in Canada, houses its office staff of twenty people, including the president, in one open work space without interior walls or partitions. Unless you see him seated at his desk, there is nothing to distinguish the president's workspace from those of twenty other office employees. This situation would be totally disarming to the typical North American CEO. This case is not exceptional. At the head office of the Japan Design Association in Osaka, the desk of the executive director is found in an office of seven desks. His is the one positioned two to three inches away from six other desks that all touch. That small amount of space, which is marginal to a Westerner, is a very powerful tool of status differentiation for the Japanese.

Enclosed spaces meant for temporary use, such as cabins onboard a ferry, can also provide some fascinating insights into the spatial behavior of people. CN Marine in Canada operates a regular ferry service between Nova Scotia and Newfoundland. On its overnight service, cabins with four berths can be reserved. The cabin, however, is reserved as a single space for a single price regardless of whether one, two, three, or four people occupy it. The North Sea ferries from England to The Netherlands are quite different. In this case, cabins—equally meant for four people—are available to passengers, who pay for a bed and thereby share a cabin with two or perhaps three strangers. This situation would upset most American tra-velers who cherish their privacy, whereas many Europeans would find our system wasteful because many beds go unused.

These are but a few examples that clearly demonstrate the cultural notions of space, the vital role that space plays in our behavioral patterns, and how these same behavioral patterns are always conditioned by the Context. However, cultural notions of space also play a role in how different societies manifest status. Private residences are good examples of this phenomenon. An upscale home in England will, quite often, reflect totally different cultural values from its North American counterpart. Typically, the English house exudes modesty in its architectural vocabulary, whether in the style of the house or the materials of construction. The strong presence of trees and shrubs—at times almost masking the house itself—further accentuates this modesty. There is a wish to not be overly loud. If visible, certain design features such as driveways and garages will again be understated. The rear of the home, however, will most likely include a superb private garden meant for the enjoyment of the family and not necessarily for public view. In the words of Hall, status has been internalized.

The American equivalent can be remarkably different. It is not unusual to see the American home adorned with borrowed architectural motifs such as Grecian columns or tiled roofs of Spanish origin or detailing originating from Tuscany, none of which is indigenous to North America. As well, it is not uncommon to elevate the house on some landscaped pedestal using trees and shrubs like a frame around a work of art. Furthermore, the presence of the automobile would be impossible to ignore given the normally imposing driveway or garage in the foreground. As a last touch, the majority of the building lot would be in the front and quite visible to the public; it would not be considered private space. In such cases, status is externalized. The official residences of the president of the United States and the prime minister of Great Britain could not express this externalized/internalized status better. By its grandeur, the White House offers a stark contrast to 10 Downing Street, a rather modest residence tucked away on a side street in London.

An argument could be made that local building codes and bylaws impose these conditions. This, however, only places our argument one step removed from the initial contention: building codes and bylaws are in themselves nothing more than reflections—albeit legal ones—of our cultural values.

Time and space are two obvious cultural values that impact designing, but there are others. We communicate in different ways, for example. Voicing and voice pitch can totally change the meaning of a spoken sentence. Nonverbal communication such as body language can have a similar impact. An innocent hand gesture in one culture can mean something radically different elsewhere. Then there are cultural values that thoroughly permeate certain civilizations. The Chinese belief in Feng Shui is one of these; it is deeply imbedded in the everyday culture of parts of Asia, much like logic is in the West.

Culture is a big part of who we are. We incorporate it—consciously or not—into everything that we do. Culture is like the air that we breathe; it's everywhere and we cannot live without it. Clearly, culture is an integral part of designing.

Lesson 3: It's About the Toast, Not the Toaster

Several years ago, I had the opportunity of meeting Tony Lepine, then the chief Designer at Porsche in Germany. Over lunch, I asked him what the difference was between a Mercedes-Benz sports car and a Porsche. I was certain that he was going to give me an answer that touched on some technical prowess that the Porsche had over the Mercedes, such as top speed, braking distance, or weight-to-power ratio. His answer was very different from what I expected. Lepine said, "If you want to look ten years older, buy a Mercedes; if you want to look ten years younger, buy a Porsche."

As we now know, designing is a process, one that culminates in the creation of an everyday thing, often in the form of a tangible object. For most Users, these everyday things are a means to an end. Curiously, that is not always the case with Designers. They often consider these same everyday things as objects— that is, material things to be admired, collected, and hoarded—at times to the point of obsession. Take a typical poster for example. It can be both an object and a means to an end. As an object, it can be appreciated for its visual attributes in much the same way that we appreciate a painting for its subject, composition, shapes, and colors. As a means to an end, we value its effectiveness in communicating a message. Much the same can be said about architecture. It is often said that architects design houses whereas people want homes. Houses and homes are not exactly the same thing. The former is an object; the latter is a means to an end. Fortunately, most people are not Designers. They do not acquire everyday things because of a strong desire to either collect or hoard them. For them, the Artifact is the promise of an experience. It is a means to an end. So, what is meant by experience in the Context of design?

Designing everyday things is one thing; designing experiences is something else, and is probably the most potent anthropological aspect of designing. It is also the most difficult because it deals with an immeasurable bond between the User and the everyday thing. Therefore, how do we incorporate experience in design? Measuring people's bodies, as we do with anthropometrics, is easy; measuring their souls and spirits is very different and extremely challenging. Theme parks are designs that are based on creating an experience. Disney World and theme cities such as Las Vegas offer more than architecture and design to the Users; they seek to create an experience for their visitors.

New Urbanism is a relatively recent concept in urban planning in the United States. It is underpinned by a return to a Main-Street-USA concept and positions experiential design on the front burner. Of course, die-hard Modernists are crying foul! From their perspective, the designs exemplified by Disney World, Las Vegas, and New Urbanism do nothing more than pander to the crass and uninformed demands of certain types of Users. The battle line has been clearly drawn between two very different Designer communities: one that is prescriptive, that is, one in which the Designer is the source of authority with only limited consultation with Users; and the other that is subscriptive, that is, one in which the Designers seeks a great deal of input from Users. (This difference in designing is discussed further in chapter 8.)

Will there be a winner? Winning is not the point. What is the point, however, is that in a marketplace that is economically democratic and where people make free choices daily about what they want to be and what they want to own, the designing of experience is the next frontier for Designers. With or without Designers, people in the end will do as they wish, leaving them to state, "It's the toast, stupid, not the toaster!"

Lesson 4: Fits and Misfits

Koen de Winter is vice president of design at Danesco, a company that specializes in contemporary housewares such as dishes and kitchen utensils. On a recent trip to China, de Winter was negotiating the fabrication of a new line of dishes including a teapot. In his discussions with one potential Chinese manufacturer, the plant manager wanted to know why de Winter had designed a new teapot. "What is wrong with the old model? Doesn't it work?" The thought that a person only designs when an everyday thing no longer works had never crossed de Winter's mind. In the West, new designs are created every day—even if the old ones are still perfectly functional.

Lesson 2 provided a general overview of culture and two significant components—time and space. When observed even more closely, culture has other facets important to designing. In the anecdote above, de Winter confronted an aspect of the unselfconscious-culture phenomenon described by Christopher Alexander.[vi] Alexander postulated that designing occurs on a kind of continuum. At one end of the continuum, there is designing as the expression of self, such as we find in self-conscious cultures. At the other end, designing occurs as the recognition of misfits, such as we find in unselfconscious cultures, in which the individual is no more than an agent who recognizes a misfit. Changes to everyday things do not occur unless something renders the existing design unfit for its purpose. The Chinese plant manager in the Danesco example was acting according to all the rules of an unselfconscious culture: why should de Winter design and make a new teapot when the old one still works?

The birch-bark canoe, an example provided in chapter 4, is another everyday thing that embodies the qualities associated with an unselfconscious culture. It has evolved over centuries because of the recognition of misfits and not because of some self-conscious need on the part of its Maker to make it different or change it. Not surprisingly, the canoe's overall form has remained more or less the same over time. Differences and changes have usually been a reflection of some external condition, such as different species of birch or a different wood for the gunwales or thwarts. All the while, the canoe-builder's wish to intentionally change the design of the canoe for reasons of self-expression never entered the picture except, perhaps, with some minor decorative elements here and there. In a way, the designing process is not unlike the Darwinian evolutionary model in which plants and animals evolve over time as a result of adaptation for survival because of changes in the environment.

The self-conscious process is quite different. Alexander observed that in this process the Designer's self-conscious recognition of his or her individuality had a profound impact on the design of the everyday thing because new designs were often the direct result of the Designer's need for self-expression. How else to explain the regular change in fashion by all major fashion Designers? Are last year's clothes worn and not usable? Then there is the annual launch of new designs for chairs at major international furniture fairs such as Milan. Are last year's chairs already obsolete? Of course not. In both cases, it is the desire for self-expression by Designers that drives the change. This does not mean, however, that Designers do not recognize misfits. They do. Rather, what it means is that change for the sake of change becomes justifiable and part of normal practice.

Moreover, the concept of self-consciousness does not limit itself to design and other obvious areas of self-expression such as the fine arts, performing arts, and literature. It finds its way into many streams of life. For example, the Western legal system is partially conditioned by the notion of self. Patents, copyrights, trademarks, and design rights—so-called intellectual property—exist to protect personal inventions and ideas that have resulted from self-expression. Most unselfconscious cultures do not possess these protective devices. In fact, they usually find great difficulty in adhering to the basic tenets of these laws. What many Westerners perceived as outright plagiarism by certain Japanese manufacturers in the 1950s was not considered as such by the Japanese. They saw it as a form of cultural and industrial flattery. Today, the business losses attributed to the fraudulent copying by Chinese and other East Asian companies of exclusive brand names such as Rolex, Cartier, and Gucci are staggering.

Similarly, many unselfconscious cultures do not perceive art and its role in society in quite the same way as we do in the West. In some cultures, the word *art* does not even exist. Bali is such a place. For most Balinese craftsmen, the idea of designs as vehicles of personal expression is a totally foreign concept and is deemed inappropriate. Balinese craftsmen often state, "We do not have art; we only do things as well as possible." Neither were the first soapstone carvings by Inuit artists of arctic Canada meant to be works of art—although these carvings are today regarded as sculptures in the tradition of Western art. However, this was not their role in traditional Inuit culture. Soapstone carvings were manifestations of Inuit mythology and served as fetishes. The nomadic Inuit people carried them on their travels. Over time, the Inuit culture was influenced by Western ethics. Contemporary Inuit carvings now exist out of Context to the original ones. Many weigh twenty-five pounds or more and would be totally unsuitable for nomadic trips.

Alexander's concept of self-conscious and unselfconscious cultures in everyday designs has been stated in less academic and scholarly terms. The phrase, "If it ain't broke, don't fix it," is often used in reaction to changes to products or technology when there does not seem to be a need for a change. This attitude clearly mimics Alexander's concept of unselfconscious cultures. At the opposite end, Raymond Loewy's thoughts, as expressed in his book *Never Leave Well Enough Alone,* were clearly in step with Alexander's design attitude of self-expression.[vii]

Lesson 5: Everyday Things or Wants—Which Come First?

Ron Hickman is a UK-based inventor. In the 1970s, he came up with the idea for the Workmate—a fold-away workbench with a unique clamping action. The idea was totally innovative, so much so that no one wanted to manufacture it because, as market studies were showing, no one wanted to buy it. The idea of a portable workbench was unknown and therefore foreign to most consumers. As a result, there was no measurable demand. Eventually, it was Black & Decker that took the risk and went forward with the idea, turned the product into a multimillion-dollar success, and made Hickman a very rich man.

The anecdote of the Black & Decker Workmate aptly illustrates a question that swirls around designing: which comes first, the Designer's idea for the everyday thing or the User's desire for the everyday thing? Hickman came up with the idea but no one wanted it. Today, the Workmate is well known and appreciated by millions of Users, and Black & Decker has an easy time selling them. What the story illustrates is the phenomenon of innovation/push, which is in contrast to demand/pull. Innovation/push is the introduction—or the pushing—of a totally new idea or design onto the market; demand/pull is just the opposite, and occurs as the result of the market influencing the design.

The original Sony Walkman is another excellent example of an innovation/push design. Before its introduction, there was no product like it. No one was walking around with a small tape player, wearing small, visible earphones, and—worse still—divorced from his or her immediate environment. Nor was anyone banging on Sony's door demanding such a device. Yet the chairman of Sony at the time believed in the idea of a portable music machine. Consequently, the company had to push the concept of a portable music machine onto the marketplace by way of astute advertising and aggressive promotion. Why? Because the concept was unknown to Users. Today, we do not give a second thought to walking around with an iPod, which, relative to the Sony Walkman, is a demand/pull product.

It is important to note that innovation/push is often the domain of Designers as stars and designs as trophy objects. It is also important to note that innovation/push products fail at a rate at least ten times that of demand/pull or greater. Apple's Newton, the predecessor to today's personal digital assistant (PDA), was a failure when launched on the market. It was the first product of this genre and, not surprisingly, found a low level of consumer acceptance. Its ultimate failure was also aided by an interface that was not very reliable. The Palm-Pilot line of PDAs, on the other hand, appeared not long thereafter and became an almost overnight success. By launching the Newton, Apple had forged the way for consumer awareness about a PDA and its eventual acceptance by the public.

In the demand/pull situation, the everyday thing is already known to the Users—at least known in some general way, much like most people know cameras, coffeemakers, or cars. The Designer does not have to get the User to accept the everyday thing but instead must attempt to determine what Users want to see improved about the everyday thing they have already accepted.

Some Designers, such as those who create new patterns and colors for towels and sheets for department stores, face the demand/pull challenge every year. Merely asking customers what they want does not do the trick. When surveyed, people are predisposed to tell interviewers what they think interviewers want to hear. Consequently, the Designers go about the survey process in a different way. First, the Designers create a variety of patterns in a variety of colors. Samples of these towels and sheets are then manufactured. Next, typical customers in strategic stores throughout the country are invited into a product showroom and asked for their preferences. The preferences are recorded. Upon leaving the room, the customers are offered a free sample set of towels or sheets, available in the same colors and patterns that were shown in the showroom. To no one's surprise, there is little correlation between what the customers in the showroom say they prefer and what they select as free samples. And equally to no one's surprise, the Designers measure the free samples taken! In this way they are able to determine more accurately the demand of the market, clearly a case where User demand pulls the design.

Aspects of innovation/push and demand/pull can be found at a more fundamental level of human behavior. British zoologist Desmond Morris observed that people reacted to an unknown stimulus in somewhat predictable ways. He noted that, at one extreme, some humans had a love of the new—that is, there was little fear in trying or doing something new. This he called neophilia. Morris found that the behavior was generally prevalent in children and young people. At the other extreme, Morris observed a fear of the new. This he called neophobia and, as could be expected, older people most often exhibited this trait. Morris observed that people who had acquired life experience—as one is prone to have with age—reacted quite differently to a new experience when compared to someone with little prior life experience. Young people will try anything once; older people tend to be more prudent and cautious.[viii]

Morris's theory helps to explain how we integrate everyday things into our lives. Some everyday things, such as chairs, have been around for generations; most people are aware of them and easily accept them. There is little fear of the new in these cases. Other everyday things, such as DVD players and PDAs, are much more recent innovations; not everyone knows about them. Consequently, Users can respond with some trepidation or fear of the new. These everyday things often bring out neophobic reactions in Users. In the end, however, we normally respond to everyday things—both known and unknown—with a combination of neophilic and neophobic reactions. It is rarely all of one or the other. And we do so in different ways over time. Most of us are much more likely to love something new—music, fashion, and everyday things—when we are younger than we are when we become older. New food, music, fashion, and everyday things are not as readily integrated into our lives.

Designers often must deal with the challenges implicit in both the love and fear of the new. High-technology products certainly pose that problem. New devices of one kind or another are launched every day. Unfortunately, a person's ability to adapt to change is not as

quick. The American Designer Raymond Loewy, realizing this phenomenon at least fifty years ago, developed his own approach called MAYA, which stands for *most advanced yet acceptable*. Loewy's perspective was clear: push the limits of innovation as long as Users find it acceptable. More recently, Peter Trussler, former vice president of design at Nortel, could not have been more to the point when he stated, "Technology changes, but values endure."

Lesson 6: Highbrow, Early Adopters, and Other Such Patterns

Michel Dallaire is an industrial Designer. As a service to a manufacturer for whom he was designing plastic bicycle accessories, Dallaire agreed to develop a new product—a simple plastic attaché case—to use the downtime of the client's injection molding machines as well as to add to the client's existing product line. The attaché case was to be produced in a variety of colors, mostly the primary colors red, blue, and yellow. This gave the client a novel product that was both inexpensive to manufacture and had all of the right design ingredients for success. Or so he thought.

With fifty or so attaché cases in hand, the manufacturer went to the most logical retail outlet for this kind of inexpensive and colorful product—a large discount department store. There, a trial sale period was arranged. At the end of the period, the manufacturer was totally shocked by the outcome. Very few of the cases had sold. Understandably, he was disappointed with Dallaire. For his part, Dallaire was neither surprised nor upset. He knew something that the manufacturer did not. Dallaire took the unsold attaché cases and flew to New York City where he met with the buyer of the gift boutique at the Museum of Modern Art (MoMA). She immediately agreed to take not only the cases that Dallaire had brought with him but also placed an order for more. But this was only the first step. Within weeks, Bloomingdale's became aware of the sales success of the attaché case and proceeded to place a large order. The rest is commercial history, as they say.

What Dallaire knew that the manufacturer didn't was the phenomenon that conditions a great deal of human behavior, including purchasing behavior. An inexpensive plastic attaché case in a vibrant color was an unknown thing to customers at a discount department store. The manufacturer had assumed that, because of the product's low cost, price-conscious people would be its logical market. But most people who shop at large bargain retail outlets such as Wal-Mart and Kmart are not normally the first consumers to adopt a new style; they, in fact, wait to follow fashion trends. What Dallaire did was to place the attaché case in an elitist boutique and let the fashion trend begin where it normally does.

The phenomenon in the Dallaire example is a simple one: generally speaking, people like what they know and do not necessarily know what they like. This observation was eloquently offered by Eric Newton, the British art critic in his book *The Meaning of Beauty*. If we know something about a particular thing—a painting, a style

of music, or a design—we are more inclined to like it than if we do not know anything about it.

The simplicity in Newton's reflection has broader implications. American social critic Russell Lynes was one of the first observers to recognize patterns in User behavior in popular taste and wrote about it in his book *The Tastemakers: The Shaping of American Popular Taste*. As described by Lynes, Users adopt everyday things into their lives in some well-recognized patterns. He observed, for example, that popular taste was conditioned less by economics than by education and other socio-cultural factors. Instead of defining groups by economically derived terms such as upper, middle, and lower class, he used the terms highbrow, middlebrow, and lowbrow. For Lynes, these terms reflected the level of acceptability of something new—such as literature, art, fashion, or music. For example, people who appreciated the latest movement in art were clearly highbrow; they did not need to be rich. Personal wealth did not in any way confer an appreciation for leading-edge art. For example, an art teacher on a modest income can be part of the highbrow community by buying a unique painting from a promising artist, while a wealthy athlete might prefer a black-velvet painting, clearly a lowbrow Artifact.

Lynes identified one other aspect of the aforementioned phenomenon. He observed that there was a migration of everyday things across different market segments over time. What was highbrow at the beginning of a cycle became middlebrow and eventually lowbrow. In other words, the changes in style, fashion, or taste often originated with the highbrow group. Depending on what the change was, it would eventually migrate to the

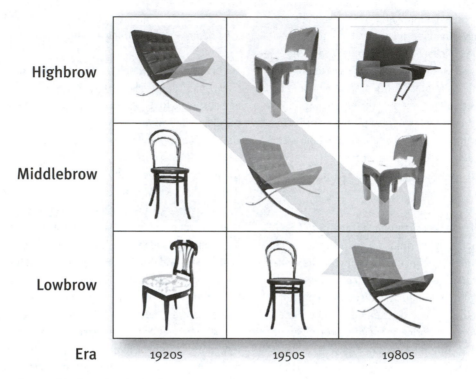

Highbrow

Middlebrow

Lowbrow

Era   1920s   1950s   1980s

Figure 7.5: The Application of Lynes's Visual Analysis to Chair Design

middlebrow segment over months, years, or decades, and then migrate once again to the lowbrow segment over months, years, or decades.

These two underlying principles from Lynes's observations apply to designing and everyday things today. Figure 7.5 shows how the design of certain classic chairs has migrated over time and over groups of Users. When Mies van der Rohe designed the Barcelona chair in the 1930s, there was no mass market for this innovative use of metal and leather. It was a strictly highbrow design. For their part, middlebrow Users of that period were most likely embracing chairs such as those made by Thonet, whereas lowbrow Users were quite happy with more traditional chairs of the day. By the 1950s, the product migration had begun. The Barcelona chair became the icon of corporate America. Reception rooms of Fortune 500 companies often had a matched set of four Barcelona chairs in the main foyer, conferring a middlebrow status to the chair. By the mid-1960s, the migration continued. Copies of the Barcelona

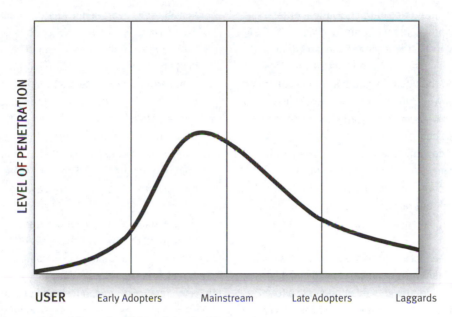

Figure 7.6: Penetration of Everyday Things into the Marketplace

chair, as well as other Bauhaus classics, became available in many retail stores and catalogs. There was nothing innovative anymore; they had become common and thus, for lack of a better term, lowbrow.

Shift back to the highbrow tastes of the 1960s, and you find the first all-plastic chairs. Trace the evolution and migration of Joe Colombo's plastic chair over the next forty years, for example, and a pattern similar to the Barcelona chair emerges. Today, we think nothing of one-piece plastic chairs, but such was not the case in the 1960s. A similar pattern repeats itself with Postmodernism designs of the 1980s. This style migrates from

highbrow to middlebrow markets (some Postmodernist-like products have found their way to Target) and ultimately to the lowbrow end (Wal-Mart perhaps). However, there is now an important difference. Principally because of globalization and instantaneous communication, the time interval for shifts in this migration is getting shorter. It is taking less time for everyday things to migrate from one category to the next.

This migratory pattern of market acceptance by the User has another dimension. Research has shown that the penetration into the marketplace of many every-day things involves recognizable stages of acceptance by four different categories of Users: early adopters, mainstream adopters, late adopters, and laggards. (See Figure 7.6.) Obviously, these stages vary according to the everyday thing, the Users, and the Context. The Dallaire example given at the beginning of this section illustrated this pattern very well. Clearly, the Users who bought the attaché case at MoMA were early adopters. They had no reluctance about being the first on the block with this innovative everyday thing, whereas the Users who frequented the large discount department store were laggards, so to speak. They were not ones to make a fashion statement but rather to follow a fashion trend already well established.

This pattern in User acceptance is repeated in many market segments—fashion, appliances, residential design, and electronics—and provides Designers with a foundation from which to work when developing a new everyday thing. For example, if a Designer were asked to design a new kettle for Wal-Mart, it would not make much sense to design something with a strong Postmodernist style. Such a style would suit the early adopters—who don't normally shop at Wal-Mart. Late adopters and laggards do. Consequently, matching the design style to the desires of this market could be the goal of the Designer.

Lesson 7: Pastimes are Past Times

In 1856, Charles F. Orvis opened a shop in Vermont. Over the next 150 years, it became the leader in the business. Today, it has over thirty-three Orvis stores exclusively offering the Orvis product line and employs 1,500 to 1,700 associates. What is more, it has a thriving catalog business and actively sells over the Internet through its award-winning Web site. What does Orvis make? Flyfishing stuff. In an age of super-trawlers catching fish on every ocean and fish farms on most continents, Orvis succeeds by selling a bit of the past. There is no way that one can justify the cost of a few trout or a salmon based on the price for Orvis equipment and clothing. Buying fish at a store is much cheaper. But then again, that is not the point of fly-fishing. Pastimes have clearly become past times...and big business!

Designers and neophilia go hand in hand. After all, designing is about change and change is often about something new. Yet, neophobia is never completely removed from the picture. This is especially the case with everyday things that are innovative, novel, and unique, which are often rejected by the User. However, some Designers—both past and present—have an antidote for this natural tendency to reject the new: mix the new with the old. Observation of styles, fashion, and trends in design over time shows that discernable patterns exist. Because they are patterns, they repeat themselves and do so most often with a combination of old and new. The Renaissance, for example, was the rebirth of classical design elements from the classical periods of Rome and Greece but executed centuries after both periods. Postmodernism revised a highly decorative approach to design, something that Modernism had previously expunged from Designers' visual vocabulary. On a smaller yet equally telling scale, the length of women's skirts over the last few decades has gone up or down with fashion as has the width of men's ties.

Mixing a judicious portion of the old with the new occurs regularly in contemporary design. The automotive industry has relied on this practice on a recurring basis. Soon after World War II, for example, the Big Three automakers in Detroit—General Motors, Ford, and Chrysler—all began introducing fins to the design of the family sedan. These were strictly decorative and in no way functional. They were also a symbolic visual reference to the airplane, which had not only played a significant role In winning the war for the Allies but also was perceived as a symbol of the future. Fifty years later, we continue to see similar patterns that mix the old with the new. It is not a coincidence that many owners of the Mazda Miata are middle-aged men. As innovative as the car was when first introduced in 1989, it was actually a visual replica of a 1960s Lotus Elan sports car—that is, something from the past. A man in his teens at that time would have most likely coveted the car but would not have been able to afford it. Today, things have changed—both for the man and for the car. The original Lotus is a collector's car, and most people still cannot afford it. Our man in his fifties can now afford a Miata and, through it, relive his youth. The same pattern repeated itself with the relaunch by Ford of the Thunderbird, which was derived from the classic '57 T-Bird, and the Mini Cooper, which is based on the original Austin Mini, an icon of the 1960s. In different ways and for different Users, these everyday things retrieved essential values and images from the past and reconfigured them for the present.

Clearly, reaching into the past in order to move forward is nothing new. Such behavior occurs for essentially two reasons. First, it provides psychological comfort for the User—that is, because the past is a known quantity. Second, it provides societal validation—that is, the comfort that comes from people having done it before. James Joyce, the Irish writer, touched on the importance of the past when he mused that "pastimes are past times." He meant that many activities that we engage in as hobbies are re-creations of activities that were essential in the past. Consider the interest in calligraphy in an age of word processing, transoceanic sailing in an age when most people travel by jet, or camping, a crude method of shelter if there ever was one. These enjoyable but nonessential activities are throwbacks to how people lived more than a hundred years ago—sailing across oceans or pioneering the west. Our pastimes are truly things of the past. (See Figure 7.7.)

Lesson 8: Law of Proximity

In 2003, the design team at Korean multinational Samsung designed and launched 360 new cell phone models in the world market. On average, the team designed nearly one original model per day, every day, including Saturdays and Sundays. By 2004, the cell phone industry worldwide was manufacturing over 400 million cell phones per year. It is reported that around 426,000 cell phones are thrown away in the United States every year.

The number of designs for any one kind of everyday thing is quite unbelievable. Want a shirt? There are hundreds on the shelves in every imaginable style and color. What about pens? Much the same. They are available as felt, ballpoint, and fountain and in a limitless assortment. Furniture is no different. Whether for the home or office, the choices are endless. Then there are cars. They come in every shape, in every color, and for every taste. Would fewer choices be that terrible? Could we not get along with fewer colors of shirts or a reduced selection of pens? Do we need one more model of SUV? Perhaps and perhaps not. The answer to the question has little to do with our needs and much more with our wants or desires.

Therefore, what are some of the possible reasons for such variety in our everyday things? Function could certainly be one. Mechanical, technological, and functional attributes could be reasons, although not convincing ones. True, some everyday things are technically superior to others and, logically speaking, improved function should eliminate inferior everyday things. That doesn't always happen. A Montblanc pen is a superb writing instrument, but there is still a place for a Bic ballpoint pen.

Perhaps we need to have everyday things available in a wide range of prices. This is clearly the case with wristwatches. They are available at all price points, from less than $10 to more than $10,000. They all tell time, and do so very accurately—even the $10 ones. Most people, however, do not acquire watches or clocks based on the selling price alone, nor do they buy watches just for the telling of time. As important as they are, function and price do not adequately explain the seemingly limitless range of designs for the same everyday thing.

The most probable answer lies much more with people and their needs and wants. The example of the watch provides a clue, but only if we consider the User—and not the watch. Why? Because watches are no longer about technology; they are about people. If this phenomenon was not evident thirty years ago, it certainly is today. It became even clearer when Swatch, the Swiss watchmaker, began marketing watches as fashion accessories. From Swatch's perspective, why shouldn't a man have as many watches as he has ties?[ix] Most people already would like us to believe that their watch—or eyeglasses or sport shoes, for that matter—are as individual and unique as they are. In many ways they are correct. In his book *Emotional Design: Why We Love (or Hate) Everyday Things*, American psychologist Donald Norman relates his astonishment when he first heard the president of Swatch state that his was not a watch company but an emotions company. For Swatch and its president, the function of a watch goes well beyond mere timekeeping.

Grant McCracken, anthropologist and member of the Institute for Convergence Culture Consortium at Massachusetts Institute of Technology, explained much the same phenomenon when he stated, "Goods carry meanings and consumers buy goods to get hold of those meanings and use them to construct self." In other words, different designs exist for the same everyday thing because people are individuals, and different everyday things feed their need to express this individuality. Thus, different people require everyday things that look different even if the function is the same. At first glance, this concept of individuality may fly in the face of the fact that people belong to one cultural group or another and share similar tastes. Isn't that why we all wear the same blue jeans? True, the blue jeans may at first appear to be the same but not so to the Users. At one level, the generic blue jeans do confer membership to a cultural group; on the other hand, there are enough differences in blue jeans on the market that everyone can remain an individual within the group.

For the Designer, the challenge is clear: how do we create self? We do so in two ways: by accentuating what self is and by differentiating our self from others. We do this every day, often unknowingly, by way of our ethnicity, education, and culture. We also do it by way of the clothes we wear, the cars we drive, the restaurants we frequent, and the cell phones we use. Each one of us—day in and day out—constantly builds and reinforces this self-image, and everyday things serve as a medium to create this self. They reflect who we are and how others see us. Manufacturers understand this phenomenon extremely well and have responded to it by flooding the market with thousands of different styles of watches, jewelry, and clothes. In the end, we become what we own.

That said, not all designs have the same level of impact on creating this self-identity. Everyday things that are physically closer to a person tend to be more closely identified with self; they generally possess a greater diversity of shape, form, and color than those that are farther away. In part, this phenomenon explains why there is a huge variety of prescription eyeglass frames, for example, but fewer models of sunglasses and even fewer models of welding glasses—although all three devices serve the same function: enhancing the ability to see under different conditions. What makes these glasses different, however, is the connection—physical and metaphysical—that exists between it and the User. Prescription glasses are meant for a unique individual. No one else but the individual User whose prescription was used to make the glasses can wear them. Sunglasses—at least the non-prescription type—are different. Most can be purchased at the local drugstore or department store. Moreover, lots of different people own the same model. Fortunately, the number of models is still large enough to make people feel that they are not wearing the same sunglasses that everyone else is wearing.

Welding glasses are also a form of eye wear but present yet another level of difference. They are available in even fewer models than either prescription glasses or sunglasses. The limited number of models is not a problem, however, because few welders are concerned that another welder is wearing the same model of welding glasses. If anything, it may be comforting to see someone else wearing the same model because it validates the product—that is, it reassures one that the glasses are of good quality since other welders are using them.

In design, the relationship between the everyday thing and its proximity to the User is known as the Law of Proximity. Simply put, the law states that in normal use, the closer physically an everyday thing is to the User, the greater the likelihood for variety in shape, form, and color. This phenomenon of proximity occurs at two levels. The first is the distance between the everyday thing and the User, such as we find in a watch that actually touches the User. This is as close as an everyday thing can be and still be seen. Shoes and clothing also fall into this category. The second level is the place for the normal use of the everyday thing, such as the home, work, and public spaces. The design of a dining chair, for example, can be significantly different for any one of these three places, even if its function remains the same—essentially as a place to sit while eating. The dining area found in a house, in a company cafeteria, and at McDonald's are very different situations requiring very different design solutions.

Watches and clocks—both timekeeping devices—also serve to illustrate the Law of Proximity very well. The wristwatch is an intimate everyday thing. It cannot be physically closer to the User than it is in normal use, strapped as it is to a person's wrist. The choice made by the User of one model over another is clearly a reflection of certain User values. The bedside alarm clock is also a timekeeping device but does not have the intimate associations that the watch possesses. The alarm clock does not physically touch the User; furthermore, several people can use it in the same place. Not surprisingly, alarm clocks are available in fewer designs or models than wristwatches. The clocks in an office also provide us with the time of day but in what is called a social environment. The range of designs is even narrower than that of bedroom alarm clocks. Clocks in airports or railway stations provide yet another level of differentiation. Like watches and alarm clocks, they are also time-keeping devices. In no way, however, are they perceived as intimate, personal, or social everyday things. From one airport to the next—across the country or across continents—these clocks are more visually similar than different. In almost every case, they are large, easily

readable, and aesthetically anonymous. They are public everyday things.

To understand the Law of Proximity better, imagine concentric spheres emanating from the person much like the spatial bubbles described by Edward T. Hall in his studies of proxemics. (See Figure 7.3.) Figure 7.8 provides an illustration of these proxemic spheres and locates various timekeeping devices within them. The difference to keep in mind between the Law of Proximity and proxemics—and it is an important difference—is that the former has to do with the relationship between Users and everyday things whereas the latter is about person-to-person relationships.

The spheres begin with everyday things that are considered intimate; these actually touch and become a physical extension of the User and are normally meant for the exclusive use of one individual. Everyday things such as toothbrushes, combs, clothing, eyeglasses, wristwatches, cell phones, and jewelry fall into this category. They are often intimate by use and thus not readily shared. It is in this category that we find the greatest diversity of form, shape, and color. Personal space follows intimate space. This is the sphere found in the home, where we have everyday things generally meant for family use. Hair dryers, coffeemakers, vacuum cleaners, televisions, furniture, and the family car are included in this category. Compared with the intimate sphere, product diversity is much reduced and, at times, is dependent on whether the everyday thing is inside or outside the home. A good example is the family car. Because people other than family members can see it, the car can become a form of externalized status.

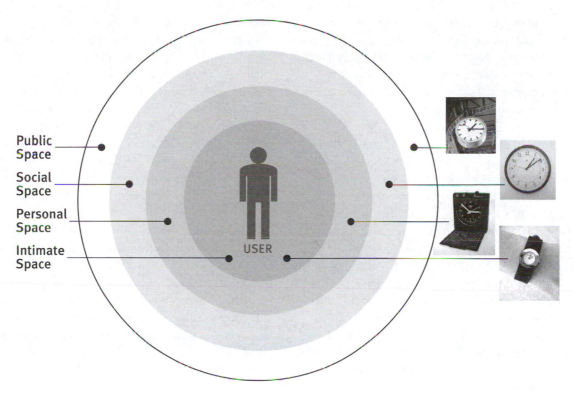

Figure 7.8: The Law of Proximity

Outside the home, we first enter the social sphere. This is the world of the office, restaurants, and hotels, for example. It is the place of everyday things such as desktop computers, contract furniture, and hotel equipment. With few exceptions, not many people identify personally with any of these everyday things. We use the same kind of PC as our co-worker, sit in the same kind of booth in a chain restaurant, or sleep in the same bed at the hotel. In all of these circumstances, we rarely ever feel that our personal identity has been violated. There are exceptions, of course, such as the corner office. In some cultures, the corner office is a well-recognized status device and a coveted space. Corner offices aside, most everyday things found in social space are more visually similar than different. In the typical office, for example, desktop computers are either putty or black; office desks are cloned models of each other; and telephones come in only a few model types and are either silver or black. There are, of course, more choices in certain everyday things, such as office chairs, but here again, the choice in available designs of chairs is not nearly as great as the designs of chairs for the home.

The sense of visual anonymity and reduced product diversity is even more apparent in public spaces such as airports, train stations, and other similar venues, including city streets. In these spaces, the need to personalize everyday things is generally nonexistent and nowhere near as great as it is for intimate, personal, and social spaces. Consequently, diversity of product form is minimal. People in public spaces have little individual affinity for these spaces or for the everyday things found there. We spend relatively little time in public spaces and have no sense of ownership. Bus shelters and the public benches are not ours; they are meant to be used by everyone, hence the adjective *public*. There is certainly no need to tailor their designs to the taste of the individual. If anything, it is more important to guarantee that the form be as generic as possible and that it be easily recognizable by everyone. A public bench is useless if no one recognizes it as such. This, however, doesn't make the public bench—or other public everyday things—less important. It is just that there is no overriding need for these everyday things to specifically please one User over another.

The Law of Proximity partially helps to explain another important facet of design: the propensity for Designers to be more involved in the design of intimate or personal everyday things rather than more complex ones, public or social. Think about it. Boutiques are filled with one designer object or another, design magazines regularly publish yet another design for the same function, and museums collect many of these same everyday things. The common ground for all of these designer objects—from exquisite carafes for olive oil and innovative corkscrews to ingenious lamps and stackable chairs—is that the closer these everyday things are to the User, the greater the need for variety because we seek to create an individual identity with them.

The need for people, especially those in the developed world, to create self is without a doubt the foremost reason why we have a proliferation of different designs of everyday things that, in the end, serve more or less the same function. It is not the only way that we create our persona; our upbringing and education also define who we are. Unlike upbringing and education, however, everyday things are visible, convenient, and readily accessible. They serve to overtly communicate what we value and who we are.

Lesson 9: Why We Like Some Everyday Things and Not Others

You are visiting a local art gallery. A good friend of yours is having an exhibition there and you want to see her work. As you go from one room to the next in the gallery, you come upon two people looking at and commenting on your friend's paintings. The discussion is vocal and intense, even heated. Descriptors of one kind or another are being used liberally. These are not two casual visitors but two people who know and who understand art. Irrespective of their expert commentary, as long as you persist in believing that they are talking about the art on the walls you will never truly understand what they are saying. In reality, they are not talking about the paintings but about themselves—their value systems, their education, and their upbringing. The paintings are only conduits that permit such a discourse in the first place because, in the end, beauty does not reside in the Artifact but In the mind.

Calling anything good—or, for that matter, bad or right or wrong—is a form of evaluation or judgment. It is how we classify and attribute value to something. We do this every day, with the food we eat, the books we read, the television programs we watch. We use this evaluation process to make choices, normally selecting what is good over what is not so good. Like the two visitors in the anecdote above, what we fail to understand is that evaluation is most often autobiographical. Why? Because impersonal value judgments are usually nothing more than personal biases. The two gallery visitors were not talking about the paintings but about themselves. We do much the same when we talk about the architecture that we like or the music that we despise or the design that influences our lives.

So, is there such a thing as good design or bad design? If there is, how is it defined as good or bad? To begin, we need to realize that designs or everyday things are neither inherently good nor bad. They are only perceived by different people as good or bad, based on each person's prior knowledge and experience. It is perception that affects whether something is judged to be good or bad. In this regard, there is no universal absolute of good and bad. Yet all of us make evaluations about good and bad on a daily basis and do so based on our prior knowledge.

Eric Newton was keenly aware of this phenomenon when he surmised that people like what they know but do not necessarily know what they like—even though they think they do.[x] When people know something about a painting, a style of music, or a design, they are more likely to view it favorably than they would if they did not know anything about it. How we perceive beauty in design is no different. People persist on referring to that chair or that house as being a beautiful design, and then go on to support their opinion by way of artistic rationale or historical precedent or theoretical foundation. The chair, they will tell you, is proportionately correct, or is a quintessential example of de Stijl, or is an honest design. However, these same people seem to forget one essential fact. Beauty does not reside in the everyday thing; it only resides in the mind of the observer. Like evaluation, beauty is autobiographical—that is, much like our aforementioned gallery visitors, what anyone likes or dislikes is very much a reflection of the values of that person.

Any attempt to find a common understanding about design needs to move beyond evaluation because everyone has a different meaning for the terms contained in the evaluation process, and most of these are highly subjective. What is beautiful for one person may not be so for someone else. A common ground appears to be nearly impossible. Therefore, should we even bother talking about good or bad design? Yes, we should, but only if we develop an approach that is more objective, more structured, and more systematic.

Evaluation is rooted in the concept of value and is therefore subjective. The value we place on almost anything is normally dependent on non-objective factors such as those derived from personal experiences. We ascribe value to all sorts of things, ranging from stocks and bonds to family heirlooms of immeasurable sentimental value. In theory, common ground for evaluation may be possible but rarely is that the case in practice. The very nature of subjectivity makes a common ground quite impossible.

If evaluation is subjective and arbitrary, description is not. Thus, it is with description that our systematic approach begins. In principle, description is the process of reporting facts in the most objective and neutral manner possible.[xi] We hear evaluations when one person considers a laptop to be heavy and another person does not. What is heavy for one person may be light for another. However, we hear a description when both people state that the laptop weighs 6.2 pounds. It is neither heavy nor light; there is no subjectivity in the statement. We can all agree on its weight as a neutral number according to a weight system that is accepted by everyone.

Not surprisingly, objectivity may appear to be paradoxical in design, perhaps even disconcerting to Designers. By definition and in the minds of many people, designs are supposed to be subjective; they are about how we see and interpret our world. This is certainly true. However, subjectivity and objectivity are not mutually exclusive. A good wine can still be measured for its viscosity. The measurement will not change the value judgment. Despite the fact that most designs are explicitly subjective, there are always conditions in every design that are objective, although we may not be aware of them. The Pyramid of Design Evaluation (see Figure 7.9) provides a model with which we can more systematically understand these various levels of evaluation in design. It is based on a hierarchy of three groups of values found in all designs: universal, cultural, and personal.

Right or Wrong

The first tier of The Pyramid of Design Evaluation consists of design properties that are both objective and universally applicable. The Laws of Nature and the Laws of Society fit into this category. Both groups of laws impact everyday things although their effects may not be at first apparent. Few Designers consciously consider gravity as they go about designing. Yet gravity cannot be ignored. A Designer of a restaurant, for example, knows that lighting fixtures will not hang magically from the ceiling without being fixed. This Designer also knows that chairs will not need to be bolted down for fear that they will fly up to the ceiling. Designers subconsciously and seamlessly incorporate gravity into their designs and don't give it a second thought.

Similarly, Designers have to conform to the Laws of Society. Architects, for example, have to build according to the local building codes. To not do so will often have dire consequences: the construction will be halted or the fire marshal will close the building.

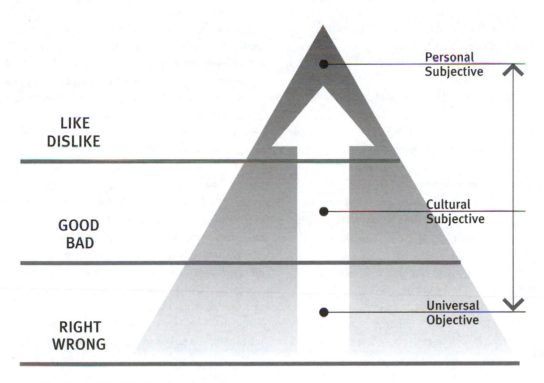

LIKE
DISLIKE

GOOD
BAD

RIGHT
WRONG

Personal
Subjective

Cultural
Subjective

Universal
Objective

Figure 7.9: The Pyramid of Design Evaluation

In The Pyramid of Design Evaluation, the objective qualities in design are either right or wrong. They are binary. Something is either structurally sound or it is not; it either meets the codes or it doesn't. Personal judgment does not really enter into the equation. These values are universal and objective. This is the first level of evaluation in our systematic model. Is the design right or wrong?

Good or Bad

The second level in The Pyramid of Design Evaluation deals with good and bad properties in design, areas that are more subjective. The right-or-wrong analysis is quite simple; it had a black-or-white quality about it. Good and bad—and like and dislike, the third level—are nuanced and exist much more as a continuum. They create a kind of gray zone prone to subjectivity and personal evaluation. Nevertheless, it is possible to be systematic about these two levels of evaluation.

Design qualities of a good-or-bad nature are normally those qualities that have found general agreement and acceptance over time no matter how subjective they may first appear to be. Furthermore, the good-or-bad qualities normally go well beyond the values of any one individual. While these qualities can never be truly quantified, they are nevertheless acknowledged and recognized as schools of thought, styles, or standards. They become cultural values that go on to define behavioral attitudes within a particular group.

The Gothic style is a good example. It is recognized and well documented. But is it right or is it wrong? Is it good or is it bad? How do we even begin to evaluate its visual qualities and make sense of its importance in the world of design? Before we can begin, it is necessary to keep certain facts in mind. First, the Gothic style in its original version only occurred in certain parts of Europe; it did not exist elsewhere in the world, at least not in its original version. Neither was the style based on some universal logic; Gothic architecture typified a unique set of European values in religious thought as well as cultural manifestations at a very specific time in history. In this Context, there is no point in discussing the Gothic style as being right or wrong. Right and wrong do not enter the picture. Gothic churches are found throughout Europe; they exist and are there for everyone to see and touch.

Can we discuss the Gothic style as good or bad? We can, on the basis that architectural historians are in general agree-

ment as to what constitutes Gothic architecture, and so we can debate whether particular examples conform well to the standards of this genre. This agreement includes the time period, the construction, the architectural style and details, and a list of other features or qualities. We can also differentiate what is Gothic from what is not and come to a general agreement about what defines Gothic style in architecture. We know what its principal attributes are. These have been studied, analyzed, documented, and shared. As a consequence, we can adroitly debate the virtues of Gothic architecture in the Context of good or bad because we have defined a visual code or standard. Generally speaking, those buildings that incorporate the codes of Gothic architecture will be deemed to be good examples whereas those buildings that do not will be considered bad examples. All along, however, it is important to note a very important aspect of the evaluation process: the person judging the Gothic style does not have to personally like it. This condition, which is critical in our evaluation model, brings us to the next and last level of design evaluation: like or dislike.

Like or Dislike

Unlike right-or-wrong or good-or-bad in design, like-or-dislike is much more of a reflection of personal values. Whereas right-or-wrong values are objective and good-or-bad values conform to a known code or standard, like-or-dislike is usually the view of one person or, perhaps, a small group. These values are totally subjective.

This explicit subjectivity does not necessarily present a problem in our design evaluation model as long as we can differentiate in our own minds between values of good-or-bad and like-or-dislike. One set of values does not automatically invalidate the other. In other words, we should be able to make a statement such as, "Mies van der Rohe's Barcelona chair is a good example of Modernist design, but I do not particularly like it," without the fear of contradiction. What may appear at first to be a paradox in critical thinking is not the case at all. The first part of our statement makes reference to the adherence—or not—of the Barcelona chair to the well-described standards of Modernism, whereas the second part expresses a highly personal and emotive point of view. In a similar vein, we could state with equal critical precision that Arad's One Off chair in stainless steel is bad Modernism but that we nevertheless like it. As a critic, one does not necessarily need to like something for it to be good, and vice versa.

Values of good-or-bad and like-or-dislike, however, have nothing to do with whether Mies's or Arad's chairs are right or wrong, much like right-or-wrong has little to do with values of like-or-dislike or good-or-bad. The rightness or wrongness of either chair can only be quantified in terms of its adherence to universal laws. As long as they do not contravene these laws, the chairs cannot be said to be wrong. We can, of course, use the good-or-bad evaluation to evaluate other qualities in chairs, such as human factors. From this perspective, Mies's Barcelona chair may qualify as an ergonomically good design because it respects the basic tenets of seating comfort, whereas Arad's One Off ignores them, making it a bad ergonomic design. Whether an everyday thing qualifies as good or bad will depend on such codes or standards.

Values of like-and-dislike, for their part, are totally personal and cannot be explained in terms other than those relating to the particular whims and fancies of the individual. Good-and-bad and like-and-dislike, unlike the amoral laws of nature, are the mirrors of human values. In this vein, we must never forget that, by definition, evaluation can never lead to understanding; only description can.

So, why in the end do we like certain everyday things and not others? This question is appropriate because few of us appear to have any difficulty in distinguishing between what we like and what we don't. Explaining why that is the case, however, is quite a different matter. Words and reasons do not come easily. Yet there are several fundamental principles that help to explain why we like certain everyday things and dislike others. In his book *Product Design: A Practical Guide to Systematic Methods of New Product Development*, Mike Baxter makes a strong case for four different types of attractiveness: prior knowledge; functional; symbolic; and inherent.

Prior-Knowledge Attractiveness. We are already keenly aware that people generally like what they know. To a great extent, past experiences will condition our reactions to everyday things. If our experience with one kind of everyday thing has been positive, then there is a strong likelihood that we will like a variation of this same everyday thing. Branding is almost solely based on prior-knowledge attractiveness; this is why it is so powerful.

Functional attractiveness. There are times when we do not have prior knowledge or experience about a new everyday thing. In these instances, the likelihood of liking the everyday thing will be based on a visceral reaction to its function. Does that chair look as if it can support my weight? Does that footbridge look structurally sound? Will that coat keep me warm? Of course, looks can be deceiving. Many of today's cars look aerodynamically efficient even if they are not.

Symbolic attractinevess. Irrespective of prior knowledge and function, symbolism can often be the prime reason we like a particular everyday thing. For example, colors are often symbolic. Some people still associate blue with boys and pink with girls. Point-and-shoot cameras usually have silver-colored bodies. If Designers wish to symbolize outdoor activities, however, the bodies will often be yellow. Aside from color, there are other features that have symbolism. Consider the Hummer 3! This vehicle is full of symbolism, from macho individualism to military might.

Inherent attractiveness. The most elusive visual attribute of an everyday thing is its visual appearance. It is elusive because the likeability of the everyday thing is established by a combination of perceptual, social, and cultural determinants in combinations unique to each individual. In the end, it appears that we like certain everyday things for no other reason than we just do! Think of Shar Pei dogs with their wrinkles. Or the Citroen 2CV with its utilitarian look. Both have cult followings.

Codes of good design. Some corporations have attempted to articulate what good design means to them. The German company Braun was one of these. With

Dieter Rams as its director of design, Braun created a code of good design for its products with ten criteria, all of which reflected the essence of rationalist thinking of Modernism. The ten criteria were:

1. Good design is innovative.

2. Good design makes a product useful.

3. Good design is aesthetic.

4. Good design helps us to understand a product.

5. Good design is unobtrusive.

6. Good design is honest.

7. Good design is durable.

8. Good design is consequent to the last detail.

9. Good design is concerned with the environment.

10. Good design is as little design as possible.

If codes of good design exist, then do codes of bad design also exist? They do, at least to some degree, and tend to categorize those everyday things referred to as kitsch. Kitsch is the antithesis of good design and is synonymous with bad taste. In his book *Kitsch, The World of Bad Taste*, Gillo Dorles provides us with an excellent overview on this phenomenon of curious designs of questionable visual quality. He provides the reader with numerous examples, from objectionable religious statuettes to works of questionable art. Keep in mind, however, that one person's meat is another person's poison. What is good design according to one set of criteria may be considered bad according to another set. In the end, good or bad is totally dependent on the knowledge and credibility of the viewer.

Summary

At this juncture in our reflections and with the lessons learned, it becomes possible to see designing in a more holistic way so that we can begin to connect the dots. We can manage to do this by layering and superimposing some of the lessons while remembering the fundamental principles that constitute The Designing Triad.

For our purposes, our connecting-the-dots model begins with the assumption that if Designers had their way, many would jump at the chance to prescribe their preferences on Users. After all, Designers are the experts. What do Users know about design? Unfortunately for Designers but fortunately for Users, the world does not easily allow for such design autocracy. The market for everyday things—tools, buildings, and signs—is essentially democratic. It is governed by freedom of choice. User behavior combined with various economic patterns provide a picture that is quite different from the stereotypical picture of designing, at least the one in which Designers are the arbiters of good taste and prescribe it to Users who willingly comply. This prescriptive, or top-down, model is preferred by many Designers, and the model remains true today, at least in principle. There will always be Designers who will create leading-edge everyday things in architecture and design. Such designs will be associated with an elite group of

Users, will possess highbrow product characteristics, will be produced in small quantities, and, consequently, will be expensive. This group of Users is clearly design-driven.

The model is changing rapidly. Figure 7.10 illustrates some of the dynamics implicit in a system that first began as a top-down model (that is, design as prescription) but that now contains a significant bottom-up component. What are some of the consequences of such a change? First, the prescriptive Designers—those designing for the Users at the tip of the pyramid—will indirectly play a role in determining the design values of Users in the larger part of the pyramid. This will occur because of the migratory patterns implicit in the designing model illustrated in the Lynes analysis. Second, there is the lower portion of the pyramid. The Users there are much more numerous and, as discussed in the Dallaire attaché case example provided, tend to follow trends rather than create them. The acquisition of everyday things by these Users is not motivated by design but is largely price-driven. In the middle of the pyramid are the value-driven Users. For these people, design is important, but so is cost. They search for a balance between the two, and that balance is value.

These three groups—design-driven, value-driven, and price-driven—are interrelated, at least operationally. The actions of one group often affect the behavior of another group. The Modernist architecture of Adolf Loos as shown in his Vienna apartment building of 1910 was revolutionary and raised many eyebrows. Clearly, it was design-driven. The presence of many similar-looking apartment buildings today in the middle of many large

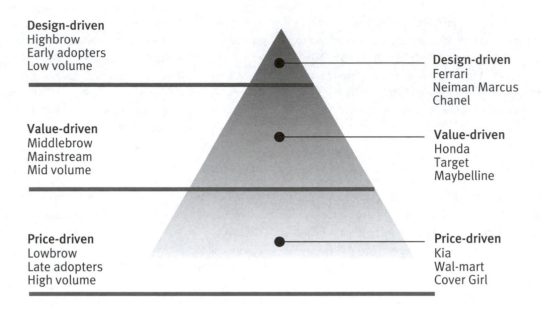

Design-driven
Highbrow
Early adopters
Low volume

Design-driven
Ferrari
Neiman Marcus
Chanel

Value-driven
Middlebrow
Mainstream
Mid volume

Value-driven
Honda
Target
Maybelline

Price-driven
Lowbrow
Late adopters
High volume

Price-driven
Kia
Wal-mart
Cover Girl

Figure 7.10: Democratic Imperative of Design

American cities goes unnoticed. Few if any eyebrows are raised. Most likely, people are more concerned about the cost of the rent than anything else.

In the end, the Loos example as well as myriad others like it illustrate that the elements of The Designing Triad are all interrelated. Touch one element and you affect all the others. Equally important is the fact that none of the elements can be studied, let alone understood, independently of the others. The nine lessons made that point exceptionally well and provided the basis for some of the more significant operational interactions that occur when de-

signing is perceived for what it is: an activity that people all over the world undertake to find the means to deliberately change an existing situation into a preferred one.

Further Reading

Adler, Mortimer J. *Six Great Ideas.*
Alexander, Christopher. *Notes on the Synthesis of Form.*
Baxter, Mike. *Product Design: A Practical Guide to Systematic Methods of New Product.*
Dorfles, Gillo. *Kitsch: The World of Bad Taste.*
Giard, Jacques. *Design FAQs.*
Hall, Edward T. *The Silent Language.*

_____. *The Hidden Dimension.*

_____. *Beyond Culture.*

_____. *The Dance of Life.*

Lynes, Russel. *The Tastemakers: The Shaping of American Popular Taste.*

Newton, Eric. *The Meaning of Beauty.*

Endnotes

[i] Hall, Edward T. *The Dance of Life.*

[ii] This implied correlation—M-time/self-conscious cultures and P-time/unselfconscious cultures—should be considered plausible rationale rather than fact. The author does not know of any research that has either proven or disproven this hypothesis.

[iii] Hall, E. T. *The Hidden Dimension.*

[iv] Ibid.

[v] The concept of landscape office planning was based on the flexibility of movable walls and task oriented furniture replacing the traditional fixed walls and status-oriented furniture, that is, large desks only for executives but not for secretaries even if the tasks of the latter demanded more desk space.

[vi] Alexander, Christopher. *Notes on the Synthesis of Form.*

[vii] Loewy, Raymond. *Never Leave Well Enough Alone.*

[viii] Morris, Desmond. *The Naked Ape.*

[ix] Norman, Donald. *Emotional Design: Why We Love (or Hate) Everyday Things.*

[x] Newton, Eric. *The Meaning of Beauty.*

[xi] The definitions of subjective and objective are those of the American philosopher Mortimer J. Adler as found in his book Six Great Ideas. Quoting Adler, "the subjective is that which differs for you, for me, and everyone else. In contrast, the objective is that which is the same for you, for me, and everyone else." Different magnitudes of objectivity are therefore possible when using this definition.

CHAPTER 8

Where Do We Go Next?

We have seen design both in the past and in the present. Why not therefore attempt to peek into its future? To do so, we need a map and, quite logically, our map should be based on the 3Ps of designing—place, people, and process—because all three underpin designing. What is more, the 3Ps are imbedded in all everyday things—good or bad. Those that we qualify as good design are so principally because the 3Ps have been appropriately integrated.

Cliff dwellings are excellent examples. They integrate the 3Ps exceptionally well in their design. So do bicycles. They provide a form of transportation effectively suited to people and place. Chopsticks also fit into this category. From simple bamboo sticks to ornately decorated ones, they have provided a simple solution to the act—if not the art—of eating. Conversely, those everyday things that we consider to be badly designed are so because some aspect of the 3Ps has been ignored. Such is the case with printed documents that use a font size that is too small to read or with tools that don't consider people who are physically challenged or with buildings that are culturally out of place.

Given the 3Ps and the other principles identified in chapter 7, is it possible to peek into the future? If we do, we might begin by asking some pertinent questions: for example, what role will the 3Ps play in designing over the next several decades? How will the aforementioned principles evolve and affect everyday things? Is our peek into the future a simple linear extrapolation of past patterns in designing? Will new principles emerge? What about unintended consequences? Most experts will tell you that envisioning the future is one thing but forecasting specific events is quite another. The goal of this chapter is to focus more on the former and less on the latter, and it will do so by using the 3Ps as the basis for a vision of the near future.

The elements of the 3Ps—place, people, and process—are not only fundamental and universal but also interdependent. They interact as a set, with any one of the elements catalyzing the other two in a way that defies predictability except in the broadest sense of the word. However, not all three elements have the same potential for impact on design and designing. There is an implicit hierarchy. Place, by its very nature, has the potential for the most extensive effects on designing, followed by people, and then process. In other words, the process is very much dependent on the action of people—the Designer, Maker, and User, much like the action of people is conditioned by place. With the 3Ps serving as guideposts, what does a peek into the future of designing foretell?

Place Is No Longer Just Here

Joe Schwartz is a former senior vice president of design and research at Herman Miller, the American company known for its leading-edge design in office and contract furniture. He worked with many of the exceptional Designers of early Modernism in the U.S., including George Nelson, Charles Eames, and Alexander Girard. It was during that same period—the 1950s and 1960s—that Joe witnessed the rise in the popularity of Scandinavian Modern furniture. Art and design historians have provided various rationales for this phenomenon in America, but Joe has his own take on the story, which is different from the experts yet equally credible.

Unlike the historians, he credits the Boeing 707, the first commercially successful passenger jet, for this significant development in popular taste. His reasoning is quite simple: The improved access to air travel permitted Americans to visit Europe more easily than they had ever been able to do in the past. Once in Europe, Americans discovered what they had never seen before: the clean and functional lines that characterized Danish, Swedish, and Finnish furniture. Once back home, these same American travelers naturally wanted Scandinavian furniture in their homes.

This story is not unusual. It parallels other examples of one society discovering and then emulating another. In 1853, Japan, which had been a closed-off society, was "opened" to the West with the visit of U.S. Admiral Matthew Perry. For the first time in two centuries, the world got a glimpse of Japanese society and its everyday things. It was no coincidence that soon thereafter, Designers in Europe began to not only visit Japan but also to be influenced by Japanese design. That was certainly the case with some of the designs of Charles Rennie Macintosh and his use of black lacquer.

The discovery of Tutankhamen's tomb in November 1922 by the British Egyptologist Howard Carter had a similar influence on design. The objects found in the tomb—jewelry, coffins, masks, and containers—were unique, had never been seen in Europe before, and inspired Designers for decades thereafter.

To varying degrees, stories such as these—the Boeing 707, Admiral Perry's visit to Japan, and the discovery of Tutankhamen's tomb—contain many of the seeds for this peek into the future. What happens tomorrow seems to depend very much on what has happened in the past. To a significant extent, this pattern has been at the center of design's evolution and there is reason to believe that it will also be the pattern for its future as well.

However, we must never forget that designing is a human activity and that it occurs everywhere. Therefore, these two factors alone guarantee that peeking into the future is not a precise science. There are too many unknown circumstances and variables to consider. Nevertheless, one thing is predictable: We will not be able to oversee the evolution of designing, at least not in any significant ways. After all, the Designer, the Maker, and the User—the central players in the designing activity—are people. In combination, they are not prone to any level of dependable predictability, and even less so over time. That said, there are patterns from past events that can provide various scenarios—general in scope but nonetheless useful.

The Boeing 707 anecdote illustrates the concept of unintended consequences very well. In this case, a technological leap, the passenger jet plane, indirectly affected an unrelated sector, popular taste in furniture. No engineer or manager at Boeing could have ever imagined such a consequence to what essentially was an engineering breakthrough. In earlier times, this kind of unintended consequence would have been extremely rare, perhaps never occurring at all. Our earliest ancestors, for example, knew their immediate environment and nothing else. Any influence came from their surroundings and certainly not from far-off cultures. Place was here and nowhere else. The world was getting smaller long before the Boeing 707. Early explorers—Vikings, Spaniards, Portuguese, French, Polynesians, and others—ventured beyond their known surroundings, and their discoveries

irreversibly changed both the people visited and the visitors alike. What the passenger jet did was to diminish even further the effects of place on a rapidly shrinking planet. Place was no longer just where one stood. Place could be anywhere.

Telecommunication has perhaps had an even greater effect on place than did the jet. Until recently, travel implied physical movement and displacement. Someone had to walk or sail or fly to a place. The mind and body had to go together from one location to the next. Thanks to telecommunication, especially satellites, the body no longer has to accompany the mind. The mind can be in another place while the body remains at home. Travel is instantaneous, or at least as fast as the speed of telecommunication.

Imagine a small Mexican village that has had very little contact with the rest of the world. It is one thing for the villagers to meet tourists visiting the community and to imagine how these visitors must live at home; it is something totally different for the villagers to get a real look at the world outside—not by actually traveling to New York or Paris or Cairo, but instead by watching television. It is not unusual to see that many of the disheveled houses in impoverished rural areas of Mexico nevertheless have satellite dishes. The villagers do not need to travel to other places because the other places travel to their village via the air waves. The experiences garnered from watching television go well beyond those provided by soap operas and cartoons. They involve catching glimpses of how other people live—what they own, what cars they drive, what their houses look like, and what they value. Invariably, they see what other people have and how to replicate this lifestyle. The typical soap opera produced in Hollywood may have a plot, but it is the context—place, people, and everyday things—that is the real message. In the past, gaining knowledge of this context would have been possible only through travel and, to a certain extent, through postcards and books. Now, people need not leave their own place to understand the context or place of others.

Historically, place was also where the designing and making activities occurred. It was people who migrated from place to place, not the designing and making. In many ways, this is how cities were born—people left rural areas in order to go to the city, the place where designing and making occurred. This pattern is now changing. People are still moving; however, so is the designing and making. During the Industrial Revolution and in the decades that followed, designing and making were centered in specific areas, normally because of the availability of materials, labor, and other associated resources. This was the era of trade dominance by Great Britain and a period when natural resources were imported from abroad, processed in the mills and factories of England, and then either consumed by the home market or exported. Such economic power was made possible because of Great Britain's colonies across the globe in Australia, Canada, India, South Africa, and Hong Kong, to name but five. Essentially, designing, making, and using were localized in one place—Great Britain.

As world economic power gradually shifted to the United States in the nineteenth and early twentieth centuries, the model repeated itself but in another place—one without the colonial infrastructure. Once again, the designing, making, and using occurred in one place—the United States.[i]

As the globe shrank, however, it made economic sense to do the making in another place if labor was cheaper there, for example, China. The designing remained in the United States as did the using, but the making often went offshore, with obvious benefits—everyday things became less expensive. Many people thought that this type of transfer, or outsourcing, would be limited to the making of everyday things. Little consideration was ever given to the possibility that designing would eventually go offshore as well. Yet, it has. American corporations are assigning more of their engineering, computer programming, systems development, accounting, and technical drawings to firms in India and China. Bill Moggridge, co-founder of IDEO, stated that his firm can hire five competent industrial Designers in China for the cost of one in San Francisco, where his office is located. Clearly, place, as a factor in designing, can change rapidly to wherever it makes sense at any given point in time.

William J. Mitchell, director of MIT's Design Laboratory, was very insightful when he reflected upon people and the cell phone. His comment went to the heart of place in our world of instant communication. Mitchell remarked that when we dial a telephone number connected to a landline, we know where the phone is ringing but we do not know who will answer it. With a cell phone, it's just the opposite: we know who will answer the phone but have no clue where the person is. Place is no longer necessarily where we think it is.

Place is not the only factor being seriously affected by the shrinking of the planet. So is the concept of time, especially with the introduction of electronic media. Marshall McLuhan was among the first persons to understand the impact of electronic media on society—more specifically, how place and time would be irreversibly changed and what effects these changes would ultimately have on society. He defined the phenomenon as the Global Village, a term that he coined. McLuhan saw that the integration of electronic media into our daily lives allowed for everything to happen at the same place and at the same time. Essentially, place and time had ceased to be very limiting factors. Consequently, the world had become almost like a single village. Everyone could be present and aware of what was going on all at once. It should be remembered that McLuhan was making these speculations well before the development of the World Wide Web, which has only reinforced his original conception of the Global Village. As we now know, the Web places us everywhere at all times. Synchronicity is no longer an issue when asynchronicity is a reality.

Place has a connotation beyond people and where they reside. Place is the physical environment that we inhabit and that sustains us. Place determines the natural resources available to use for building our Artificial World—the wood that we hew, the minerals that we mine, and the oil that we drill. It is all of these things and more. Not that much more, however, because these natural resources are finite. They can only sustain humanity if we use them in the most thoughtful way. There is no doubt whatsoever that people will have to develop an increased regard for this place we call earth and the

resources we find here. We cannot continue to act as if the resources are infinite and, as William McDonough and Michael Braungart fittingly state, to continue to design everyday things that conveniently pay us a visit on their way to the landfill.[ii]

In his book *The World Is Flat,* Thomas Friedman, author and *New York Times* columnist, presents a contemporary picture of the Global Village as it affects design and economic growth and development. Friedman refers to three phases of globalization—Globalization 1.0, 2.0, and 3.0. Globalization 1.0 was about "countries and muscle" and how power of one kind or other—muscle, horse, or steam—positioned countries. It ran from the time of Columbus to around 1800. The world shrank from large to medium. Globalization 2.0 took it one step further; it shrank the world from medium to small. This was the era of greater world trade and the influence of multinational companies as reductions in the costs of transportation and communication made all corners of the planet readily accessible. Globalization 3.0, which started around 2000, is moving to the next level, that is, shrinking the planet from small to tiny. And if Globalization 1.0 was about countries and Globalization 2.0 was about companies, Globalization 3.0 will be about the individual, which is the focus of the following section.

People and Process, or the Democratization of Designing

Every Tuesday and Saturday in SoHo, a big truck pulls to the curb on the east side of Broadway to have its cargo unloaded. From out of the truck emerge not fresh New Jersey tomatoes or Long

Island sweet corn, but rather stacks of dress shirts in soft colors, slim-cut black skirts, and elegant women's jackets that look—from a distance—like they have just come off a Milan runway. All the pieces of clothing have two things in common. They come from a million-square-foot warehouse owned by a company called Zara, in the town of La Coruna in the Spanish province of Galicia. And, in all likelihood, three weeks before they were unloaded, they weren't even a glint in their designer's eye.[iii]

Author James Surowiecki recounts the above story in his book *The Wisdom of Crowds* as a telling example of how the designing and making of everyday things are changing. The fashion industry has traditionally functioned on a cycle of seasonal changes in which manufacturers attempt to guess the desires of the marketplace, proceed to fill the stores with apparels that they believe will sell, but—more often than not—are resigned to clear their shelves with end-of-season sales. Zara is different. It does not operate on the seasonal calendar but on perceivable shifts in the marketplace whenever they occur. And because it controls the designing and making processes, Zara can react to these shifts in the market literally overnight. Its Designers can quickly create the necessary fashion apparels and the factory can just as quickly manufacture and deliver them to its stores. If the items turn out to be best sellers, more are produced and delivered; if not, production ceases. In other words, everyday things are designed, made, and used in a quantity appropriate to the market at any point in time.

The Zara example clearly shows that changes in the designing process are not limited to place and time only. The operations that comprise designing—the people-process combination—are also changing in ways that are as significant as place and time. In its earliest configuration, designing was a very integrated activity—that is, it was an activity undertaken by one person who was the Designer, Maker, and User. By extension and quite logically, designing was democratic—that is, the Designer, Maker, and User were acting as one person and therefore could seamlessly incorporate the demands of each without the imposition of any one onto the other two.

Over the span of three million years or so, that situation evolved. With the separation of the Designer, Maker, and User as we have today, some areas of designing have become more autocratic. The fashion design industry—at least in the traditional sense but unlike the Zara example above—is certainly one of these; fashion Designers often act as if they can impose their desires and wishes—no matter how fanciful and outrageous—onto the public. How else to explain garments that are designed for women who are nearly six feet tall and weigh one hundred pounds or less.

Architecture can also be autocratic, especially in those cases in which star architects consider it only natural that their opinions should override those of the clients. In part, this attitude explains why architects are not involved to any great extent in the housing industry in America. In both cases, the Designers are not incorporating the needs and wants of the Users as they might in a designing process that is more democratic.

Perceptible changes to a more democratic designing process are beginning to appear. The current state of the Designer, Maker, and User as separate and different entities is being challenged. There are signs that the autocratic model is giving way to a more inclusive and participatory model, one in which Designers, Makers, and Users are once again more integrated. The change, however welcomed by some people, will not be a return to the good old days. Much more likely, it will provide an opportunity for the individual to play a more active role—to have a voice, so to speak—in how the Artificial World is being designed. It is, after all, the Users' world; it is therefore only logical that they have a role in its development and evolution.

The democratization of designing is not a recent phenomenon. We first began to see its potential during the Industrial Revolution with the emergence of manufacturers, or Makers, and their capacity for large-scale production of everyday things. As a consequence, no longer was the production of Artifacts limited to the needs and the means of royalty, nobility, and members of the upper class. With mass-production, everyday things became more popular. People other than the elite could now acquire everyday things—clothing, furniture, dishes, cutlery—or at least mass-produced versions of them. Designing was beginning to influence a much larger segment of the population. Makers were part of the wave of democratization but not so the Designers. They were generally left out of the designing process. The majority of Makers did not perceive the need to incorporate the Designer, at least not as a separate entity. In practice, most manufacturers acted as both Makers and Designers. The designing portion of the activity was relegated to visual mimicry—that is, the borrowing of design styles with little logical or rational relation to function or the developments in functional designs. There appeared to be little or no appreciation for formal qualities or style. Exceptions aside, Designers were not yet the independent force that they would soon become.

Designers emerged as independent agents of change in the late nineteenth and early twentieth centuries and did so for a simple reason: it was the perception of many Designers—especially those who were leaders of the Art Nouveau movement—that industrialization was creating a world of everyday things devoid of humanity. Industrialization was making the world too mechanistic. These Designers were not against industrialization per se; on the contrary, their desire was to be included in the designing process in order to contribute a level of humanity that they thought was missing in everyday things. They would eventually accomplish their goal with designs from Hector Guimard and his light standards and entrances for the Paris Metro (see Figure 1.8), Antonio Gaudi and his many buildings in Barcelona (see Figure 6.2), and Louis Comfort Tiffany and his glassware and lamps. The Deutscher Werkbund was also cognizant of the divide that existed between the "inventing and accomplishing spirits" and sought to bridge the gap between Designers and Makers.

Over the next decades, many Designers—especially the leaders—gradually developed more independence from Makers and Users although they still remained involved in the designing and making process. Many also became more autocratic and more prescriptive in their intervention in the designing process. Like physicians who prescribe medication, these Designers acted as if it was their prerogative to prescribe what was good in architecture, graphics, products, and all kinds of everyday things. By the late 1990s, this prescriptive attitude seemed to have reached its peak. The market was filled with designer objects of one kind or another. Some of these everyday things actually carried a Designer's name, such as Ralph Lauren or Giorgio Armani; others did not go that far but made a clear allusion to design with terms such as International Design or *ergonomic design*.

It should be mentioned that the Designer name, or signature, did play a useful role, at least at the beginning, because it provided information about the provenance of the design—who designed the everyday thing and who made it. To know that your lounge chair was an original design by Charles and Ray Eames and that it was made by Herman Miller was important information. However, the Designer names on everyday things soon went beyond matters of provenance; they came to validate the need to belong, a human need that Abraham Maslow identified in his Hierarchy of Needs (see chapter 3). By acquiring one everyday thing instead of another, people are able to display their membership in an elite group, thereby asserting their values and status. In many cases, the everyday things acquired may not be the best values in terms of function; however, they are the most appropriate in terms of reinforcing a person's need to belong to a particular group and announce it to others.

Many Makers and Designers—independent agents who work in concert—often considered the User a passive bystander in the designing process. For all intents and

purposes, Users appeared to have no direct role in the designing process. Of course, Users had been part of the designing process in the past but certainly not in a deliberately active way. For example, architects based their measurements for doors and stairs on anthropometrics, and product Designers had integrated the User in the designing process via user-centered design. The inclusion of Users was even more evident in business, where the customer—or User—was always right. If nothing else, this attitude had been instrumental in the development of marketing. However, many Designers had been wary of and uncomfortable with certain aspects of marketing. Its principles seemed to be nothing more than pandering to Users. Designers—especially those who shared a similar ethos with artists—did not see the need to pander to Users. Moreover, Designers did not trust marketing to accurately predict or help forecast innovation in design, which was central to the Designers' role.

With housing construction rising at an unprecedented rate, the opportunity for Designer involvement in the design of the typical house had never been greater than it was in the 1990s in America. Yet the prescriptive attitude of many architects combined with a building industry much more attuned to providing whatever the market wanted guaranteed that the architect or Designer would be excluded from the picture. As previously noted, most houses in America are still not designed by architects—a market that constitutes of a very large segment of the building industry.

In some industries, such as automotives, the User had always been accustomed having choices. These existed in the form of different models, trim, accessories, and color. When buying a new car, Users were expected to make design choices. Designers never totally prescribed to Users. Years later, some computer manufacturers also adopted this strategy and allowed for choices by the Users, who could select processor speed, hard-drive memory, and other operating features. Even builders and developers of homes got into the game and did so by allowing the buyers of houses to be involved directly in the designing process before the house was built. The buyer could make room changes and select from an assortment of architectural details and finishes, both exterior and interior.

In other industries, the inclusion of Users in the designing process went beyond their merely selecting from a list of options or choices. This desire was accompanied by an attitudinal change in Designers and Makers alike. Nike, the sports-shoe manufacturer, was one of these Makers. As an alternative to buying shoes from one of its many lines of products, Nike deliberately set out to engage Users by providing a Web site where they could design their own shoes on-line. Of course, Users were not really designing their shoes, at least not in the true sense of the word; what they were doing was personalizing their shoes by selecting soles, uppers, colors, and monograms from a list of pre-determined options that the Nike Designers had provided. However, the cat was out of the bag. Users could now play a direct role in the designing process. What is more, allowing Users to participate directly in the designing process empowered them. Prescription was giving way to subscription.

Empowerment and participatory design will not stop with the sportswear industry. This is only an innocent beginning in the bigger scheme of things. In the fall of 2007, there was a political coup in the country of Myanmar. The military, which was behind the coup, quickly attempted to shut down communication to the outside world. In such circumstances, the last thing the leader of a coup needs is to have the world as an audience. Yet, images of soldiers beating protestors got out almost instantly via the use of the cameras built into many cell phones. Well before any of the major networks could get a news team to the spot, people were sending still pictures as well as video clips of the atrocities all around the world. The fidelity of these pictures was perhaps less than perfect, but the point was made: the world had an army of reporters as long as cell phones were available. Major networks are well aware of this potential. The BBC news site on the Web, for example, declares to its viewers, "Send us your pictures and videos." Obviously, it understands the empowerment implicit in participatory news reporting. The so-called Arab spring of 2011 was more of the same but with an added twist; that is, the uprisings in Tunisia, Egypt, Syria, and Libya were all fueled by one type of social networking or another.

The active participation of the User is quickly becoming a mainstay in designing. In part, it began with the involvement of experts who represented the User and who traditionally had never been involved in designing—experts such as psychologists, sociologists, and anthropologists. It continued with the direct intervention of Users, as shown in some of the examples above. The role of the Designer as a gifted individual is not necessarily over;

however, it is changing. More and more, people know that they can have a say in the designing process. Just as patients have become more assertive in asking questions of their doctors, seeking second opinions, and playing a role in their wellness, so do consumers of everyday things take a more active role. Many Designers play the prescriptive role because of a sense of entitlement and their having had permission to do so in the past. The pre-scriptive role will continue in those areas where public safety and welfare is paramount. In most other domains of designing—graphics, product, fashion, and homes—the User will play an ever-increasing role in the designing of everyday things. After all, consumer purchasing drives around 70% of the American economy. As long as people have this level of financial clout, they are in a position to demand a more active role in designing. The examples of the housing market and Nike certainly provide the poten-tial for a shift from prescription to subscription.

Kevin Kelly, co-founder of *Wired* magazine, said there is no reason not to believe that soon "everyone will write a song, author a book, make a video, craft a Weblog, and code a program...What happens when the data flow is asymmetrical—but in favor of creators? What happens when everyone is uploading far more than they down-load?"[iv] It seems that in some respects, we have returned to our earliest days on this planet, when everyone was Designer, Maker, and User.

A world where people are more directly involved in the designing process as Designers, Makers, and Users bring with it certain benefits. For example, people who design artifacts also understand the making of artifacts and their maintenance. This is certainly not typical today. Few of us can repair a toaster, let alone a car. More impor-tantly, the more intimate the involvement is of a person in the designing process, the stronger the bond between the User and the Artifact. As superficial as this attribute may be at first—after all, people bonding with everyday things may not appear to be normal human behavior—it could encourage people to hold on to their everyday things longer rather than encourage consumerism. The latter situation was certainly Victor Papanek's observa-tion, one that he made in his revealing book, *Design for the Real World*, when he stated that we as a society can-not continue to buy things we don't need, with money we don't have, to impress people who don't care. In other words, we cannot dispose of so many everyday things at the pace and the regularity that we do. If we do, our ac-tions as Designers, Makers and Users will no longer be sustainable.

This being the case, how do we begin to address the situ-ation of insatiable consumption when resources are fi-nite? How do we integrate an ethos of sustainability into the designing process? Before anything else, it is impor-tant to know what is meant by sustainable design be-cause interrelated concepts such as green design or climate change or environmentalism can easily obfuscate the picture. To be effective, we need to share the same lexicon if we are to understand the various facets of sus-tainability. On that note, DuPont, the American multina-tional and a leader in good environmental and sustainable practice, has produced several publications, one of which, *Green Glossary*, provides succinct and con-cise definitions for some of the more common terms used in sustainable design.[v] Several of the more important terms appear below.

- Cradle-to-grave: A term used in life cycle analysis (LCA) to describe the entire life of a material or product up to the point of disposal. The term also refers to a system that handles a product from creation through disposal.

- Ecology: A branch of science concerned with the interrelationship of organisms and their environments.

- Ecosystem: An interconnected and symbiotic grouping of animals, plants, fungi, and microorganisms that sustain life through biological, geological, and chemical activity.

- Environmental Impact: Any change to the environment, whether adverse or beneficial, wholly or partially resulting from human activity, industry, or natural disasters.

- Global Warming: A process that raises the air temperature in the lower atmosphere due to heat trapped by greenhouse gasses, such as carbon dioxide, methane, nitrous oxide, CFCs, and ozone. It can occur as the result of natural influences, but the term is most often applied to the warming predicted to occur as a result of human activities (that is, emissions of greenhouse gases). (Note: Some experts now use the term *Climate Change* instead of *Global Warming* because the climatic changes that have resulted from greenhouse gasses have created changes in weather patterns beyond warming.)

- Green Design: A design, usually architectural, conforming to environmentally sound principles of building, material, and energy use. A green building, for example, might make use of solar panels, skylights, and recycled building materials.

- Life Cycle Analysis (LCA): The assessment of a product's full environmental costs, from raw material to final disposal, in terms of consumption of resources, energy and waste.

- Pollution: Generally, the presence of a substance in the environment that, because of its chemical composition or quantity, prevents the functioning of natural processes and produces undesirable environmental and health effects. Under the Clean Water Act, for example, the term has been defined as the man-made or man-induced alteration of the physical, biological, chemical, and radiological integrity of water and other media.

- Recycling: Process by which materials that would otherwise become solid waste are collected, separated or processed and returned to the economic mainstream to be reused in the form of raw materials or finished goods.

- Renewable Resources: A resource that can be replenished at a rate equal to or greater than its rate of depletion; i.e., solar, wind, geothermal, and biomass resources.

- Sustainability: Practices that would ensure the continued viability of a product or practice well into the future.

With a shared lexicon in place, we can now move to some of the underpinning qualities that define sustainable design. Let's use a simple example to make the point. Many people buy and eat salmon. Generally speaking, fish protein is good for you; it is low in fat and is a good source of Omega-3 fatty acids.[vi] In most instances, the salmon that you buy in your local grocery store is raised in fish farms, in a practice known as aquaculture. So far, so good. Raising salmon would appear to be a sustainable venture because we can raise as many salmon as the market needs. It is naturally renewable, hence sustainable. However, there is an inevitable twist in the story. Because salmon are carnivores they are fed a diet of feed made from wild fish, and it takes anywhere from two to three pounds of this feed to obtain one pound of salmon. Therefore, does it make sense to use three pounds of one kind of fish to produce one pound of another kind of fish? Unless the fish that is used for feed populates at a rate higher than its conversion into feed there is a strong possibility that the fish stock used for feed will be quickly depleted. In essence, we are using more to create less. Is this practice sustainable?

At one level, the answer to the question is complex. There are many facets in the life-cycle analysis (LCA) to consider with aquaculture, such as infrastructure costs, operations, and transportation. At another level, the answer is quite simple. Using three pound of fishmeal to create one pound of edible fish is not sustainable, much like withdrawing three dollars from your savings account for every one dollar you deposit is not sustainable.

Sustainability is directly connected to our use of the Natural World in order to create an Artificial one. Moreover, sustainability is not only about the present but, more importantly, about the future, as explicitly stated in 1983 by United Nations (UN) by way of the World Commission on Environment and Development, known as the Brundtland Commission. It defined sustainable development as "... development that meets the needs of the present without compromising the ability of future generations to meet their own needs." The indigenous people of North America shared this view long before the UN declaration. An ancient Native American proverb states, "We do not inherit the Earth from our ancestors, we borrow it from our children."

Sustainable design is not limited to the use of our natural resources, such as our forests, minerals, water, and other assets in our Natural World. To be effective, sustainable design must also include other elements that comprise the overall picture of human existence in the Artificial World. There are three such elements: people (cultural and social values); planet (natural resources within an ecological balance); and profit (economic viability). All three elements are interdependent. Focusing on one or two all the while ignoring the third will not prove effective. It is for this reason that sustainable design is challenging. It will not happen by accident; rather, it will happen by design.

Sustainable design is not a recent phenomenon. Its ideology has a modest beginning in the words of your parents when they voiced, "Want not; waste not." Their intention was obvious: you should not waste what Nature has provided. Similar versions have been practiced in the developing and developed worlds as well. As mentioned above, indigenous people lived in a way that was sustainable. The birch-bark canoe described in chapter 4 is an excellent example of a sustainable design. It was designed and made locally using local materials that were biodegradable. Once past its usable life it could be disposed with little harm to the environment.

Early colonists such as the Shakers were equally sensitive to a sustainable way of life. They adopted a lifestyle that reflected a waste-not, want-not ethos. Like native people, they relied on the Natural World for their livelihood. Materials found locally were used for their buildings, furniture, and clothing. Life was simple and Shakers frowned on any sense of overt materialism. This approach to design was in many ways similar to the approach of early Modernists such as Adolf Loos. His distaste for waste made him, at least in today's terms, a closet environmentalist. In his seminal article of 1908 entitled "Ornament and Crime,"[vii] Loos railed against the waste of material and capital involved in unnecessary decoration. Like environmentalists today, Loos was convinced that the reduction of waste was the way of the future. Clearly, individuals and groups in the past were cognizant of society's connection to nature and therefore the need to live within the constraints of Nature.

This legacy of conservation left to us by our predecessors has taken almost one hundred years to surface as a common call to action, and for good reasons. In the United States, for example, buildings account for 36% of the country's total energy consumption, 65% of electricity use, and 30% of greenhouse gas emissions.[viii] Yet, we are just now beginning to address sustainability in buildings. And what of the millions of automobiles and cell phones mentioned in previous chapters? What ultimately happens to these products when they are discarded? As William McDonough and Michael Braungart so fittingly remarked in their book, *Cradle to Cradle: Remaking the Way We Make Things*, all of these everyday things conveniently pay you a visit on their way to the landfill.

Some corporate executives and government officials claim that resources will always be plentiful; that sources for energy will never run out; and that even if they do, technology will come to our rescue. Many consumers rally around the mantra, "He who dies with the most toys, wins," was a popular saying in the 1970s and 1980s. Less is no longer more, as Mies van der Rohe believed; more is more.

According to other experts, however, the picture is bleaker. They portray a world with finite resources that is being depleted at an unsustainable pace. In their opinion, the developed world is consuming resources at a rate that cannot be sustained. At the same time, developing countries such as China and India are beginning to exert their right to a standard of living equal to that found in the West. And why not? Why shouldn't every citizen of Africa or Asia have access to the same clothes, homes, and automobiles that we do? Some environmental experts will emphatically declare that this goal is not possible unless we have the natural resources of another three planets like Earth[ix] . . . and we don't!

These polar opposites—depletion of resources, on the one hand, and technology to the rescue, on the other—create two very different pictures and leave us in a quandary. Who is right? The eco pessimists or the techno optimists? In the end, the environmental situation of the future will not be a simple one of either/or. The challenge ahead is too complex for such simplistic ideology. Yet, design can play—in fact, must play—a role in how society integrates sustainable principles in its practice.

It is difficult to argue against the irrefutable logic of more fuel efficiency, or a reduction in material consumption, or less pollution all around. Early on in the environmental movement, this logic spawned the well-known three Rs of sustainability: reduce, reuse, and recycle. The challenge for Designers has moved well beyond such a facile practice, as good as it is. The situation now requires more deliberate and focused actions beginning with two important considerations: embracing shared principles of sustainability and integrating these principles into day-to-day design practice. Several such principles of sustainable design are now in current practice; however, three are of particular interest to Designers. These are: The Natural Step, LEED, and ISO 1400. Each one will be described briefly below.

The Natural Step

As we know, actions speak louder than words. The Natural Step, an international advisory and research organization, provides a blueprint for designers who choose to incorporate sound environmental practice into their everyday lives. Since 1988, this organization has addressed substantive and fundamental issues about sustainability. Its mission statement, ". . . to accelerate global sustainability by guiding companies and governments onto an ecologically, socially, and economically sustainable path," goes to the heart of the issue: the Earth and its ecosystems.[x] Designers should not be discouraged by the daunting scope of the problem or by the lack of easy fixes.

The Natural Step focuses on three fundamental principles. They are:

- Society depletes the Earth's bounty at a rate that is faster than resources can be replenished. This is especially the case for oil, coal, and many metals.

- The rate of production of everyday things by society is greater than the rate that natural processes of the Earth can reclaim them.

- Society is also using the Earth's resources at a rate that is greater that the natural rate for replenishment. Not only are we are overharvesting, overfishing and overmining, but we are also eliminating the potential for sustainability by over-building and overpaving.

The Natural Step advocates four practices:

1. Eliminate our contribution to systematic increases in concentrations of substances from the Earth's crust. This means substituting certain minerals that are scarce in nature with others that are more abundant, using all mined materials efficiently, and systematically reducing dependence on fossil fuels.

2. Eliminate our contribution to systematic increases in concentrations of substances produced by society. This means systematically substituting certain persistent and unnatural compounds with ones that are normally abundant or break down more easily in nature, and using all substances produced by society efficiently.

3. Eliminate our contribution to systematic physical degradation of nature through over harvesting, depletion, foreign introductions, and other forms of modification. This means drawing resources only from well-managed ecosystems, systematically pursuing the most productive and efficient use both of those resources and land, and exercising caution in all kinds of modification of nature.

4. Contribute as much as we can to the goal of meeting human needs in our society and worldwide, going over and above all the substitution and demateri-alization measures taken in meeting the first three objectives. This means using all of our resources efficiently, fairly, and responsibly so that the needs of all people on whom we have an impact, and the future needs of people who are not yet born, stand the best chance of being met.

The Natural Step also provides a methodology or framework. Simply described, there are four strategic levels to the framework.

1. Phase One: Building Awareness and Understanding
To be effective, decision makers and stakeholders must be working from a common understanding of sustainability and from a holistic understanding of the context.

2. Phase Two: Conducting a Baseline Assessment
Phase Two is the creation of a baseline or sustainability analysis of the major flows and impacts of a business or organizational system. Such a baseline identifies critical issues, their impact and, most importantly, the opportunities for change.

3. Phase Three: Creating a Vision and Strategic Plan
This phase would most likely be the most stimulating and challenging for designers. This is where key decision makers and stakeholders develop a persuasive vision accompanied with a strategic plan to address the issues identified in Phase Two. The true challenge is moving beyond an immediate solution

to an existing problem to one that effectively addresses long-term sustainability.

4. Phase Four: Supporting Effective, Step-by-Step Implementation
Follow-through is critical. A compelling vision and a credible strategy are meaningless if not implemented. This phase consists of two stages. First, means of implementation such as training, techniques, and tools are provided. Second, these need to be followed by the measurement of progress towards goals including modifications.

The Natural Step provides a rational and logical process with which we can recognize, measure, and address our environmental situation. And there is no reason why Designers cannot be part of the solution. At the very least, they should not be exacerbating the problem.

LEED
LEED is an acronym for the Leadership in Energy and Environmental Design. Developed in the United States by the Green Building Counsel, LEED "provides building owners and operators with a framework for identifying and implementing practical and measurable green building design, construction, operations and maintenance solutions."[xi] In other words, LEED provides a kind of toolkit for architects, designers, engineers, and builders who wish to implement a form of best practice in sustainable design, construction, and performance of buildings and similar structures. It is considered a benchmark for the design construction in the USA and is being used abroad more and more.

LEED recognizes that not all buildings are the same; consequently, these differences are reflected in the criteria for certification. The important ones are:

1. New Construction, which deals with new building construction, construction of core and shell only (i.e. structure, envelope, and HVAC), schools, buildings for retail, and healthcare.

2. Existing buildings, including their operations and maintenance. Existing buildings on a university campus would be a good example.

3. Commercial spaces, with a special focus on interiors that provide environments that are both healthy and productive. Office buildings fall into this category.

4. Retail spaces, equally with a special focus on interiors that provide environments that are both healthy and productive. Shopping malls fall into this category.

5. Existing healthcare facilities, especially renovated buildings as well as long-term care facilities, medical offices, and research centers.

6. Green Home Design and Construction, that is, standards that promote the design and construction of high-performance green homes.

LEED also focuses on the measurement of several key areas. Some of the important ones are:

1. Human and environmental health. This criterion is centered on the User interface aspects of the building.

2. Sustainable site development. The building and its site are interdependent. Consequently, attention must be paid to drainage, sunlight, erosion, and other similar site/building interfaces.

3. Water savings. Water, much like energy (below), is a significant factor when considering green building design. Buildings in the US are responsible for around 13% of water consumption.[xii]

4. Energy efficiency. Of all artifacts, buildings are among the ones that consume the most energy. According to the U.S. Green Building Council, "Buildings in the United States are responsible for 40% of energy consumption."[xiii]

5. Materials selection. The judicious selection of materials for a green building is obvious, but other factors need to be considered such as material life (how long will the material last under normal conditions?), transportation (what distance has the material traveled to get to the building site?), and possibility for recycling (can the material be recycled once it has been used?).

Furthermore, LEED provides certifications when buildings meet or exceed the criteria for a building type. The four standard are: certified, silver, gold, and platinum. Platinum is, of course the highest level. Buildings awarded these levels of standards often affix a plaque on the building to that affect.

LEED is a good first step in sustainable design for architecture and interior design, but it is not a panacea. For example, LEED is not mandatory; architects, developers and builders do not have to conform to LEED standards. Moreover, buildings designed to meet LEED standards may be more expensive, at least in the short term. This fact often deters people from applying LEED standards. In the long term, however, the costs drop as up-front investments in environmental systems are amortized.

Many experts are of the opinion that a true ecological appreciation cannot be assumed by way of LEED certification. In their concern, they see the LEED standards as a mere checklist for good environmental behavior. As a case in point, is an 8,000 sq. ft. house meant for two people sustainable, even if it has solar panels, bamboo floors, triple glazing, and meets LEED standards? That size of house for two people is not sustainable. Why? For the same reasons that you cannot use three pounds of fishmeal to produce only one pound of salmon.

ISO 1400 Environmental Management Standards
ISO is the abbreviated name for the International Organization of Standardization, a group composed of representatives from various national standards organizations and based in Geneva, Switzerland. Although its membership is voluntary, the ISO has an impact in most parts of the world. Its principal goal is the establishment

of worldwide commercial and manufacturing standards, which allows manufacturers from different countries and in different industrial sectors to integrate better their design, production, and distribution of their products. Simply stated, everyone is singing from the same hymnal, which is a principle that underpins globalization.

The ISO has created and promoted a great variety of standards. ISO 1400 Environmental Management Standards is one of these; it provides the basis for management of environmental standards and is the standard that most closely addresses issues of sustainability and how products are manufactured. It is commonly referred to as an Environmental Management System or EMS. Three principles underpin ISO 1400. They are: a) minimizing the environmental impact of production; b) compliance with existing environmental laws, standards, and guidelines; and c) continuous improvements of the first two principles. It should be noted that ISO 1400 does not address the design of products per se, but how products are manufactured.

As an environmental management tool, ISO 1400 provides four steps or phases in order to meet the goals of good environmental stewardship. These are:

- Plan—establish objectives and processes required: This first step requires a review and analysis of the existing production situation. That is, we need to know what the existing situation is in order to change it to a preferred one, which dictate the new goals and objectives.

- Do—implement the processes: The goals and objectives in the previous step now become the basis for a plan to make environmental management more effective. This may include a change in production and material, the purchasing of new manufacturing equipment, and the hiring of qualified personnel.

- Check—measure and monitor the processes and report results: The implementation of new processes and changes in production are meaningless if there isn't a feedback loop. It is imperative that that the changes are producing the desired results.

- Act—take action to improve performance of EMS based on results: Meeting a first level of changes is good; improving on these is even better. In fact, continuous improvement is one of the goals of ISO 1400.

Many of the world's leading manufacturers have incorporated ISO 1400 into their manufacturing operations. In North America (USA and Canada), for example, over 3,600 companies had met the standards of ISO 1400.[xiv] In Europe, the number was significantly higher—over 23,000 companies had met the standards.[xv]

Are Things Changing?
Critics of sustainable design, even within the design community, are quick to tell us that such a practice is not feasible or, worse, that it is too costly. And if that

isn't enough, they say there is not a large enough demand for everyday things produced using sound sustainable practice. Fortunately, patterns in the marketplace are beginning to tell a different story. Perhaps we are still in the early days of change, but if the following list of initiatives is any indication, there is good reason to believe that things in the corporate world are beginning to change.

- DuPont will remove and recycle carpet from a corporate office at no charge to the customer if new DuPont carpet is installed.

- Herman Miller, the office furniture manufacturer, has made a commitment to sustainable design. The Aeron chair, the company's most popular office chair, has a recyclable content that is close to 85 percent. Herman Miller's commitment to sustainable design goes beyond products. In attempting to deal with a pesky insect problem at their plant in The Netherlands, company officials were informed that bees would be just effective as pesticides in controlling these insects but more environmentally responsible. Beehives were installed and now visitors to the plant receive jars of honey.

- Even at its full selling price and with no rebates or dealer incentives, Toyota cannot keep up with consumer demand for its fuel-efficient hybrid Prius. Two years after the vehicle's launch, there was still a waiting list of around 22,000 eager buyers. In fact, Toyota was so caught off guard with the demand that in September 2004, it had to increase the production of the car three times to a level that now stands at 15,000 per month—twice the initial production quota.

In each of these cases, the companies demonstrated their understanding of the triple bottom line of good, sustainable practice: people, planet, and profit. For these leaders, the fiscal bottom line of the old business model is no longer enough.

Where there is a will, there is a way. When the tenets of Modernism first appeared, the idea of integrating aesthetic qualities at every level of design was unheard of. Today, it is common practice. Designers do it without even blinking. And this is what they must do about sustainable design. Designers must realize that they play one of the most important and critical roles in the stewardship of our planet. If Designers don't make design sustainable, who will?

Summary

Designing always included place, people, and process. It did at the time of the earliest stone tools much like it does today with cutting-edge technology. The elements have not changed. What has changed, however, is the role and interaction of each element. From a period when the Designer, Maker, and User were one person, we have gradually evolved to a point where the three players are independent but interact very much in an interdependent way. Remove or ignore any one of the three players and the other two are impacted—sometimes only minimally but at other times quite significantly. As we move forward in the twenty-first century, these interplays have three new rules of engagement.

First, place is no longer local but global. There is nothing new here, but the impact is greater than it has ever been and will only increase. Second, now is no longer here but everywhere. The concept of time being where we are is no longer important. Third, the concept of prescription, or autocracy in designing is giving way to a model more akin to subscription, or democracy, in which the User becomes an active participant in the designing process.

Further Reading

Diamond, Jared. *Collapse: How Societies Choose to Fail or Succeed*.

Friedman, Thomas. *The World Is Flat*.

Hamel, Gary. *The Future of Management*.

Kelley, Tom. *The Ten Faces of Innovation*.

McDonough, William, and Michael Braungart. *Cradle to Cradle: Remaking the Way We Make Things*.

McLuhan, Marshall. *Understanding Media: The Extensions of Man*.

Papanek, Victor. *Design for the Real World*. New York: Bantam Book, 1973.

——————. *The Green Imperative: Natural Design for the Real World*. New York: Thames and Hudson, 1995.

Pink, Daniel. *A Whole New Mind: Why Right-Brainers Will Rule the Future*.

Schumacher, E. F. *Small Is Beautiful: A Study of Economics as if People Mattered*. London: Abacus, 1974.

Surowiecki, James. *The Wisdom of Crowds*.

Swaback, Vernon D. *The Creative Community: Designing for Life*. Victoria, Australia: The Images Publishing Group, 2003.

Endnotes

[i] When countries such as Britain and the United States first began to export everyday things, they tended to do so to countries that had similar markets. For example, British auto manufacturers exported their cars to countries who shared a similar car culture. It was only with globalization that countries such as China began designing, making, and exporting everyday things that were not part of their own culture. For example, the Chinese manufacture and export Halloween decorations to the United States, despite the fact that few Chinese celebrate Halloween.

[ii] McDonough, William and Michael Braungart. *Cradle to Cradle: Remaking the Way We Make Things*.

[iii] Surowiecki, James. *The Wisdom of Crowds*.

[iv] Friedman, Thomas. *The World Is Flat*.

[v] Reprinted with permission of DuPont. ©2005. DuPont. All rights reserved.

[vi] As healthy as salmon may be it should be noted that some farmed salmon can have unacceptable levels of PCBs and dioxins.

[vii] Loos, Adolf. *Trotzdem, 1900–1930*. Wien: G. Prachner, 1982.

[viii] Lockwood, Charles. "Another Green World," *Hemispheres Magazine*, January 2005.

ix McKinney, Michael L. and Schoch, Robert M.
   Environmental science: systems and solutions.

x The Natural Step, www.naturalstep.org

xi http://www.usgbc.org/DisplayPage.aspx?CMSPageID
   =1988; accessed September 17, 2011.

xii http://www.usgbc.org/DisplayPage.aspx?CMSPageID
   =124; accessed September 17, 2011.

xiii Ibid

xiv http://earthtrends.wri.org/searchable_db/results
   .php?years=2002-2002&variable_ID=567&theme
   =5&cID=33,190&ccID=5; accessed August 25, 2011.

xv http://earthtrends.wri.org/searchable_db/results
   .php?years=2002-2002&variable_ID=567&theme
   =5&cID=10,16,17,24,28,45,48,50,59,62,63,70,73,83,
   84,89,91,103,108,109,111,117,131,138,146,147,151,152,
   161,162,166,173,174,187,189,202,209,222,223&ccID=2;
   accessed August 25, 2011.

CHAPTER 9

Designing Your Journey

Everyone is a Designer, or at least that is what was stated in chapter 1. As we have already learned, the capability to design is a human quality. Everyone can design to some degree or other. Children do it all the time, as do adolescents and adults. However, we have also come to recognize that some people do it more often and certainly do it better than most. These are the people who we call Designers. This section of the book will explore the options and directions in the transformation of the amateur Designer, who resides in each one of us, to the many types of professional Designers in contemporary society. Let's begin by getting some sense of the design professions, especially the more common ones such as architecture, landscape architecture, industrial design, interior design, visual communication design, and engineering.

Is Designing the Same for All Design Professions?
There are Designers of all types. They range from floral Designers at a flower shop in a local mall to the architect and engineer who designed the mall in the first place.

Clearly, the design activity associated with floral design is very different from the one associated with the design of a building. Yet, there continues to be a perception that designing is designing, whether it is the designing of a corporate image for a multinational, the interior of a hotel's lobby, or the housing for a laptop computer. While this attitude of a one-size-fits-all design may have been possible one hundred years ago when our world was technologically much simpler, it is certainly not the case today. The different areas in which we find design as a principal activity—fashion, automotive, interior, branding, architecture, aviation, medical devices, etc.—have become too diverse, too complex and too challenging for this generalist approach. This being the case, how is a person educated and trained to be a Designer for these and other areas? There are several approaches to consider.

The professions that have designing as a central focus of their activity is a long one. For our purpose, the list will be reduced. We will examine more closely architecture, landscape architecture, industrial design, interior design, visual communication design, and several branches of engineering. Together, these professions are responsible for the design of most of our built environment—from our houses and cities to laptops and airplanes.

As a group, many design professions—especially architects, landscape architects, industrial designers, interior designers, and visual communication designers—share a similar set of skills and body of knowledge. In fact, there is a strong philosophical and pedagogical lineage—a kind of mutual design DNA—among all of these design professions. Fine arts is even part of this DNA. Architecture, for example, is often perceived as the definitive expression of the fine arts—the ultimate sculpture, if you will. As we learned in chapter 6 when discussing Modernism, there is a close connection between fine arts and design because of the way art and design evolved over centuries, from craftsmen and artisans to early designers and architects, most originating from various movements in fine arts (Figure 9.1).

Design education, both in Europe and in North America, followed the path charted by the fine arts. For example, the earliest schools of design in England such as the Normal School of Art (now the Royal College of Art) were educating designers in the ways of the artist or craftsman. During the same era, Henry Cole, the English design activist, perceived design as an alliance between fine arts and manufacturing. Much the same direction developed in France with l'École des arts décoratifs, fundamentally a school of decorative arts, and in Germany with the Bauhaus, an institution with an arts-and-crafts foundation. In the United States, the pattern did not stray much from the European model. Most design programs were situated and nurtured within schools of art. By the time the 1950s rolled around, design education was well ensconced in the domains philosophically occupied by architecture and the fine arts.

Most schools of design in the US still function within an arts environment. This is certainly the case with The Design School at Arizona State University. It is situated in the Herberger Institute for Design and the Arts. So are the design schools at Carnegie Mellon University, the Ohio State University, and Pratt Institute. However, there are many schools of design that function outside the arts. This is certainly the case with The D School at Stanford University, which is a stand-alone school, and several industrial design programs found in engineering such as the ones at the TU Delft (The Netherlands), the University of Leeds (UK), and Carleton University (Canada). There are even MBA programs with a strong design bias such as the one at the University of Toronto. Schools of architecture as well as schools of engineering are somewhat different from schools of design; it is not at all unusual for these design professions to be located in dedicated colleges.

Given this early evolution in the arts, most design professions now share similar intrinsic design values, or ethos. These values underpin the designing activity and are present in almost every design, although not in equal measure. The shared values are:

- Delta Knowledge: Delta Knowledge is a type of knowledge based on the notion of modeling what does not yet exist. This is what Designers do a

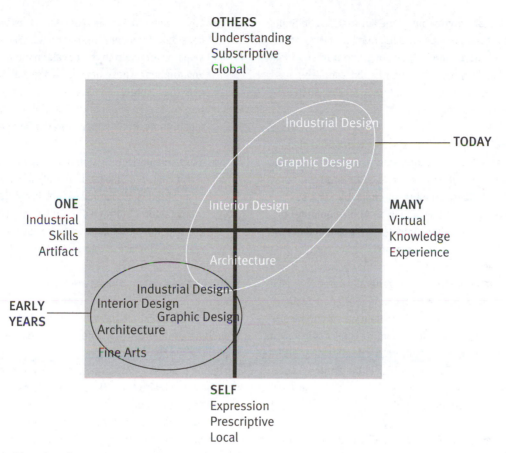

OTHERS
Understanding
Subscriptive
Global

Industrial Design

Graphic Design

———— **TODAY**

ONE
Industrial
Skills
Artifact

Interior Design

MANY
Virtual
Knowledge
Experience

Architecture

**EARLY
YEARS**

Industrial Design
Interior Design
Graphic Design
Architecture
Fine Arts

SELF
Expression
Prescriptive
Local

Figure 9.1: Situating the Design Disciplines

great deal of the time; that is, they imagine and model a new reality.

- A Visual Language: Designers make constant use of visual language as a form of communication.

The visual language was discussed at length in chapter 2.

- Aesthetic Codes: Historically, many early Designers were members of groups—such as the

Deutscher Werkbund, the Futurists, or de Stijl—
that were established to create and promote
specific aesthetic codes or standards, commonly
called styles. The same phenomenon—or
some aspects of it—continues today, such as
Postmodernism.

- Self-expression: Most Designers would also
  agree that self-expression—whether explicitly,
  such as self-expression in a Ron Arad chair or
  Frank Gehry building, or implicitly, such as
  corporate-expression in an Apple computer or
  a Herman Miller chair—is important and is part
  of the shared design ethos.

- Innovation: Designers generally agree that innovation is an essential element of good design,
  whether we are talking about an ergonomically
  sound power drill, an inviting retail environment,
  or an inventive solution to a public transportation
  challenge. Copying, which is the antithesis of
  innovation, is reviled by Designers; it is generally
  considered unacceptable.

- Human Context: There is always a human context
  in design, one other than the one that the
  Designer brings. Users have always been central
  in the designing activity, but this has become
  even more significant with the advent of Universal
  Design[i] and user-centered[ii] research within the
  unbridled freedom of choice that exists in the
  marketplace.

- Environmental Factors: For design, environmental
  considerations are centered on the direct responsibilities attached to the development of the built
  environment. These have grown exponentially
  over the last few decades as the world's population continues to expand, material consumption
  mushrooms, but within a world of finite resources.

- Economic Impact: Design plays an important and
  significant role in local, national, and global economic arenas. Economic growth is a reflection of
  many factors, but high on the list are building
  construction and manufacturing output, both of
  which are inextricably attached to designing.

Together, these design values are the glue that binds
various design disciplines together (see Figure 9.2).
Over time, these values have not dramatically changed.
What have dramatically changed are the operational
imperatives in the designing activity itself—how the
designing process is undertaken and how designs
become available to the ultimate User. These changes
have been remarkable since around the 1960s, when
designing began going mainstream. That said, the
modes of operation for architecture, landscape architecture, interior design, and fine arts have not shifted as
radically over the same period of time—all four disciplines continue to operate in a kind of one-off, top-down
model. By contrast, design, especially industrial and
graphic design, now function in a very different operational world. In the end, one-off production and top-
down considerations continue, but mass production and

	Delta Knowledge	Visual Language	Aesthetic Codes	Self-expression	Innovation	Human Context	Environmental Factors	Economic Impact
Architecture	●	●	●	●	●	●	●	●
Graphic Design	●	●	●	●	●	●	●	●
Industrial Design	●	●	●	●	●	●	●	●
Interior Design	●	●	●	●	●	●	●	●

Figure 9.2: **Same Ethos;** Different Operations

a bottom-up approach have now become as important and relevant.

That was not always the case, however. Mass production, mass merchandising, and a user-driven agenda were not the operational concerns of the industrial and graphic designers who created the professional practice of design in the 1850s and the years thereafter. Early Designers often came from architecture, fine arts, set design, and the crafts. Most of them designed in a way that was similar to their first profession. For example, products and furniture often became nothing more than small-scale buildings. Some of Frank Lloyd Wright's furniture reflected his architectural bias toward small-scale objects. Today, this approach is no longer appropriate

(see Figure 9.3). While many of design's intrinsic values remain relevant, many of design's operational methods have changed. They include:

- One-off versus Mass Production: One of the most notable operational differences between architecture and interior design, on one hand, and graphic and industrial design, on the other, is the volume of production. Architecture and interior design almost always deal with one-off production; graphic design and industrial design most often do not. The design parameters implied by mass production are very different from the one-off model. Mass production imposes a set of operational imperatives that, from the beginning,

	One-off	Mass Production	Mobile	Immobile	Dimensional Tolerances	Artifact Life	Market Cost	Making Cost
Architecture	●			●	Low	Long	High	Low
Graphic Design		●	●		High	Short	Low	Med
Industrial Design		●	●		High	Short	Low	High
Interior Design	●			●	Low	Med	Med	Low

Figure 9.3: Same Ethos; **Different Operations**

situates the designer in a completely different creative realm. It is no wonder that many of today's designer chairs are very expensive and made in limited numbers. Most continue to be the result of the one-off operational model of architecture and fine arts.

- Mobile/Immobile: Working drawings for an interior or a building often have some reference to north as a cardinal point. Why? Because the building's location on the site is critically important. It positions the building with respect to the rising and setting of the sun, a factor that determines both the quality of light and the solar heat generated in the building. As valid as these concerns are for architects and interior designers,

they are irrelevant in the normal designing activities of industrial and graphic designers. The rising and the setting of the sun have no impact whatsoever on the site location of smart phones or books. In fact, site location—as a permanent location—is not an issue.

Moreover, mobile/immobile can mean much more for some Designers. It can directly impact the making or building processes. In the United States, for example, there are thousands of homebuilders, some small and others large. Consequently, a homebuilder can be found in nearly every town and certainly in every city. The same cannot be said for automobile manufacturers or the manufacturers of most other everyday things. There are more cars than homes in the United States, yet there are only three major American car manufacturers. Why? Because cars and other mobile everyday things can be designed in one place, manufactured in a second, and then shipped to a third. The majority of homes cannot.

- Dimensional Tolerance: Most interior designers and architects are extremely pleased if a wall is built to within one-half inch of the prescribed dimension. For graphic and industrial design, such a dimensional tolerance is unacceptable. In graphic design, the tolerance for spatial error is much finer. For example, if the words HAT and RED are spaced far apart, they form two distinct words; placed closer together, they become HATRED, a word with no connection at all to either HAT or RED. And what about a piston in the engine of a modern car? The engineer has to work within dimensional tolerances of thousandths of an inch, not one-half.

The effects of dimensional tolerances can also exceed mere physical boundaries. The concept of dimensional tolerance can have a contextual or emotional fit. As Professor John Meunier, former Dean of the College of Architecture and Environmental Design at Arizona State University, contends, "Architecture is about long life and loose fit; interior design is about short life and tight fit." In other words, architects have to design buildings in such a way that they can have the capacity for several design iterations in their spaces. Think about it. Commercial spaces in buildings can be restaurants one year and a beauty salons the next. The building hasn't changed, but the spaces within it have.

- Artifact Life: Most buildings have a life span of fifty years or more, whereas most everyday things do not. This is especially the case in the computer industry, where products come and go in the space of twelve to eighteen months. The implicit long life in architecture cannot be assumed for most other kinds of designs; and the operational methods associated with long-life artifacts may or may not be relevant to short-life artifacts.

- The Market Cost: The market cost of an everyday thing is what it costs the User to acquire it. It is financially much easier to buy a new iPhone app than it is to buy a new house. Kids can buy smart phone apps every day, but not houses. Not only that, most consumers own more smartphone apps than houses. The cost of any everyday thing therefore plays a direct role in the consumption of any everyday thing. As self-evident as this logic may seem, the ramifications of this distinction are not self-evident. Over time, consumers will acquire and dispose of more inexpensive everyday things than costly ones. And this pattern affects every aspect of the designing process, from user behavior and designing to making and disposal. Nothing goes untouched. For designers it also means that architects and interior designers tend to deal with artifacts of higher market costs whereas graphic and industrial designers focus on artifacts with lower market costs.

- The Making Cost: The User rarely ever knows the indirect costs associated with the making of an everyday thing but for the Designer and the Maker, they are significant. Indirect costs include expenditures such as overheads and investments required to make the everyday thing in the first place. In some sectors, such as the building industry, the indirect costs are relatively low compared with the market cost of the finished product; in the automotive industry, indirect costs are exceptionally high. A conventional homebuilder, for example, needs to invest only moderate sums to construct houses, such as the cost of a backhoe and an onsite trailer. For the automobile manufacturer, the tooling costs for a new car can easily be in the hundreds of millions of dollars.

Over time, design professions have evolved; they have continued to share some aspects of their identity all the while changing others. That said, the design ethos has remained more similar than different. Generally speaking, the design disciplines still make extensive use of the visual language, and aesthetic codes and self-expression continue to be important.

What has changed, however, are the operational models in design. In some cases, these have become dramatically different. As a case in point, one-off designs are very different from designs for mass production.

Consequently, the design approach that an architect takes in designing a unique building will be different from the automotive designer creating a mass-produced car or the visual communication designer developing a web site.

Keep in mind that in no way should these differences be perceived as a criticism of the operational models of one design discipline or another. The operational models for architecture, for example, are extremely well suited for this discipline. Nevertheless, architecture's operational model may not be suited at all for graphic design. New ones—ones that are more appropriate to each discipline—have evolved and taken the place of what existed in the past. This evolution is not at all surprising; if anything, it is completely natural.

Are there exceptions to this general rule of discipline-specific operational models? Of course there are. But even these exceptions follow certain rules. Frank Gehry was educated as an architect and was mentioned earlier in the book. His claim to fame is his many innovative buildings, such as the Guggenheim Museum in Balboa (Spain) and the Disney Concert Hall in Los Angeles. Gehry has also designed chairs and jewelry. Was he educated as a furniture designer or as a jeweler? Not explicitly. What Gehry did was modify the operational methods of architecture, add some personal ingenuity, and apply these to two new domains: furniture and jewelry. Could he do the same and design a jumbo jet? Or a high-speed train? Most likely not, or at least not in a substantive way. The design of jets and trains is operationally very dissimilar to the design of buildings.

It's All About Change

Besides these ethical and operational premises, what else do you need to consider when creating your personal design journey? Having a good sense of the context of design in the future is critically relevant because designing will be different ten years from now than it is today. As we are obviously aware, the world is in a constant state of change. And design is no exception. Consequently, any action on your part needs to be conditioned by two types of changes: those are occurring now and that can be integrated relatively easily into your plans; and those that may occur in the future, which are not as well defined and therefore require some judicious speculation on your part. In the end, the goal is to connect the dots, so to speak.

Let's begin with the notion of change. Charles Darwin, the English naturalist who proposed the evolutionary theory of natural selection, best situated change for living species. He considered natural selection in animal species to be the result of adaptability to place over an extended periods of time. From his perspective and in the context of your designing journey, your ability to adapt to change as your working environment changes will most likely be the most significant factor for success. It will not be a high GPA or a more expensive computer or deep financial pockets, but your ability to change. More importantly, the last thing that you will want to do is to resist change. You will want to engage it, take advantage of it, and even initiate change.

Furthermore, change is more than a localized condition. Change is a global phenomenon and affects everyone.

How does this globalization of change impact your designing journey? Daniel Pink, the author of *A Whole New Mind*, best described the situation when he observed that if it can be done faster, computers will do it, and if it can be done cheaper, it will be sent offshore. In other words, don't rely on today's design skills as an indicator of what will be in demand tomorrow. Model making, which for a long time was a staple as a manual skill for industrial designers, is now being done by computers via 3-D printing. Much like a great deal of graphic design is now totally dependent on computers. And more and more basic design work, including software programming and technical drawing, is being done offshore by very competent engineers and designers and at a much reduced cost. Lesson 1: Embrace change.

What to Do?

With change as a common platform, where do we go next? Are there other steps that need to be considered? The answer is yes. There are several steps, beginning with a most logical one: what design discipline do you wish to pursue? Is it interior design? Or architecture? Or graphic design? As logical and psychologically comforting as this question appears to be, you may have already forgotten the previous lesson on change. Why? Because no one knows if these design professions will even exist in ten years. What we do know, however, is that societal challenges such as housing or transportation or healthcare will continue to exist. In part, this may be the reason why Barbara Morgan,[iii] the NASA teacher astronaut, has changed the question she often asked of her high school students. It is no longer, "What do you want to be?" Instead, she now asks, "What do you want to do?"

Morgan realized that our career focus should be centered on issues, which are greater in scope and offer more possibilities than a mere vocation. Societal issues such as housing, transportation, poverty, and the environment will not go away. In her opinion, looking at issues first and then acquiring the skills and knowledge to resolve them makes more sense then merely picking a profession that may no longer exist in ten years. It also provides the future designer with a greater mission or purpose.

IDEO is one of the world's largest and most effective design consultancies. It too is concerned about what needs to be done rather than the validation of one design profession over another. In this respect, IDEO uses very different terms when referring to the designer and the designing process; terms such as the Anthropologist, the Director, the Storyteller, the Hurdler, and the Collaborator. These terms all denote what these people do and not some narrow definition of territory within design such as graphic design, interior design, and industrial design. Lesson 2: It's about knowing what you want to do.

Moving Upstream

The designing and making of almost anything—automobiles, electronic equipment, structures, and airplanes—includes many participants, from the executives who manage the business at the upstream end of the operation to the people on the assembly line or building site at the downstream end. Traditional design is usually located somewhere in the middle. Should it remain there? Or should it consider moving? And if it does consider moving, should it move downstream or upstream? Moving downstream means that designing comes closer to the making process. This direction is very comforting to many designers because there is a hands-on quality to designing. However, moving downstream comes at a cost. First, downstream activities provide the least possibilities for a designer to affect change. Second, many downstream activities are either being done by computer or being sent offshore. Let's not forget what Daniel Pink stated above. Therefore, design needs to move upstream if it is to be an active part of change. There is no reason that a designer cannot be the CEO of a corporation. Or, as it is happening in many companies, with the Chief Design Officer, such as Jonathan Ive at Apple or Todd Wood at Research in Motion. Both Ive and Wood were educated as designers. In principle, there is no reason why a designer cannot be at the corporate helm. Lawyers and businesspeople do it all the time.

To be at the helm comes with certain conditions, however. It will mean that Designers will have to move beyond the narrowness implicit in their design education and adopt an interdisciplinary, if not a transdisciplinary, approach. No longer will more courses in color, typography, history and even CAD be sufficient for upstream design success. Instead, designers will need to be well versed in subject areas such as psychology, business, marketing, and finance, as well as operational areas like research, sustainable design, and computer simulation. Lesson 3: Move upstream.

Soft As Well As Hard Skills

Most of the design skills taught in schools of architecture, design, and engineering are what psychologist call *hard* skills. That is, they are skills that can be quantified and measured. However, they are not necessarily difficult to master, as the word hard erroneously implies. What are some of these *hard* skills? Obvious ones are computer skills by way of applications such as AutoCAD and PhotoShop. There are other *hard* skills, such materials and processes for industrial designers and achieving LEED certification for some graduate architecture students. To one degree or another these skills are all measureable, and terminate in a grade of some kind. That grade becomes part of a student's grade point average (GPA), which is the holy grail of *hard* skills.

As well entrenched and as desirable as this desire for *hard* skills may be, the reality in the workplace is that *soft* skills are often deemed to be a better gauge of career success. What are soft skills? They include communication, collaboration, critical thinking, and cooperation, which, amusingly enough, are not often taught in schools of architecture, design or engineering. Moreover, students become focused, if not obsessed with their GPA, which is essentially a measure of *hard* skills. And why not? Surely, a student with a high GPA will always have the upper hand when seeking a job, will they not? Not always. Perhaps that is the case in areas like engineering and law, but design? An extremely reputable communication design firm recently hired the top graduate from a well respected graphic design program. The person lasted only three months on the job. Why? Because the employees of the firm always work in teams. Consequently, cooperation and collaboration are essential skills. Like many graduates of design schools, the new employee had been trained in the fine-art tradition of design; that is, self-expression. In his four years at uni-

versity, he had never worked in a team, and therefore never learned the *soft* skills of cooperation and collaboration. Lesson 4: Over time, *soft* skills will outlast *hard* skills.

There Is No Easy Path

It is easy to believe that successful people like Bill Gates of Microsoft fame were in the right place at the right time, and that his abilities were some fortunate combination of innate talent, fate and happenstance. On second thought, is success really all about innate talent? Or being at the right place at the right time? There is no simple answer to these questions, but there is insight from studies undertaken about highly successful people.

Malcolm Gladwell, the author of *Outliers: The Story of Success*, relates the stories of successful people and how they became successful. Despite the diversity of professions exemplified by the individuals mentioned—from musicians and athletes to scientists and computer programmers—two qualities surfaced as the prime reasons for success.

First, being born in the right era does have some credence. For example, Gladwell points out that it may not be a coincidence after all that Bill Joy, Bill Gates, Steve Jobs, and Eric Schmidt—individuals who all became leaders in the computer revolution of the 1980s—were all born in 1955. Paul Allen, who was a founder of Microsoft, was born in 1953, just two years earlier. Significant societal changes, such as the computer revolution, occur at specific times in history. To directly take part in that change, it certainly helps to be the appropriate age. Had

Joy, Gates, Jobs, Schmidt, and Allen been born ten years later, we would probably not know them.

Unfortunately for you, you cannot control the year that you were born and what societal changes will occur ten, twenty or thirty years from now. But you do have control over the second quality that was discovered about successful people. In the many studies cited by Gladwell in his book, one trait stood out time and again with successful people. The trait was 10,000 hours. That is, successful musicians, athletes, scientist and, dare I say, designers, became successful not because of innate talent but sheer hard work. In other words, successful musicians, athletes, scientists and designers may begin with some innate talent, but what ultimately differentiates them from others is hard work, and lots of it. Lesson 5: 10,000 Hours

Employer or Employee?

Generally speaking, contemporary public education, including the establishment of modern colleges and universities, was mostly the result of industrialization. That is, industrialization created a need for educated workers and employees. As a result, academic programs of one kind or another were established to provide employers with a qualified work force. Therefore, it is not surprising that, generally speaking, higher education is underpinned with an ethos that is employee biased. That is to say, schools, colleges, and universities educate people to become productive workers, i.e., employees.

Such a direction was definitely valid in the age of industrialization, an age defined by the making of everyday things. That age, however, is no longer what it used to be, at least not in many of the developed countries including the US. Go to Wal-Mart or walk through a BMW dealership or visit IKEA and you will soon see that most of our everyday things are no longer made here. Being educated to be a future employee should not be immediately dismissed, but neither should the alternative: being educated to be an employer. And in this regard, please do not wait for the colleges and universities to take the first step in educating you as an employer. A few institutions have by providing courses and programs in entrepreneurship. But the initiative ultimately rests with you. As a design student, you must seek out those courses and those academic experiences that will direct your focus towards entrepreneurship. In the end, you and only you are responsible for the steps that you take to become an entrepreneur. Lesson 6: Employer or employee: it's your choice.

A Few Last Words

Projecting into the future is always risky; it certainly does not come with guarantees of any kind. No one knows what will happen tomorrow, let alone ten years from now. If there is one guarantee, however, it is that tomorrow will be different from today. This being the case, how do we survive, let alone thrive, in our personal design journey? Darwin gave us a first clue earlier: change is a constant; it's as inevitable as day and night. Therefore, meet it on its terms by changing yourself .

Further Reading

Blaich, Robert, and Janet Blaich. *Product Design and Corporate Strategy*. New York: McGraw-Hill, 1993.

Gladwell, Malcolm. *Outliers: The Story of Success*, New York: Little, Brown and Company, 2008.

Kelley, Tom. *Ten Faces of Innovation*. New York: Currency Doubled Day, 2005.

Pink, Daniel. *A Whole New Mind: Why Right-Brainers Will Rule the Future*. New York: The Berkeley Publishing Group, 2006.

Endnotes

[i] Universal Design is a design direction that evolved as the result of the Americans with Disabilities Act (ADA) of 1990. Because the ADA required that public buildings and places be accessible by all people, certain features of buildings had to be modified or designed anew. As a case in point, people in wheelchairs had to have access to public buildings. Whereas stairs would have been sufficient prior to the ADA, now ramps or other means of entry must be provided as well.

[ii] Generally speaking, user-centered research is focused on the observation and the subsequent revelations that come from studying Users in context. For some Designers, however, user-centered research is anathema to the traditional design process because the needs of the Users appear to precede the self-expression of the Designer. For these Designers, such a design direction is tantamount to putting the carriage before the horse.

[iii] Barbara Morgan is a high school teacher and a NASA teacher astronaut. She visited the International Space Station in August 2007.

Bibliography

Adler, Mortimer J. *Six Great Ideas.* New York: Macmillan Publishing, 1981.

Alexander, Christopher. *Notes on the Synthesis of Form.* Cambridge, MA: Harvard University Press, 1964.

Ambaz, Emilio. *Italy: The New Domestic Landscape.* New York: The Museum of Modern Art, 1972.

Banham, Reyner. *Theory and Design of the First Machine Age.* Cambridge, MA: The MIT Press, 1980.

Basalla, George. *The Evolution of Technology,* Cambridge, UK, The Cambridge University Press, 1988.

Baxter, Mike. *Product Design: A Practical Guide to Systematic Methods of New Product Development.* London: Chapman & Hall, 1995.

Bayley, Stephen, ed. *The Conran Directory of Design.* New York: Villard Books, 1985.

Benedict, Ruth. *The Chrysanthemum and the Sword,* London: Rutledge and Kegan Paul Ltd., 1967.

Birdsall, Derek, and Carlo M. Cipolla. *The Technology of Man.* London: Wildwood House, 1980.

Blaich, Robert, and Janet Blaich. *Product Design and Corporate Strategy.* New York: McGraw-Hill, 1993.

Blake, Peter. *Form Follows Fiasco: Why Modern Architecture Hasn't Worked.* Boston: Little, Brown & Company, 1977.

Branzi, Andrea. *The Hot House: Italian New Wave Design.* Cambridge, MA: The MIT Press, 1984.

Bryant, Kathleen M. *Stories in Stone,* in *Arizona Highways.* Phoenix: August 1999.

Burchell, S. C. *Age of Progress.* New York: Time-Life Books, 1960.

Bush, Donald J. *The Streamlined Decade.* New York: George Braziller, 1975.

Caplan, Ralph. *By Design.* New York: Fairchild Publications, 2005.

Carr, Geoffrey. *The Story of Man: The Proper Study of Mankind.* London: The Economist, December 24, Christmas Survey, pp. 3-12.

Coulton, J. J. *Ancient Greek Architects at Work: Problems of Structure and Design.* Ithaca, NY: Cornell University Press, 1977

de Bono, Edward. *The Mechanism of Mind.* Harmondsworth, UK: Penguin Books, 1973.

Diamond, Jared, *Guns, Germs, and Steel: The Fates of Human Societies.* New York: W. W. Norton, 1997.

_____ *Collapse: How Societies Choose to Fail or Succeed*. New York: Penguin Books, 2005.

Design Center Stuttgart. *Mobel aus Italien*. Stuttgart, Germany: Design Center, 1983.

Dorfles, Gillo. *Kitsch: The World of Bad Taste*. New York: Universe Books, 1968.

Dormer, Peter. *Design Since 1945*. London: Thames and Hudson, 1993.

Dreyfuss, Henry. *Designing for People*. New York: Simon and Schuster, 1955.

Edwards, Betty. *Drawing on the Right Side of the Brain*. Los Angeles: Jeremy P. Tarcher Inc., 1989

Eidelberg, Martin, ed. *Design 1935-1965: What Modern Was*. New York: Harry N. Abrams, 1991.

Ekuan, Kenjii. Japanese Design and Modern Technology in *DD Bulletin*. Copenhagen: Danish Design Council, June 1982.

Ferebee, Ann. *A History of Design from the Victorian Era to the Present*. New York: Van Nostrand Reinhold, 1980.

Friedman, Thomas. *The World Is Flat: A Brief History of the Twenty-First Century*. New York: Picador, 2007.

Garrison, Webb. *445 Fascinating Word Origins*. New York: First Galahad Books, 2001.

Gay, Peter. *Age of Enlightenment*. New York: Time-Life Books, 1960.

Giard, Jacques. *Design FAQs*. Phoenix: The Dorset Group, 2005.

Giedion, Siegfried. *Mechanization Takes Command*. New York: W. W. Norton, 1969.

Gilles, Wim. *The Context of Industrial Product Design*. Ottawa: Carleton University Press, 1999.

Gladwell, Malcolm. *Outliers: The Story of Success*. New York: Little, Brown & Company, 2008.

Greenough, Horatio. *Form and Function*. Berkeley, CA: University of California Press, 1947.

Grillo, Paul Jacques. *Form, Function and Design*. New York: Dover Publications, 1975.

Hall, Edward T. *The Silent Language*. New York: Anchor Books, 1959.

_____. *The Hidden Dimension*. New York: Anchor Books, 1966.

_____. *Beyond Culture*. New York: Anchor Books, 1976.

_____. *The Dance of Life*. New York: Anchor Books, 1983.

Hamel, Gary. *The Future of Management*. Boston: Harvard Business School Press, 2007.

Heskett, John. *Industrial Design*. New York: Oxford University Press, 1980.

Hiesenger, Kathryn B. *Design Since 1945*. Philadelphia: Philadelphia Museum of Art, 1983.

Hollis, Richard. *Graphic Design*. London: Thames and Hudson, 2001.

Horn, Richard. *Memphis: Objects, Furniture, and Patterns*. Philadelphia: Running Press, 1985.

Huygen, Frederique. *British Design: Image & Identity*. London: Thames and Hudson, 1989.

Ikko, Tannaka, and Koike Kazuko, ed., *Japan Design*. San Francisco: Chronicle Books, 1984.

Jones, John Chris. *Design Methods,* 2nd ed. New York: Van Nostrand Reinhold, 1992.

Julier, Guy. *Dictionary of Twentieth Century Design and Designers*. London: Thames and Hudson, 1993.

Kelley, Tom. *The Ten Faces of Innovation*. New York: Currency Doubleday, 2005.

Kubler, George. *The Shape of Time: Remarks on the History of Things*. New Haven, CT: Yale University Press, 1962.

Levitt, Steven D. and Stephen J. Dubner. *Freakonomics: A Rogue Economist Explores the Hidden Side of Everything*, New York: William Morrow, 2005.

Lidwell, William, Kristina Holden, and Jill Butler. *Universal Principles of Design*. Gloucester, MA: Rockport Publishers, 2003.

Lister, Robert H. and Florence C. Lister. *Those Who Came Before*. Tucson, AZ: Western National Parks Association, 1993.

Loewy, Raymond. *Never Leave Well Enough Alone*. Baltimore, MD: Johns Hopkins University Press, 2002.

Lynes, Russell. *The Tastemakers: The Shaping of American Popular Taste*. New York: Dover Publications, 1980.

Mang, Karl. *The History of Modern Furniture*. London: Academy Editions, 1979.

MacCarthy, Fiona. *British Design Since 1880*. London: Lund Humphries, 1982.

Massey, Anne. *Interior Design of the Twentieth Century*. London: Thames and Hudson, 2001.

McClellan III, James E., and Harold Dorn. *Science and Technology in World History*, Baltimore, MA: The Johns Hopkins University Press, 1999.

McCracken, Grant. *Culture and Consumption*. Bloomington, IN: Indiana University Press, 1988.

McDonough, William, and Michael Braungart. *Cradle to Cradle: Remaking the Way We Make Things*. New York: North Point Press, 2002.

McFadden, David Revere, ed. *Scandinavian Modern Design: 1880-1980*. New York: Harry N. Abrams Inc., 1982.

McLuhan, Marshall. *Understanding Media: The Extensions of Man*. New York: Signet Book, 1964.

_____ and Quentin Fiore. *The Medium Is the Massage: An Inventory of Effects*. New York: Bantam Books, 1967.

Meggs, Phillip B. *A History of Graphic Design*. New York: John Wiley and Sons, 1998.

Mitchell, C. Thomas. *Redefining Designing: From Form to Experience*. New York: Van Nostrand Reinhold, 1993.

Morris, Desmond. *The Naked Ape*. London: Corgi Books,1969.

_____. *The Human Zoo*. London: Corgi Books, 1971.

Newton, Eric. *The Meaning of Beauty*. New York: Penguin, 1967.

Norman, Donald A., *The Design of Everyday Things*. New York: Basic Books, 2002.

_____. *Emotional Design: Why We Love (or Hate) Everyday Things*. New York: Basic Books, 2004.

Ortiz, Simon. *A Good Journey*. Turtle Island, 1977.

Pacey, Arnold. *Technology in World Civilization*, Cambridge, MA: MIT Press, 1991

Papanek, Victor. *Design for the Real World*. New York: Bantam Book, 1973.

_____. *The Green Imperative: Natural Design for the Real World*. New York: Thames and Hudson, 1995.

Petroski, Henry. *The Evolution of Useful Things*. New York: Vintage Books, 1992.

Pevsner, Nikolaus. *The Sources of Modern Architecture and Design*. New York: Oxford University Press, 1968.

_____. *Pioneers of Modern Design*. Middlesex, UK: Penguin Books, 1981.

Pile, John F. *Design: Purpose, Form and Meaning*. New York: W. W. Norton, 1979.

Pile, John. *A History of Interior Design*. New York: John Wiley & Sons, 2000.

Pink, Daniel. *A Whole New Mind: Why Right-Brainers Will Rule the Future*. New York: The Berkeley Publishing Group, 2006.

Postrel, Virginia. *The Substance of Style*. New York: HarperCollins, 2003.

Pulos, Arthur J. *American Design Ethic*. Cambridge, MA: The MIT Press, 1983.

_____. *The American Design Adventure*. Cambridge, MA: The MIT Press, 1988.

Pye, David. *The Nature and Aesthetics of Design*. New York: Van Nostrand Reinhold, 1982.

Raizman, David. *History of Modern Design*. Upper Saddle River, NJ: Prentice Hall, 2004.

Rybczynski, Witold. *Home: A Short History of an Idea*. New York: Penguin Books, 1986.

_____. *One Good Turn: A Natural History of the Screwdriver and the Screw*, New York: Scribner, 2000.

Oliver Sacks. *An Anthropologist on Mars: Seven Paradoxical Tales*, New York: Vintage, 1995.

Schumacher, E. F. *Small Is Beautiful: A Study of Economics as if People Mattered*. London: Abacus, 1974.

Simon, Herbert. *The Sciences of the Artificial* (3rd edition). Cambridge, MA: The MIT Press, 1996.

Surowiecki, James. *The Wisdom of Crowds*. New York: Anchor Books, 2005.

Sparke, Penny. *Ettore Sottsass Jnr*. London: The Design Council, 1982.

_____. *An Introduction to Design & Culture in the Twentieth Century*. London: Allen & Unwin, 1986.

Sprigg, June and David Sprigg. *Shaker Life, Work, and Art*. New York: Stewart, Tabori and Chang, 1987.

Swaback, Vernon D. *The Creative Community: Designing for Life*. Victoria, Australia: The Images Publishing Group, 2003.

Tenner, Edward. *Our Own Devices: How Technology Remakes Humanity*, New York: Vintage Books, 2004.

Thybony, Scott. *Canyon de Chelly National Monument*. Tucson, AZ: Western National Parks Association, 1997.

Tilley, Alvin R. *The Measure of Man and Woman: Human Factors in Design*. New York: John Wiley & Sons, 2002.

Venturi, Robert, Denise Scott Brown, and Steven Izenour. *Learning from Las Vegas*. Cambridge, MA: The MIT Press, 1972.

Von Vegesack, Alexander, ed. *100 Masterpieces from the Vitra Design Museum Collection*. Weil-am-Rhein, Germany: Vitra Design Museum, 1996.

Wilk, Christopher. *Thonet: 150 Years of Furniture*. New York: Barrons, 1980.

Wingler, Hans M. *The Bauhaus*. Cambridge, MA: The MIT Press, 1969.

Wolfe, Tom. *From Bauhaus to Our House*. New York: Farrar, Straus and Giroux, 1981.

Woodham, Jonathan M. *Twentieth-Century Design*. New York: Oxford University Press, 1997.

Yoshida, Mitsukuni, et al. *Japanese Style*. New York: Kodansha, 1980.

Lexicon

Many books include a glossary. *Design FAQs*, my first book, did not. Rather, it provided the reader with a lexicon. This was done because the term lexicon refers to words that are part of our language, in this case, the Designer's language. Design is no different from other professions; it has developed a language particular to its needs and peculiarities. Consequently, access to the profession often begins by learning the appropriate language, or the lexicon.

Aesthetics is an area of study in philosophy concerned with the appreciation of beauty or good taste. Aesthetics deals with all of the senses; in design, aesthetics is especially concerned with visual qualities.

Anthropometrics is the science of measuring the human body. It's one of the primary goals of effective design, which is to fit the everyday thing to the person, not vice versa. It should not be confused with ergonomics.

Art Deco was a movement in art and design inspired by the Paris *Exposition des Arts Décoratifs et Industriels* in 1925. Art Deco found favor especially in Great Britain and the United States in the 1930s. Art Deco had strong geometric overtones, and made significant use of exotic and expensive materials.

Art Nouveau developed throughout much of Europe between the 1880s and World War I. It had two distinct directions. One was characterized by the use of amorphous lines as found in nature and came to be known as Curvilinear Art Nouveau. Designers in France and Belgium were strong proponents of this direction. The other stylistic direction occurred in Austria, Germany, and Scotland. It was based on geometric lines and became known as Rectilinear Art Nouveau. In both types, Art Nouveau designers were making a strong visual counterstatement to the reigning mechanistic styles found in public buildings, such as the Eiffel Tower.

Artifact is the everyday thing that normally results from the designing process in The Designing Triad. Normally, the artifact is tangible and can be anything from a simple tool to an urban complex.

Arts and Crafts was a short lived yet significant English design movement in the 1890s, which was led principally by William Morris. One of its basic tenets was the rejection of industrial methods because of the removal of the artisan in the production process.

The Bauhaus was situated in Germany and became the first school of art, architecture, and design to advocate a curriculum that reflected what would eventually become known as Modernism. Although it had a very short history—from 1919 to 1933—its influence has impacted most design programs the world over.

Classic is a stylistic term often associated with the use of classical architectural and design forms, such as columns. The term can also be used to describe designs that have stood the test of time, such as the Volkswagen Beetle and the No. 14 Café chair by Thonet. The term is often associated with good taste.

Context is where the designing process occurs in The Designing Triad. It is a combination of natural and artificial qualities associated with location and can include culture, geography, climate, and other such factors. Context is also referred to as *place* in the 3Ps.

Corporate design is a business strategy that involves the integration of design in order to create a cohesive presence for a corporation. It first appeared at the turn of the twentieth century, with Peter Behrens and the German company AEG. Corporate design is now common practice in leading corporations such as Apple, Ford, VW, and Target.

De Stijl identifies a group of Dutch artists, architects, and designers who explored a minimalist visual language based on simple geometry, primary colors, and black and white. The work of Gerrit Rietveld epitomized De Stijl in architecture and design.

Designer is one of three participants in The Designing Triad. The Designer can be an individual or a group. Normally, the Designer is perceived as the source of the idea that underpins and drives the designing process.

The Designing Triad is a simplified model of the designing process. The name is derived from the three significant participants in designing: the Designer, the Maker, and the User. The Designing Triad also includes the Context and the Artifact.

The Deutscher Werkbund was an association of politicians, manufacturers, architects, and designers founded in Germany in 1907. Its members believed that German national interests would be better served if all of the partners involved in industry would work in concert.

Ergonomics is the study of people in a specific activity and environment. It is generally considered part of human factors. The term should not to be confused with anthropometrics.

Feng Shui is a Chinese belief in which formal organization is based on harmonious living with energy. In the Western and Modernist context, Feng Shui would be considered non-rationalist.

Fordism is a term used to describe the manufacturing innovations introduced by Henry Ford, especially mass production and the assembly line.

Form follows function is a rule of thumb that has become a truism of Modernism. It has often been attributed to Louis Sullivan, Frank Lloyd Wright, or The Bauhaus but its first appearance was in Horatio Greenough's book, *Form and Function*.

Functionalism is a term coined as the result of the influence of Frank Lloyd Wright, especially in the context of 'form follows function.'

Human factors is an area of study focused on the human interaction with design. It is a term used in the USA. It refers collectively to anthropometrics and ergonomics.

International Style is a term sometimes used to describe Modernism after 1930.

Kitsch normally refers to everyday things in bad taste.

Maker is one of three participants in The Designing Triad. As the name implies, the Maker is responsible for the making or execution of the Artifact in the designing process.

Memphis refers to a group of designers founded in Milan in 1981 and whose raison d'être was the disenchantment with Modernism. It became a beacon for the Postmodernist movement in design in Italy. Some of its members included Ettore Sottsass, Jnr. (sic), Andrea Branzi, and Michele de Lucchi.

Modernism was the most influential art and design movement of the twentieth century. Founded on functionalism and rationalism, its philosophical roots began in northern Europe. Its early leaders included Walter Gropius, Ludwig Mies van der Rohe, and Marcel Breuer.

Postmodernism is the art and design movement that immediately followed Modernism. In part, it was a reaction to the rational and functional nature of Modernism, and questioned Modernism's fundamental tenets through a greater level of subjectivity and expression in design. If Modernist designers proclaimed that less is more, Postmodernist designers considered less to be a bore.

Rationalism is a term often used interchangeably with Modernism or Functionalism. Its meaning pertains to the most economical use of material, space, and the visual language.

Streamlining was a design movement that occurred not long after the 1929 crash of the stock market in the United States. At a time when European designers were becoming more focused on rationalism in design, American product designers pursued a direction that accentuated a visual style based on the advances in aerodynamics, even in everyday things that were essentially stationary.

Swiss school refers to an influential graphic design school of thought with very strong Modernist ideals (from the 1930s to present). The term includes the ideology in typographic style of several designers such as Hans Keller, Max Bill, Herbert Bayer, and Armin Hoffman.

It had a strong adherence to the grid and sans serif fonts such as Univers and Helvetica. It was very prescriptive in nature and continues to influence certain aspects of contemporary graphic design.

Universal design is a recent design movement (from 1985-present), focused on the premise that design should accommodate as large a segment of the population as possible. It is at times erroneously identified with designing for the handicapped or the elderly. The American Disabilities Act (ADA) was a catalyst for its application, but some Scandinavian countries, especially Sweden, had recognized its principles before 1985.

User is one of the participants in The Designing Triad. The User is the person or the group that will use the Artifact that results from the designing process.

Visible language is a reference to the graphic qualities implicit in typography and letterform.

Visual literacy is the human capacity to create, interpret, and understand messages via visual images.

Visual communication is the use and application of visuals signs as a means of conveying a message. The signs can be letters but also include all forms of two-dimensional figures.

Visual language is the communicative properties imbedded in everyday things, especially in shape, form, and color, and that leads the viewer to react in more or less predictable ways.

Index

C

Index

Volkswagen, 121, 216

Volvo, 105

W

Wagner, Otto, 86

Wal-Mart, 158, 208

Walnut Canyon cliff dwellings, 69

wants vs. needs, 50–51

water, 3–4

Watt, James, 78

Wedgwood, Josiah, 80–81

Wegner, Hans, 104

Westman, Carl, 105

Westminster Palace, 124

White House, 149

White House at Canyon de Chelly, 67–68

A Whole New Mind, 205

Wired magazine, 184

Wirkkala, Tapio, 106

Wisdom of Crowds, The, 180

Wolfe, Tom, 118

Wood, Todd, 206

Workmate, 152

World Is Flat, The, 179

World War II, 103–104, 110–111

World Wide Web, 179

Wright, Frank Lloyd, 69, 101–102, 217

Wright Brothers, 54, 84

writing, 24, 90–91

Y

Yavapi, 71

Z

Zanuso, Marco, 110

Zara, 180

zoomorphs, 70